PLANNING·ENVIRONMENT·CITIES

Series Editors: Yvonne Rydin and Andrew Thornley

The context in which planning operates has changed dramatically in recent years. Economic processes have become increasingly globalized and new spatial patterns of economic activity have emerged. There have been major changes across the globe, not just changing administrations in various countries but also the sweeping away of old ideologies and the tentative emergence of new ones. A new environmental agenda emerged from the Brundtland Report and the Rio Earth Summit prioritizing the goal of sustainable development. The momentum for this has been maintained by continued action at international, national and local levels.

Cities are today faced with new pressures for economic competitiveness, greater accountability and participation, improved quality of life for citizens and global environmental responsibilities. These pressures are often contradictory and create difficult dilemmas for policy-makers, especially in the context of fiscal austerity. New relationships are developing between the levels of state activity and between public and private sectors as different interests respond to the new conditions.

In these changing circumstances, planners, from many backgrounds, in many different organizations, have come to re-evaluate their work. They have had to engage with actors in government, the private sector and non-governmental organizations in discussions over the role of planning in relation to the environment and cities. The intention of the *Planning, Environment, Cities* series is to explore the changing nature of planning and contribute to the debate about its future.

The series is primarily aimed at students and practitioners of planning and such related professions as estate management, housing and architecture, as well as in politics, public and social administration, geography and urban studies. It comprises both general texts and books designed to make a more particular contribution, in both cases characterized by: an international approach; extensive use of case studies; and emphasis on contemporary relevance and the application of theory to advance planning practice.

PLANNING·ENVIRONMENT·CITIES

Series Editors: Yvonne Rydin and Andrew Thornley

Published

Philip Allmendinger
Planning Theory

Ruth Fincher and Kurt Iveson
Planning and Diversity in the City: Redistribution, Recognition and Encounter

Patsy Healey
Collaborative Planning (2nd edn)

Ted Kitchen
Skills for Planning Practice

Peter Newman and Andrew Thornley
Planning World Cities

Michael Oxley
Economics, Planning and Housing

Yvonne Rydin
Urban and Environmental Planning in the UK (2nd edn)

Geoff Vigar, Patsy Healey and Angela Hull with Simin Davoudi
Planning, Governance and Spatial Strategy in Britain

Forthcoming

Cliff Hague, Euan Hague and Carrie Breitenbach
Regional and Local Economic Development

Patsy Healey
Making Better Places: People, Planning and Politics in the 21st Century

Other titles planned include
Introduction to Planning
Urban Design

Planning, Environment, Cities
Series Standing Order
ISBN 0-333-71703-1hardback
ISBN 0-333-69346-9 paperback
(*outside North America only*)

You can receive future titles in this series as they are published. To place a standing order please contact your bookseller or, in the case of difficulty, write to us at the address below with your name and address, the title of the series and the ISBN quoted above.

Customer Services Department, Macmillan Distribution Ltd
Houndmills, Basingstoke, Hampshire RG21 6XS, England

Planning and Diversity in the City

Redistribution, Recognition and Encounter

Ruth Fincher and Kurt Iveson

First published 2008 by
PALGRAVE MACMILLAN
Houndmills, Basingstoke, Hampshire RG21 6XS and
175 Fifth Avenue, New York, N.Y. 10010
Companies and representatives throughout the world

PALGRAVE MACMILLAN is the global academic imprint of the Palgrave Macmillan division of St. Martin's Press, LLC and of Palgrave Macmillan Ltd. Macmillan® is a registered trademark in the United States, United Kingdom and other countries. Palgrave is a registered trademark in the European Union and other countries.

ISBN-13: 978-1-4039-3809-1   hardback
ISBN-10: 1-4039-3809-1   hardback
ISBN-13: 978-1-4039-3810-7   paperback
ISBN-10: 1-4039-3810-5   paperback

This book is printed on paper suitable for recycling and made from fully managed and sustained forest sources. Logging, pulping and manufacturing processes are expected to conform to the environmental regulations of the country of origin.

A catalogue record for this book is available from the British Library.

A catalog record for this book is available from the Library of Congress.

10   9   8   7   6   5   4   3   2   1
17   16   15   14   13   12   11   10   09   08

Printed and bound in China

Contents

Preface

This book offers a new framework for thinking about the planning of cities. The framework seeks to highlight the social obligations and opportunities of planning. Planning is a form of governance and management of urban built environments and facilities which now accepts how diverse urban populations are and how varied are the ways in which people live in cities. Since the early 1960s, when critical perspectives began to emerge of those forms of planning that neglected this complex variation in urban living – in the writing of authors like Jane Jacobs and Richard Sennett, whose work from decades ago remains highly influential – planning thought has rejected approaches that treat urban citizens as homogeneous, as simply part of an overall and ill-defined 'public interest'. The argument of this book is that we should plan cities, acknowledging this diversity, with reference to the social norms of redistribution, recognition and encounter.

It might surprise readers that we have chosen norms, or social logics, as a means to make an argument about how to plan for diversity in cities, as much discussion in the last decade, about planning and its acceptance that urban populations are complexly differentiated, has focused on planning processes rather than planning ambitions or broad social goals. The discussion has been about the need for consultation in planning conducted in partnership with communities and individuals of variety. Planning discussion has rarely, in recent years, combined evaluations of and proposals for the processes of planning practice with reference to the overall norms of planning. With this book, we argue that there is a need to look at both sides of the planning coin – the conceptualization of broad social goals of the activity as well as the form and effectiveness of planning practices. We focus on the former matter, the conceptualization of the broad social goals of planning, to right the balance in recent planning discussion.

Readers may also be surprised that the book is not organized according to the social 'groups' usually named in equal opportunity policies, which is the approach in public policy that seems most commonly associated with the pursuit of social justice. This book might have had separate chapters on planning for a range of social groups, such as women, youth, the elderly, people with disabilities, communities of a range of ethnicities, gays and lesbians, and might have described and evaluated planning approaches that have emphasized their needs. Social groups indeed have a strong presence in this book, but are not its central organizing feature. Our decision not to organize this book around varied social groups reflects our awareness of the important critiques of such a practice. The identities of most individuals are not captured, nor their needs expressed, by any one social label. So, whilst in the book we discuss planning for and with many social groups, in a range of contexts, we do so in full awareness that such groupings can be troubling if they are used as the sole basis for social planning practice and can marginalize some people who are labelled as being within the groups as much as supporting the interests of others within the groups. In fact, in many of their urban encounters, individuals may act outside the 'group identity' with which we might commonly align them. And there is another reason that we moved away from a focus on social groups. A focus on social groups as the principal feature of planning for diversity in cities tends to draw attention away from matters long of concern to planning thinkers with an interest in planning for social justice – especially the matter of reducing disadvantage.

In proposing the conceptual framework offered here for planning, then, we wanted to shift the ground a bit – to include matters of planning process and practice, and to consider the varied social groups of cities, through an approach that is more overarching. By claiming the norms of redistribution, recognition and encounter as central to planning, we can consider both these important matters – planning practice and social groups in cities – with reference to normative and evaluative ways of thinking that have considerable longevity in critical planning thought. For, of course, none of our three norms is new to planning. We have just put them together in this book in a new way, in one place.

As you read the book, you will see examples of planning practice from numerous countries, evaluated with reference to these three social norms. The book may be read just to see the conceptual framework it proposes in its more conceptual chapters, and our critical reflection about that framework in the book's conclusion. Or it could be read for its many examples, in its example chapters, that draw on the work of planning scholars in different places. But we hope that you, the reader, will find invigorating the juxtaposition of concept and example offered in the book, and will take with us a step away from classifying people in bounded and static social groups and a step towards planning for the diversity of cities through the use of important social norms as a basis for conceptualizing, designing and implementing planning actions.

In writing this book, we have been fortunate to have the assistance and support of a number of people. Our colleagues near and far, Margo Huxley, Brendan Gleeson and Kate Shaw, have read the manuscript in its various stages and have offered suggestions that have helped us enormously. Haydie Gooder has been a wonderful research assistant, making comments of particular insight as well as finding many references and drafting the index. Steven Kennedy, as publisher, and Yvonne Rydin, as series editor, have given constructive criticism frequently. We are most grateful to all these friends and supporters, and of course blame none of them for the deficiencies of the final product. Our partners, Michael Webber and Nancy Griffiths, have rehearsed the arguments with us time and time again, and have come along to many of our inter-city meetings – well, they have come to the cities if not to the meetings. We dedicate this book to our children, Sophie and Tom, and Benji and Tilly (Tilly having been born in the very week that the final manuscript was submitted), with our hopes that the cities in which they will live their lives will benefit from the thinking of planners about redistribution, recognition and encounter.

RUTH FINCHER AND KURT IVESON
Melbourne and Sydney
October 2007

1 Introduction

In the industrialized countries of the West, by the 1960s, assumptions that had been largely taken for granted in planning thought and practice were being scrutinized critically from a range of directions. Richard Sennett's assault on the practice of urban planning in the United States, in *The Uses of Disorder*, is a celebrated example. And, of course, Sennett's book, when it was published in 1970, was but the latest in a series of blistering attacks on urban planning in America that were beginning to have (and indeed continue to have) a profound influence on planning debates in the United States and beyond – Herbert Gans's *The Urban Villagers* and Jane Jacobs's *The Death and Life of Great American Cities* among them. Hugh Stretton's *Ideas for Australian Cities* presented his vision of urban planning as a means to improve life for inhabitants of cities and was a major Australian contribution to the discussions.

These works, and many other revaluations of planning, were written to address quite different historical and geographical contexts. They certainly did not speak with one voice, either with regard to their diagnoses of planning's ills or with regard to their suggested remedies. But, in retrospect, it is possible to say that their cumulative effect was to challenge the assumption that expert planners knew what was best for cities and their diverse populations. Many planners in these different contexts may have assumed that their actions would improve urban life and further the 'public interest' through the application of expert knowledge. But their scholarly critics were identifying and reflecting upon the concerns being raised by some of the very people who were supposed to be benefiting from the application of planning expertise. From inner city urban renewal programs replacing decaying workers' housing with tower blocks, to new developments in rapidly expanding suburban fringes, to bold experiments with 'new towns' built from scratch on the basis of modern town planning principles, the outcomes of urban planning were being lambasted by a chorus of critical voices.

1

Among these voices were working-class people, immigrants and people of colour who keenly felt the loss of communities and net-works that were being destroyed along with their inner city houses. Among them also were women resisting the isolation of the domes-tic spaces to which they were being assigned in planned suburban developments. For these groups and others, the reality of urban life seemed not to live up to the utopian promise of planning.

Over the following decades, a broader argument gained momen-tum. Planning came to be faulted increasingly for its failure to take account of the *diversity* of cities and their inhabitants. The voices of dissent were widely interpreted as being the voices of groups whose particular views, experiences of the city and expectations had been marginalized in the planning process, which seemed to be premised on (and which sought to impose) a homogeneity across the diverse urban field. In grappling with this critique, the most discerning thinkers were sympathetic – but only up to a point. For example, Stretton's 1970 book certainly voiced a need for planning to take more account of the particular needs of women and children. But if the homogenizing impulses of the planners were being identified as a problem, Stretton was also clear that the response could not be a simple embrace of 'diversity'. 'Any decent intellectual', argued Stretton, 'despises the difference of more and less and reveres the difference of originality' (1970, p. 11). Addressing attacks on the conformity of planned suburbs, he noted: 'Before we all got the same houses, the contrasts of mansion and slum did not signify individual differences of desire, nor a tenth of the free choices we have now' (1970, p. 11).

The point here is that some forms of homogeneity might not be a bad thing, and that some forms of diversity are not necessarily desirable. The job of the critical thinker about urban planning is, in part, to distinguish between desirable and undesirable forms of diversity and homogeneity. This argument continues to be perti-nent for how we think about planning in cities of diversity. In the 40 years since the first attacks on the homogenizing assumptions and practices of planning, the diversity of cities and their inhabit-ants has become a core topic of concern for planning thought and practice, and for urban theory in general. And yet, reflecting back on the ways in which the diversity of cities has been conceptualized in these discussions, Loretta Lees (2003a, p. 613) has observed that '[the] diversity of different "diversities" is often under-theorised'.

Her point here is similar to Stretton's. If planning is to craft more just cities in a context of diversity, then this cannot be simply a matter of 'accommodating' or 'embracing' diversity as such. Rather, it is a matter of disentangling the different kinds of diversity which characterize city life and distinguishing between those forms of diversity which are just and those that are unjust, in order to promote what we will refer to through this book as a 'just diversity'.

Our aim in this book is to offer such a normative framework for planning practice – one that offers a set of 'social logics' for local planning efforts which respond to different kinds of diversity, and which might thereby assist planners to develop some 'rules of thumb' that can guide their actions. The three social logics are: **redistribution**, through which attempts are made to plan for the redress of disadvantage; **recognition**, through which efforts are made to define the attributes of groups of people so that their needs can be met; and **encounter**, through which the interaction of individuals is planned for in order to offer opportunities for increased sociality. But before introducing this framework in detail, let us situate our approach within broader discussions about diversity that have taken place in contemporary planning scholarship.

Diversity and the 'communicative turn' in planning

In developing our normative framework for working towards a just diversity in this book, we are consciously charting a different course to some of the existing planning frameworks for dealing with the issue of diversity. Much of the recent planning literature seeking to address this issue has placed considerable emphasis on styles of engagement with different groups of citizens in the planning process itself. These groups might include women and men and children, same sex or heterosexual couples, people with disabilities, people of varied ethnicities and identities, people of different class or income groups, etc. (and, of course, many people may belong to more than one of these groupings). The role of planners in facilitating the participation of these different groups of citizens in matters of urban policy has become a key concern for planning scholarship and practice. An acknowledgement of the heterogeneity of urban populations underlies these approaches to planning, which emphasize the need for planners to facilitate the inclusion of voices of diverse publics and population groups in decision-making processes.

As Heather Campbell (2006, p. 97) has argued, proponents of the so-called 'communicative turn' in planning theory and practice have paid particular attention to matters of procedural fairness, in an attempt to ensure that planning decisions are the product of 'open, uncoerced reasoning between free and equal citizens'. Here, the planner is positioned as a facilitator of respectful or reasonable communication among different groups whose interests might conflict, and the focus has been squarely on the engagement of planners with citizens to produce outcomes. As such, the need for planners to consult has been widely promoted, and making consultation more effective and inclusive has been a focus of democratically motivated planning practice and research, which properly insists that planning should be a social process of interaction between stakeholders, rather than a technical process of design and implementation by experts (Healey, 1997, p. 65). Sandercock (2003, p. 34) has stressed the contested nature of this democratic planning process, rejecting 'the modernist certainty about what's right for others. In its place is just one radical postmodern certainty – a belief in the virtues of a participatory, inclusive and always agonistic democratic process.'

Now, some critics of 'communicative' or 'collaborative' or 'deliberative' planning have pointed out that planning procedures – no matter how well-intentioned or formulated – often fail to live up to theorized ideals of procedural fairness and uncoerced reasoning in situations in which citizens are not really free and equal. This may be because planners themselves unconsciously or consciously privilege those points of view and forms of knowledge that cohere with their own operating frameworks (McGuirk, 2001). Or, as Susan Fainstein (2005, p. 125) points out, it may be because:

> if the powerful lose their advantages as a consequence of open communication, they are likely to either suppress unpleasant truths or to marginalize the tellers of them. Social power includes the capacity to control and channel communication and is extremely difficult to counter simply through voice.

Beyond the fact that planning on the ground might not live up to some normative ideal of communication, the very ideals espoused in the communicative turn also have some important limitations. In particular, it is of some concern that planning scholarship and practice have overwhelmingly paid attention to matters of process in responding to diversity. The normative foundations of urban planning and policy ought not be restricted to these matters of process, as important as they may be. To put it bluntly: to create more just cities, planners need a framework for *making judgements between* different claims in the planning process, as well as for *facilitating* them. That is to say, planning frameworks must enable planners to make calculations about 'what should be done', not just about 'how it is done'. In voicing this concern, we join a range of scholars who are critical of the emphasis on procedure and process over ends and outcome in much of contemporary planning scholarship and practice. Speaking from his North American base, for example, Michael Dear has lamented the fixation of contemporary planning thought and course curricula on the processes through which stakeholders might negotiate outcomes. Sometimes, he says, 'it seems to matter little what kind of decision is being reached' (2000, p. 132). He goes on to argue for more explicit attention to be given to the nature of different planning outcomes through the formulation of progressive visions of the city:

> There have been very few explicit attempts to connect contemporary planning discourse with its progressive, utopian roots. ... I am pinpointing the need to restore the reform tradition to a prominent position and thereby to forge a politically-aware and socially-conscious planning agenda relevant to a postmodern era. The planner's ability and responsibility to forge substantive visions of the urban future have been all but forgotten in the rush to become articulate, technically-proficient facilitators.

Also writing from an American perspective, Susan Fainstein (2005, p. 125) is critical of those whose focus on communication in planning theory leads them to 'back away from a concern with ends and aim their spotlight virtually entirely on the planner's mediating role rather than on what should be done or on the context in which planning operates'. Such concerns are not specific to the North American situation. Speaking more generally from her position in the United Kingdom, Heather Campbell (2006) has also emphasized the need for planning scholarship and practice to come to grips with issues of substance and value as well as process. Likewise, in Australia Gleeson and Randolph (2001, p. 3) have argued that social planning 'remains rather weakly developed, intellectually and professionally. Much of this social planning work focuses on issues of process and participation. ... Important as they are, these do not amount to an urban planning view on social disadvantage; its causes and policy remedies.'

As Campbell is keen to point out, to call for planners to develop and work towards some vision of 'what is to be done' is not to call for a return to some model of the planner as an expert, who seeks to undemocratically impose their will on a diverse urban field. In fact, quite the opposite is true. In the absence of an explicit set of values about the goals of planning processes, there is a danger that planners will once again wrongly claim the very neutrality which characterized the planner-as-expert approach:

> The recent history of planning thought has seen the replacement of the planner as instrumental rationalist by the planner as facilitator. Inherent in both these positions is an emphasis on the neutrality of the planner and hence on appropriate procedures and due process, although of a very different nature in each case (Campbell, 2006, p. 103).

For the planner as instrumental rationalist, the fantasy of neutrality was sustained by claims of superior technical knowledge and expertise, on whose basis planners could claim to be acting in the 'public interest' (while other groups were perceived to be acting on the basis of their particular interests). For the planner as facilitator, the fantasy of neutrality is sustained by the claim that they can somehow avoid imposing any values, coming to decisions instead by enabling all groups to articulate and negotiate their particular interests. The point here is that for planners to acknowledge their role in the *politics* of difference as political players rather than neutral observers and facilitators, they must also articulate the value frameworks through which they exercise judgement when faced with the different kinds of difference which characterize urban life. In policies, formal politics and activist movements, people do attempt to craft forms of just diversity in their cities rather than leaving the emergence of outcomes to the chance of some unscripted political moment. In this they exercise judgement. As such, the grounds upon which such judgements are made are of crucial importance.

In order to address these questions of 'what is to be done', there is a need for planners to engage with both emerging theorizations of the city beyond the technical planning literature (Fainstein, 2005) and emerging theorizations of justice and their potential application to the planning field (Campbell, 2006). These are the challenges we take up in this book. Our goal in engaging with these literatures is to develop a framework for envisaging what should be done, by outlining a set of norms or 'social logics' that are self-consciously progressive in orientation. The book, then, is not an ethnography of planning practice. Rather, we see the framework on offer here as a different kind of intervention in debates about planning, which might usefully sit alongside the valuable writing on the micro-politics of planning practice. Even as we understand that the point of implementation is important, we have sought instead to return to the intellectual territory of what planning is seeking to achieve. Without clear goals, good implementation strategies and processes are as limited in their potential as are goals lacking appropriate processes for implementation and deliberation.

Having said this, we are also keen to suggest ways in which students, practitioners and scholars of planning might incorporate these norms in their thinking about what is done in planning processes on the ground. As such, our approach in this book is to isolate some tenets or social logics currently used in attempts to work towards just diversity in cities, accepting that these suggest useful templates for improving practice even though all diversity is situated in context. This book aims to showcase and compare some of these efforts to shape cities, drawing to the fore the working principles (logics) evident in these efforts. We also aim to distil the sorts of 'decision rules' or 'rules of thumb' that have been used to work towards these normative goals in practice across different contexts.

It will by now be clear that we are taking a particular view of 'planning' here which is much broader than the application of local laws and zoning strategies to the resolution of land-use conflicts. Planning in this book is able to be likened to urban governance or urban management, which we see as a public sector activity for the most part – with groups of citizens and private sector firms engaged in (and, of course, sometimes contesting) practices led by the public sector and its policies. By taking up the idea of planning as part of urban governance and management, we are able to range well beyond the physical regulation of land use and to consider urban social policy and management questions. Note, however, that planning in this book, while it may be at the general (though often very local) level of urban management and governance, is also seen as having a principal concern with the way people's opportunities are influenced by the characteristics of the built environment and the provision of facilities within it. Planning, as we consider it here, is urban governance with a particular orientation to the links of social conditions to the built environment. In addition, we give priority in this book to the social goals of planning – to the manner in which the norms of planning can be rethought socially now that we recognize the diversity of urban populations.

We turn now to consider the conceptual basis of the three social logics for planning for just diversity that are offered in this book – redistribution, recognition and encounter.

Just diversity and the 'right to the city': *redistribution, recognition* and *encounter* as three social logics of urban planning

Reflecting on the question of 'what is to be done', Susan Fainstein (2005, p. 126) argues that '[t]he "what" for urban planners is the "right to the city" described by Henri Lefebvre'. She goes on to argue that Lefebvre's concept of the 'right to the city' is useful because it:

> raises questions of who owns the city, not in the sense of direct individual control of an asset but in the collective sense of each group's ability to access employment and culture, to live in a decent home and suitable living environment, to obtain a satisfying education, to maintain personal security, and to participate in urban governance.

Lefebvre's original articulation of the 'right to the city' (first published in 1967) is very much of its time and place – 1960s Paris, where the working classes and migrants were finding themselves increasingly banished to the *banlieues* on the outskirts of the city, and denied access to certain parts of the city. Lefebvre's speculations on the right to the city are pre-occupied with this process of socio-spatial marginalization and functional segregation, and his particular recommendations reflect this context. His work on the right to the city was informed by a strong critique of the technocratic will to plan cities as if they were machines, made up of separate parts with programmable functions and quantifiable characteristics (Lefebvre, 1996; see also Elden, 2004, p. 144–57).

But despite the particular context in which it was developed, Lefebvre's notion of a 'right to the city' has struck a chord among those concerned with achieving spatial justice. While Lefebvre was clearly critical of particular forms of planning, his work seems to have inspired a number of reformulations of planning. In invoking Lefebvre's notion of the 'right to the city', Fainstein is one of a number of contemporary thinkers in the planning and urban studies fields who have continued to draw insights from the concept (see for example Amin and Thrift, 2002; Deutsche, 1999; Harvey, 2003; Isin, 2000; and Mitchell, 2003 among others). The appeal of the concept beyond the context of its initial formulation derives from the importance that Lefebvre ascribed to space for progressive politics and social justice. Spatiality, insisted Lefebvre, was not simply symptomatic of social relations, but formative of them. And as such, attempts to address injustice and inequality would have to change space. The notion of a 'right to the city' emerges from this view that social justice must involve certain rights to urban space. According to Isin (2000, p. 14–15), Lefebvre's notion of a right to the city is therefore important as 'an expression of urban citizenship, understood not as membership in a polity – let alone the nation-state – but as a practice of articulating, claiming and renewing group rights in and through the appropriation and creation of spaces in the city'. Here, then, the 'right to the city' does not just refer to rights of access to the physical spaces of cities. Rather, it refers more broadly to rights to access and participate in urban life, a right to use and shape the city as an equal, a right 'to habitat and to inhabit' (Lefebvre, 1996, p. 173).

How might we develop the notion of a 'right to the city' to usefully inform contemporary planning efforts to work towards a just diversity? If we concentrate on the core promise of the right to the city – the notion that all urban inhabitants have a right to full participation in urban life as equals – then we may turn to recent debates in critical theory and feminist political philosophy for inspiration. These debates have worked through the relationship of two core normative principles of justice – those of redistribution of resources towards the poor, and of recognition of social diversity. From this discussion we draw inspiration, and we use the discussion to name two of the social logics of this book.

Published in a series of articles by Nancy Fraser, with responses by Iris Marion Young and others, we see in this spirited intellectual conversation the ways that questions about the principles under-lying contemporary notions of social justice have arisen from the critique levelled by analysts of the cultural politics of identity at political economies of inequality focused on class. Redistribution is often understood to be the remedy for inequality rooted in class, and recognition the remedy for the failure to treat all social or identity groups as equivalent in their diversity. These principles of designing justice, recognition and redistribution, form a defining point of departure for this book on planning cities for diversity, and frame its first two chapter pairs. The principles pose funda-mental questions for the social planning of cities, even if their spa-tiality is rarely articulated by those engaged in formulating them philosophically. Spatial questions aside for the moment, consider the argument between Fraser and others about how these princi-ples may be used to conceive better outcomes that we might see as acknowledging diversity more fully and justly.

Fraser (1995) begins the debate on the intellectual road she is still travelling, working out how to combine a 'cultural politics of difference' with a 'social politics of equality' (1995, p. 69) on the assumption that both are needed in a proper conceptualization of justice. Separating the two matters analytically, she develops a dis-tinction as well between the types of remedy that might be consid-ered when redistribution or recognition is required. This distinction in types of remedy is between 'affirmation' and 'transformation': affirmative remedies correct a particular outcome without altering the broader social arrangements giving rise to it; transformative remedies restructure causal processes and thus remove the prob-lem itself (1995, p. 82). To cut a very long discussion short, Fraser concludes from an application of these ideas to some dilemmas of gender and race that:

> the scenario that best finesses the redistribution–recognition dilemma is socialism in the economy plus deconstruction in the culture. But for this scenario to be psychologically and politically feasible requires that people be weaned from their attachment to current cultural con-structions of their interests and identities (1995, p. 91).

Young (1997) takes Fraser to task for polarizing economy and cul-ture, seeing it as 'theoretically and politically more productive to pluralize categories and understand them as differently related to particular social groups and issues' (pp. 148–9). Young herself has pursued this theoretical strategy in distinguishing 'five faces of oppression – exploitation, marginalisation, powerlessness, cultural imperialism, and violence' (p. 151) in her book *Justice and the Politics of Difference* (1990). Accordingly, she would like to depict issues of recognition as having material consequences, and issues of redistribution as having the consequence of inscribing a lowly status for certain identities or social groups. This she sees as less likely in a theorization based on a dichotomy.

From this initial flurry of disagreement, Fraser responds that her case is in fact one of refuting the dichotomous distinction that Young accuses her of making. Her concern is that in contemporary thinking 'the two paradigms of justice do not communicate' (1997a, p. 127). That many discussions of difference, and of forms of democracy that respect it, fail to pay sufficient attention to economic inequality is a point made also by Phillips (1997), citing Benhabib (1996). Fraser has continued her work on ways of merging the analytically separated but materially intertwined forms of injustice, arguing that the analytical distinction is required to signal the relative decline of claims for 'egalitarian redistribution' in political conflicts today (2000, p.107) in favour of, and displacing onto, claims for the recognition of identity groups. Working towards an integrative framework, Fraser (2003; 2004) proposes that a way forward can result from seeing recognition without its need to foster group identity, which it then reifies, and rather in terms of its definition of individuals as being of equal social status, as 'peers in social life' (2004, p.129).

Interestingly, Fraser's (2004, p.127) discussion of 'what institutional arrangements can ameliorate injustices of status and class simultaneously?' proposes a process rather than a set of decision rules. A 'parity of participation' principle is proposed, following which:

> justice requires social arrangements that permit all (adult) members of society to interact with one another as peers. ... First, the distribution of material resources must be such as to ensure participants' mutual independence and 'voice'. ... The second condition requires that institutionalised patterns of cultural value express equal respect for all participants and ensure equal opportunity for achieving social esteem. ... (2004, pp. 127–8).

Now, this position gives the impression of a reversion to a focus on process, at the expense of principles and particular interpretations of what justice means – another dichotomy between process and principle. But, in fact, it calls for processes of deliberation to have a particular thematic structure and for the decisions they make to have this thematic orientation too. Perhaps, if Young were now to reply, she would find this formulation still too abstracted from the integrated contingencies of particular contexts. Certainly it is a formulation that is simpler than the situated contexts of any urban conflict – but it has the benefit of articulating the principles that can guide discussion in the forums through which that conflict is considered. Indeed, Healey's (1997) collaborative planning merges the distinction between process and judgement somewhat as well, for despite its argument that spatial planning attempts are to be assessed according to the qualities of their processes (p. 71), she lists a series of criteria for making judgements about processes, one of which is about people appreciating difference in others, and another of which is about the redistributional opportunities of all stakeholders being included.

The concept of 'parity of participation' is particularly useful in helping us to elaborate upon the notion of a 'right to the city', with its emphasis on the conditions which might enable urban inhabitants to participate in urban life as peers/equals. And yet, there is another sense in which the notion of 'parity of participation' might itself be expanded upon through a closer engagement with contemporary theorizations of *urban* citizenship. Cities are places that people experience differently, inhabiting them in a range of ways. They are formed by the movements and mobilities of people, the playing out of their biographies in their time and space that is constrained and enabled by many relations of power, including those expressed through the built form of the city. Whilst not wanting to see the city as a physical or administrative container, then, we support Keith's point of wanting

> to reject ... the dualism that is so central to Lewis Mumford's great work *The City in History* through which he contrasts the urban as container with the urban as movement. The corporeal walker through urban space is always ... linked to the street through which that body inscribes their route (Keith, 1996, p. 145).

This understanding leads to a view of the 'right to the city' which recognizes the variety in the people and groups who will find their homes and workplaces there, have needs there, and seek access, opportunity and mobility there. Whether or not they will all seek to participate in the political decisions of the local planning forums, where they might be labelled as types of persons or as belonging to particular groups and thus as legitimate claimants to provide input, diverse people and groups will all seek some form of *encounter* with the city and its other inhabitants. Thus our view of the 'right to the city' is one which attributes to people their own spatiality – a life path peculiarly circumscribed for them by the spaces, places and governance structures of the city – which we interpret as a right to encounter. Indeed, if people have that 'parity of participation' proposed by Fraser (2004), they will not only have the opportunity to 'be themselves', they will also have opportunities to become someone else through exploratory encounters with the strangers with whom they share the city (Deutsche, 1999; Amin and Thrift, 2002).

Such a view draws partly on the broader, normative ideals about the need to foster in cities 'spatial openness and hybrid spaces', 'eroticism of the new and unfamiliar via ... "disorderly" streets and bazaars', 'publicisation of difference and strangers via open public events such as festivals and games' and 'access to public institutions and well-being in place' (Amin and Thrift, 2002, p. 139, quoting Iris Marion Young). But it also recognizes that inclusionary encounter is not the necessary outcome of providing large public spaces in cities. Amin (2002) shows this in his examination of multicultural interaction in British cities, in which he rejects the seductive notion that the freedom of association and encounter in large public spaces always develops a cosmopolitan urban civic culture. Such public spaces function either as spaces of transit rather than destination or are used by particular groups (like skate-boarders) whose presence might preclude others from comfortably lingering there. While not rejecting large-scale public festivals and public spaces, Amin concludes that 'micro-public' sites of compulsory daily interaction and conversation are those in which the accommodation of diversity, and successful multiculturalism, flourish. These include workplaces, schools, community organizations – in fact organized social interfaces of groups of people.

As a third social logic for the book, then, adding to those of redistribution and recognition so thoroughly debated in the philosophies of Fraser and Young, we use the notion of 'encounter'. If the forming of diversity by planning is to have a spatial context, an understanding that lived spaces can be improved by measures to increase redistribution and recognition also requires awareness of the public interactions in the confined spaces that constitute a city. Identification as a legitimate citizen and acceptance of redistributed private benefits are matters, when they occur in urban contexts, that are accompanied by encounter with others in public spaces and public interactions of a range of kinds. Possibilities need to be maximized, when trying to craft a just diversity in cities, for people to have available to them 'networks of enrolment' (Amin and Thrift, 2002, p. 29) that are momentary as well as enduring. Combining collective political debates (that, we say, generate recognition or form identity) with opportunities (through, we say, redistribution) to enhance capacities, with socializing (we say, from encounter) are the dimensions of the 'right to the city' outlined by Amin and Thrift (2002, pp. 146–9).

Including encounter as a normative social logic for planning is a way of grounding our discussion of diversity in one basic reality or defining feature of urban life. For urban life, by definition, juxtaposes and mixes people in workplaces, residential areas, public and private spaces of different kinds. The discussion of crafting diversity in this book is about doing so in urban contexts – like other geographers and urban planners we are seeking to root the seductive but broad claims of philosophers in the specific realities of the environments about which we conduct our empirical research and make our situation-specific observations and interventions.

Looking at particular situations makes it clear, however, that redistribution, recognition and encounter, the social logics of our focus in discussing planning and its contribution to the forming of diversity, are not independent of each other. We use them as three entry points, three organizing features, of the book. But in the examples through which we develop our discussion it is very evident that the three normative social logics are linked in these real-world situations. Redistribution is rarely possible without effective recognition and encounter. For example, the allocation of additional resources to creating recreational facilities for young people in an area, thus redistributing those resources to a group in need, will be ineffective if the variations between local young people in what they require are not recognized in the facilities' design, and if the facilities are not planned so as to draw the young people together in such a way as to maximize their socializing, interaction and understanding of each other. Recognition is rarely possible without redistribution and encounter. For example, acknowledging the cultural particularities of a recent immigrant group by giving planning permission for them to build a place of worship near their residential area, will be an ineffective strategy of recognition if the emphasis of their 'difference' marginalizes them in their town by making others resentful of the benefits extended to them, resulting in the group's members failing to obtain work in the town (a material or distributional matter) and having poorer quality public interaction with others in the town (a matter of encounter). Encounter is rarely possible without effective redistribution or recognition. For example, groups utterly without material resources, like the homeless, who spend time in public spaces of a kind intended to foster social interaction, are less likely to be recognized appropriately by other citizens and to have positive interactions with them than if they were individuals of less marginal economic status.

Nonetheless, in noting the interdependence in most realities of the three norms we identify, we take Fraser's view that the analytical categories of redistribution, recognition and encounter are useful for the matters to which they draw our attention, even as we recognize their indivisibility. The alternative approach, what Fraser terms 'post-structuralist anti-dualism', which holds that the matters are so intertwined in any particular reality that it is worthless to try to separate them out, is, in our view, less useful analytically (Fraser, 2003, p. 60).

We have observed that the absence of a spatial interest is something characterizing much philosophical discussion of the relationship of norms like redistribution, recognition and encounter (though the work of Iris Marion Young does engage with questions of social justice in cities). Another matter which requires additional thought, in a book about the crafting of strategies from using social logics in planning, is the conceptualization of the state, as most urban planning occurs in or in association with the institutions and practices of governments. Consider now the conceptualization of the state, in the forming of diversity in cities.

Conceptualizing the state

One criticism levelled at Fraser's work in forging a theory that couples redistribution and recognition as norms of social justice has been her lack of attention to proposing a conceptualization of the state. As Feldman (2002, p. 410) has it: 'what remains less developed in Fraser's work is the particular role of the state and "the political" in struggles over distribution and recognition'. This lack of attention to the state as itself a site, through its institutional practices, for creating injustice as well as providing some possibility for rectifying injustice, has occurred, according to Feldman, as a consequence (perhaps unintended) of the interest of critical theorists in identifying the exercise of power in places where it is unexpected. 'When the state is lost as an object of critique, it is also found as an uncritically embraced, undertheorized instrument for confronting the injustices of civil society' (Feldman, 2002, p. 411). For this book, concerned with strategies for crafting diversity in cities through urban planning, a conceptualization of the state is needed, to ground our analysis, in the same way as a spatially aware interpretation of such strategies is needed to locate our work in the context of cities.

The state, the principal institutional actor in urban planning, is seen in this book as the site both of injustices and their remediation in cities. It is within the departments and instrumentalities of government that much planning is undertaken – whether it is in national strategic policy about the conditions of cities, or in local governments organizing forums of citizens to provide input in local planning decisions, or in regional or other government instrumentalities concerned with provision of infrastructure to large areas. Not only does the state encompass the work undertaken by elected officials and paid workers in government, but it includes also the work that goes on in communities in association with, or in response to, such governmental efforts. So, we include in our concept of the state the partnerships or even oppositional movements that might engage with particular government departments or legislation.

An important perspective on the state, as we think about it in this way, comes from Mountz (2003). She stresses the importance of envisaging the state bureaucracy as made up of people making decisions in their everyday workplaces: 'behind each decision are individuals acting within varied institutional and geographical contexts'

(2003, p. 625). Her conceptualization of the state is thus that its bureaucracies are an 'everyday social construction' to which those activities and individuals defined as 'outside' the state connect in a variety of ways (p. 626). As we move later in the book to investigate the actions of planners and urban policy-makers in particular settings, as they participate in the implementation of the planning strategies of redistribution, recognition and encounter, we see these planners often working within bureaucracies, and often working at the local level in bureaucracies influenced profoundly by the decisions of national or regional institutions of government. We note these planners and urban policy-makers negotiating with their counterparts in other sections of the state apparatus, often in other locations. Conceptualizing the state as a set of working bureaucracies, the sites of people's everyday working lives, allows us to appreciate the importance of the activities of planners and urban policy-makers in any part of the state apparatus, rather than underestimating their activities. This is the significance, as Mountz (2003, p. 625) says, of correcting the tendency to conceptualize the state too abstractly, as unpeopled.

The state is also, of course, a terrain of struggle and conflict over the means and priorities of governance – and the devising of strategies for crafting diversity in cities involves it centrally. It is not just a unified bureaucracy that sets up 'process' – a value-free organizer of frameworks within which decisions can be made after input from citizens outside government. Neither is it everywhere and always oppressive and in search of social control, as some interpretations of the 'dark side of planning' suggest (see Huxley, 2002, p. 141). Rather, the state is a place of politics; its activities are contested from within as well as without, it is the site of possibilities both repressive and liberating, and of outcomes to be determined through the exercise of power relations. Any of its processes may not be seen as value-free in their implementation in any urban reality, though the basic outline of these processes may seem innocent enough.

In writings of political theorists about redistribution and recognition, it is very clear that states are principal sites of the establishment and maintenance of status distinctions between people and places. These status distinctions can be of a material or a cultural kind – they can seem amenable to improvement by redistributional means or by recognition, both of these occurring in cities through appropriate forms of encounter. Hayward (2003) has described the role of the American state in establishing divisions and differences, social and physical, in American cities, reaching back to the early twentieth century. Her emphasis is particularly of how racial differentiation of the American urban population has been constructed by repeated examples of 'the state-sponsored racialization of place' (p. 503). She says:

> Consider the all-too-familiar characterization of particular urban areas as comprising the 'black sections' of a given city. ... State actors helped forge the black American ghetto through the legal institution of racial zoning during the early part of the twentieth century, then through the enforcement of racially restrictive covenants, and, finally, through zoning laws that, although not explicitly racially targeted, function to maintain established patterns of racial segregation. Constructing racialized places in which its citizens live and work – in which they experience the social world and develop their interpretations of it – the state has been instrumental in racializing the processes through which people perceive their relations with others and form their social identities (Hayward, 2003, p. 503).

The routes chosen for highways, and the placement of high-rise housing projects under urban renewal regimes in the mid-twentieth century, reinforced the spatial differentiation of the urban population in American cities (Hayward, 2003, p. 504). Class and race have remained segregating features. More recently, municipal governments in American cities have legislated to prevent the homeless from occupying urban public spaces.

Activism from within and from outside governments has chipped away at some of these racializing and segregating practices of the American state, as they affect places, over the years. In the mid-twentieth century, as Hayward notes (p. 504), federal programs controlling mortgage investments in urban areas were responsible for 'red-lining' inner urban neighbourhoods through the use of 'Residential Security Maps, which outlined in the color red, signalling the highest possible investment risk rating and marking as an unsound investment – neighborhoods characterized by mixed primary uses, high population density, relatively old building stock, and minority, especially black, residents' (p. 504). Since that time, federal governments have actively worked against the practice of red-lining by imposing, under the Community Reinvestment Act of 1977, sanctions on institutions failing to comply with their public obligations (Marshall, 2004). But the question is whether this redistributional work, the product of efforts to shift the terms of engagement of the state with places and their occupants, continues to stigmatize the areas and people so identified, despite the affirmative action being undertaken. In Young's terms, is redistribution, in this context, reducing the status and recognition of the group receiving the resources? Hayward concludes that actions of the state that continue to treat such areas separately, will continue to racialize the areas even as they seek to redistribute resources towards them. She discusses proposals to shift decision-making about urban areas away from very local authorities – to unsettle the differentiation between black and white areas of American cities by having more metropolitan-scale government, where people vote and make decisions for areas far bigger than their own residential communities.

On a different scale, here that of government-provided shelters for the homeless, degrading criteria were imposed on shelter users in Portland, Maine in the late 1980s, that they identify themselves as members of an eligible category such as mentally ill or substance abuser (Feldman, 2002, p. 429). In this case, following a major protest involving the establishment of a tent city through which residents could establish a group presence and more positive relationships with residents of the city, forms of classification of this stigmatizing kind were removed and some distributive benefits gained by homeless people in this locality.

It is clear in how many cases the state's rules and procedures are classifying, stigmatizing and segregating even as they may be redistributive. The state is a major site from which this occurs, and in which battles to avert such institutional behaviours are fought through protests, legal challenges, lobbying of bureaucrats and elected officials and the like. In our conceptualization of the state it is important that it be understood as a set of political institutions and practices that can be pushed towards affirmative and even transformative change, as well as producing injustices.

Now, in different countries, the institutional settings in which urban policy-makers and planners are positioned vary, allowing them access to create improved circumstances in cities at certain spatial and political scales and not at others. Or, as Healey (1997, p. 34) has it, there are different governance cultures in different places, which influence (for example) the degree to which collaborative or communicative planning orientations are adopted in planning practice, as well as the different decision rules and forums developed legislatively. Through the rest of the book, the institutional arrangements of the state in different contexts, the terrains of political action that craft forms of diversity in cities, will be described as we discuss particular examples, with reference particularly to their orientation towards redistribution, recognition and encounter.

Our approach is particularly concerned with the nature of action that can be taken at the 'local' scale in pursuit of redistribution, recognition and encounter. We take this approach not because we claim that the 'local' scale is a privileged scale politically, as though action taken at the local scale is somehow more democratic. We also recognize the geographical connections that shape (and take shape through) localities, such that efforts to change the lived reality of a locality cannot restrict themselves to action within that locality. Our choice is more pragmatic. We recognize that 'planning', as we conceive of it, is often institutionally organized at the local scale, and that planners often find themselves engaged in projects designed to transform localities. As will become evident, the ways in which these locally situated actions seek to negotiate and transform trans-local processes will play a significant role in their ability to facilitate redistribution, recognition and encounter.

The rest of the book

In what follows, in the rest of the book, three chapter pairs will consider the social logics of planning cities for diversity – one pair will focus on redistribution, one on recognition and one on encounter. In the first chapter of each pair, we will discuss the conceptualization of the social logic in question, and in the second chapter of each pair we will consider in detail examples of the ways that particular social logic has been used (not always entirely successfully) in planning practice in a range of contexts. The example chapters will draw heavily on cases and situations of planning practice discussed in the literature – by drawing on the work of eminent urban analysts from a number of countries around the world our case examples can be wider in their scope. In addition, our detailed use of examples from the research of others underscores how useful it is for planners to be informed about internationally varying practices, and to learn in their own practice by networking widely. We are aware that even as we have taken this approach, there are significant planning issues which have not been given any sustained attention in the book. It is our hope that the framework offered here might usefully be applied (and indeed amended) in the analysis of issues we have not examined.

The trivalent conceptual framework that we have developed posed particular challenges for the organization of this book. As we noted earlier, while the three social logics are separated for analytical investigation in the book, this is done in full acknowledgement that in reality the logics are not separable. That is, a planning action that is redistributive will often include, as well, attention to recognition and encounter; the conceptualization of such a planning strategy may define redistribution with reference to recognition and encounter. In fact the best redistributive planning will do this, enhancing its interpretation of what redistribution for a just diversity consists of, in that situation. Stressing this point, we have organized those chapters in the book that present examples of the implementation of these three social logics, in a way that showcases the interconnecting of these social logics of planning, in practice. So, in each 'example' chapter, there are three examples. If that chapter, for example, is illustrating planning focussing on the social logic of recognition, then one illustration will be an example of planning informed by that particular social logic (of recognition) alone, a second will be an example of planning informed by recognition and also by redistribution, and a third will be an example of planning informed by both recognition and encounter. We acknowledge that the relationship between the three social logics and the realities they seek to describe, and indeed the relationship between the social logics themselves, presents challenges. But the task of interrogating the complex situations in which planning action is required demands the development of a conceptual tool-kit that has flexibility as well as clarity. This is what we hope our three social logics, and our exploration of their use, will offer.

The table below sets out the particular examples considered in the chapters of the book (Chapters 3, 5 and 7) that illustrate the use of the social logics in planning and policy practice.

Table 1.1 **Examples demonstrating the use of the three social logics in urban planning and policy practice**

Example chapter		Examples	
	Redistribution:	*Redistribution and recognition:*	*Redistribution and encounter:*
3. Planning for redistribution	Urban renewal	Local child care planning	Deinstitutionalization
	Recognition:	*Recognition and redistribution:*	*Recognition and encounter:*
5. Planning for recognition	Child friendly cities	Planning for immigrants	Contesting heteronormativity
	Encounter:	*Encounter and redistribution:*	*Encounter and recognition:*
7. Planning for encounter	Festivals	Public libraries	Drop-in centres

2 Conceptualizing Redistribution in Planning

In this first chapter pair, Chapters 2 and 3, we consider redistribution as a social logic of planning that contributes to building a just diversity in urban life by fostering 'rights to the city'. In our view of a just diversity, very great and increasing differences between rich and poor are the result of unjust structures of distribution and are of significance for planning because they confer better rights to the city on the rich than on the poor. The primary aim of redistribution in planning, then, is to *reduce* this particular difference. In shining a light on redistribution, our focus is consistent with a long tradition of planning thought and practice, which has sought to position planning as an alternative to the unfettered operation of markets in distributing resources, infrastructure and services in cities.

In this chapter, we build our case for redistribution as an important social logic of urban planning by examining the spatial dimensions of material differences among urban inhabitants. Here, we are referring to both physical and social space. In shaping the location and accessibility of services and infrastructure, urban planning and policy-making always have distributive consequences. Our aim is to develop a framework that can be applied to evaluate critically a range of remedies that seek to address the systematic reproduction of differences between rich and poor, by promoting urban spatial arrangements which do not disadvantage some people relative to others.

Redistributive planning

Redistributive planning in cities seeks to reduce disadvantage and inequality. A contemporary idea of redistribution, on which we draw here, stems from the post World War 2 period of the formation of the welfare state in Western societies. The political and economic values that underpinned the emergence of planning for the reconstruction of European cities at that time acknowledged and sought to ameliorate the differential access of people to resources, envisaged economic improvement and full employment as something to which the public sector could contribute, and sought administrative reform through forward-looking planning that included people democratically (Gleeson and Low, 2000, p. 18). The welfare state and the practice of a 'mixed economy' emerged from these values. The thinking of economist John Maynard Keynes was particularly influential here. He attributed an important role to the state in collective planning for public prosperity, seeing this as compatible with a market-led economy and individuals' rights as citizens. It was the responsibility of the state to redistribute public funds in a range of ways to ensure that all citizens were provided for and equality of opportunity was gradually achieved. Economic stability and collective welfare were the aims. Through the operation of fair and impersonal procedures, formal equality for citizens (and, implicitly, homogeneity) was to be achieved (Brodie, 2000, p. 111).

In a major theoretical treatise, Jessop (2002) has positioned post World War 2 planning for social and economic redistribution as part of the 'Keynesian welfare national state' in a political-economic ideal type he terms 'Atlantic Fordism' (a general social regime of governance and capitalist economic production occurring in the United States, Canada, north-western Europe, Australia and New Zealand). We can draw out three key features of the Keynesian welfare national state from Jessop's account (though of course there are variations to the ideal type in different places) (Jessop, 2002, pp. 71–2). First, urban and regional policies were initiated generally from national levels of government in an attempt to level economic and social conditions. The national level of the state dominated local and regional levels for the design of social and economic policies. Second, nations' economic policies were developed on the understanding that national economies were relatively closed. Social policies had as their principal object the nation's citizens and households, and particularly saw the latter in terms of the patriarchal nuclear family. And third, welfare policies were state-led. The state was strong, as public institutions and their bureaucracies had a large role to play in establishing the societies envisaged. Infrastructure planning was particularly important in economic and social terms:

> [The state's] activities here included promoting the general infrastructural conditions for nationwide diffusion of mass consumption (for example, electricity grids, integrated transport, modern housing), promoting economies of scale through nationalization and/or supportive merger policies, engaging in contracyclical demand management, legitimating responsible collective bargaining, and generalizing norms of mass consumption through public sector employment and welfare expenditure. Urban and regional policies oriented to reducing uneven development helped to secure the conditions for mass production, mass distribution and mass consumption … the state's provision of collective consumption helped to socialize and to lower the social reproduction costs of labour power (Jessop, 2002, p. 77).

Following fiscal and political crises in the 1970s and 1980s, in which people in a range of social movements objected to the top-down and homogenizing forms of nation-state provision, and in which other groups objected to the costs of redistributive welfare state provision, a shift in the form of the state to a competitive 'workfare state' may be identified in the countries of 'Atlantic Fordism'. The three key features of the welfare state have given way to different approaches in these new regimes. First, the national economy is now increasingly considered (and indeed encouraged) to be open rather than closed, such that economic policy is focused on achieving international competitiveness. There has been an associated discursive shift away from '"productivity" and "planning" in favour of an emphasis on "flexibility" and "entrepreneurialism"' (Jessop, 2002 p. 133), and the subordination of social to economic policy. Second, within the area of collective consumption, provision and payment of services by the state was replaced by mixtures of private provision and public payment, and in some sectors by privatization of both. In governance of this service provision there is 'increased reliance on public–private partnerships, multi-agency cooperation, and participation of the third sector' (Jessop, 2002, p. 162). Third, the political terrain of state action shifted over this period, compared to what it was earlier. Now, political activism within and outside the state, trying to design and implement redistributive measures, would confront a different set of expectations about the 'normal' approaches to be taken by governments.

Sixty years after the end of the Second World War, the Keynesian model of state-led collective planning has been replaced by a vilifying of bureaucracy and a growth of anti-government ideologies, according to some analysts of the public sector. New governance strategies of privatization and the contracting-out of public services provision are widespread. In the 'enterprising states' which have emerged in this recent period, the provided-for, if uniformly treated, citizen of the welfare state has been replaced by the citizen as a 'self-enterprising agent' who must take on obligations and comply with myriad rules if s/he is to receive assistance from governments (Considine, 2001, p. 9).

The trajectories of the national welfare state outlined above have had profound consequences for the ways in which urban planning thought and practice has approached the goal of redistribution. It was through its concern with the public interest over the decades following the Second World War that urban planning, along with numerous other policy domains from which it is inseparable, was located by some analysts and practitioners in the moral landscape of reducing disadvantage and was seen as arranging the social and physical landscapes of cities and environments to improve the circumstances of 'the public'. Thus, looking back a few decades:

> ... it is not hard to find in the literature of planning a thread of concern for justice – being fair to people who seem to have suffered hardship through no fault of their own; putting right the unfair consequences of market transactions; a concern with the poor, old people, disabled people, aborigines, black people, migrants, young children and, in so far as they are discriminated against by market society, women (Low, 1994, p. 116).

At this time of redistributive national thinking, with its implications for cities and welfare states, the focus was economic or material. The scale of operation was national, or at the level of states in nations that were federations. The emphasis was on reducing income and wealth disparities between social groups, and reducing poverty. This was to be achieved by state-funded provision of housing and public facilities, with pensions paid to individuals in need (on the basis of age, unemployment, etc.), the precise form of these welfare state provisions varying between countries. Class differences were understood to be significant.

Now, of course, there were some significant limitations in this way of approaching redistribution. If one looks at planning practices at the time when Keynesian welfare states were in place, it is not hard to find examples where apparently redistributive planning did *not* create urban landscapes of reduced disadvantage. Indeed, despite the lofty intentions of national policy settings, the practice of planning and the implementation of public policy often worked to disadvantage some people and some areas. According to Sandercock (1998), planning informed by redistributional goals often worked on behalf of a 'public interest' that proved to be one defined by 'the assumptions and priorities of the privileged' (1998, p. 198). The 1960s regimes of urban renewal in a number of parliamentary democracies are frequently cited as examples of redistributional planning which worked in practice to further disadvantage the poor. There were significant blind spots in these approaches towards other axes of difference in urban populations. As Fraser has noted (2003, p. 2) of this period, 'with questions of difference usually relegated to the sidelines, claims for egalitarian redistribution appeared to typify the meaning of justice. There was no perceived need to examine their relation to claims for recognition.' Or to investigate their links to spatial practices of encounter, we might add. Residents of cleared areas were often not consulted about their particular ways of life or aspirations, and too often found themselves spatially segregated in new housing estates located at some considerable distance from the inner cities from which they had come (we consider the practice of urban renewal in more detail in Chapter 3).

The limitations of redistributional planning approaches associated with the Keynesian welfare state can be understood as a product of the ways in which planners and policy-makers came to decide what the 'public interest' in any question of public policy might be. The idea of a uniform citizen, receiving benefits in collective consumption alongside his/her fellows, was an idea central to the idea of the 'public interest' associated with the Keynesian welfare state. Accompanying the contestation of these equalizing assumptions and practices of the welfare state by post World War 2 social movements, there have been profound theoretical critiques of the assumptions that a 'public interest' can be found at all, in policies or practices like urban planning, as in other forms of institutional intervention. We have referred to these in Chapter 1, and the way they are present in the intellectual tussle between Fraser and Young. These critiques of a uniform public interest are drawn particularly from feminist theories of difference and citizenship. This has been one basis from which questions of the recognition of difference and identity have stepped to the fore in many discussions of justice, overtaking redistributive questions about moves towards greater economic equality. From this conceptual position, it is clear that a range of people – perhaps particularly those without proficiency in the principal language of their society or place, young people, same-sex couples and women of the full range of class backgrounds, are under-represented in our social institutions and citizenship practices. We are no longer in a situation where redistribution can be considered without its links to recognition, as was pointed out in Chapter 1, and without its links to spatial and social questions of encounter.

In light of these critiques, Sandercock has argued that planning thought and practice needs to recognize the presence in cities of 'multiple publics', thereby working towards a politics of inclusion in cities and regions. Focussing on a democratic planning process, she says:

> ... a heterogeneous public is still a *public*, where participants discuss together the issues before them and come to a decision according to principles of justice which they also must come to some agreement on. In theory we can imagine the possibility of a 'togetherness in difference'. Different groups might be understood as always potentially sharing some attributes, experiences and goals with other groups. ... In practice, the emergence of all sorts of coalition politics over the past decade ... indicate that this ideal of togetherness is far from unachievable (Sandercock, 1998, p. 199).

Others are less inclined to do away with the concept of a 'public interest' than Sandercock appears to be. They worry that the critique of the public interest for planning has robbed it of an important rationale and goal. Indeed, if the coincidence of the critique of a uniform public interest and the rise of competition rather than equality as a motivation for government action in post-Keynesian economic and social policy is sometimes interpreted as the former being blamed for the latter, then this is perhaps not surprising. For example, Campbell and Marshall (2000, p. 309) regret the uncertainties for planning in Britain that have resulted from the critique of the uniform public interest they say it served, and they regret as well the focus of the last decade on the procedures of fair planning rather than its outcomes. They call for a 'rehabilitation' of the idea of the public interest as 'shared values which transcend a mere summation of individual preferences', allowing 'emphasis to be given to an "outsider" perspective in making an evaluation of public policy' (2000, pp. 308–9). This call for a disinterested expert to decide the nature of the public interest is unlikely to be supported by feminist analysts or by those, like Sandercock (1998; 2003) interested in inclusive, democratic planning processes and practices. Nonetheless, both positions would seem to support the notion that it is important to articulate how a public realm in cities can continue to be fostered, even as we define it in more nuanced ways through the conceptual frameworks now available to us.

If planning is to work to reduce unacceptable inequality between people and places, its task is clearly complex. Its guiding moral notion of 'the public interest' must now be interpreted as that of the interest of 'multiple publics' or a 'heterogeneous public'. The centrality of economic capacity, of class, to the differences that many in planning seek to ameliorate now takes on a more nuanced hue. Class relations and positions will be recognized as taking diverse forms in the range of contexts in which they appear. In addition, of course, contemporary planning for redistribution is positioned within a regime of economic and social policy and governance in which equality has been outflanked by competitiveness in the list of desirable outcomes, and in which the private sector has a major role in provision of services. We recognize the complexity of contemporary contexts for urban planning and policy-making with the transformation of Keynesian welfare state economies which framed earlier efforts at redistribution. We wish here to contribute to conversations about the conceptual tools planners might find helpful to diagnose social circumstances and negotiate better outcomes.

The spaces requiring redistribution in the contemporary Western city, via urban policy and planning, are those spaces – both physical parts of urban built environments and areas of urban policy – limiting the opportunities available for disadvantaged people and therefore causing their material conditions and liberties to deteriorate. What are the ways in which urban planning and policy strategists may negotiate their situation within the 'entrepreneurial state' and the dismissal of the relevance of 'the public'?

How does urban planning for redistribution sit within modes of regulation and governing that highlight the individual rather than the collective as the unit of agency? Of course these spaces requiring redistribution and the degree to which policy philosophies and discourses dismiss equality in favour of competition will vary between contexts – between systems of governance and places. But they do include the question of the equitable spatial distribution of urban infrastructure and what planning is doing (or could be doing) to see that it is 'adequately' provided (within contemporary modes of governance). There is also the matter of the growing spatial concentration of rich and poor people, within some urban areas and types of housing. Part of the success of urban planning practice, where it has been used to reduce disadvantage, has been in its capacity to locate change at the appropriate scale. National-level, top-down, policy intervention, or even national-scale infrastructure provision, are not all that is needed for redistributive urban planning. Local initiatives are also effective and necessary, as will be evident later in this chapter and in Chapter 3.

Important concepts: locational (dis)advantage and accessibility

Central to urban policy and planning in their attempts to be redistributive have been two related concepts that see the relationship of people to the urban environment in particular ways: locational disadvantage (or advantage) and accessibility. Use of these concepts brings planning to a more local operational scale than the national or state-scale referred to in the previous section. Both these concepts are rooted in the recognition that equity, equality or social justice are spatially constituted and expressed. Both are grounded in a commitment to provision of services for collective consumption, though in their recognition that every individual is spatially located in ways that affect their wellbeing, these concepts also provide for individuals' wellbeing and progress. The way that space is used and manipulated to the advantage and disadvantage of particular groups, how groups of people are defined and separated by spatial planning solutions, or are clustered together, are core components of the spatial manifestation of inequality. Whether or not the features of physical and social space provide 'enabling structures' for people, to enhance their mobility or opportunities across the city, or to participate in its activities in a range of ways, is also a significant matter. Planning and the spatial social sciences bring to public policy and to discussions of social justice this recognition of the embeddedness of inequality, advantage and disadvantage in the organization and production of space. (In much of the literature and policy work about locational disadvantage and accessibility, however, economic improvement for poor people and areas has not been conceptualized in terms of the class relations of the society in question. Rather it has been analyzed by examining (often mapping) the income levels of population groups in places, and the causes of these patterns have not been sought. This means that transformative strategies have not been sought either – rather, amelioration of the inequality has been proposed, with the underlying causes of the inequality left unexamined).

Locational disadvantage and accessibility refer to different scales of relationship between a person or group and a set of facilities they might need or wish to use. *Locational disadvantage* or advantage refers generally to a place – a locality or region – that is disadvantaging or advantaging for residents by virtue of the facilities it contains. *Accessibility* refers generally to a facility or set of facilities themselves, to which a person or group may wish entry but which may be located at a prohibitive distance from that person or group. So – areas can have the property of being locationally advantaged or disadvantaged; facilities or services may be accessible or inaccessible. With both ideas, the spatially distributed mix of people, facilities and places or locations is the defining feature.

Locational disadvantage or advantage

The concept of locational advantage (or disadvantage) draws on the idea that where a person lives affects their opportunities, and contributes substantially to their wellbeing or difficulties. Though locational (dis)advantage can be a property of a place or of a person – it is loosely used in this regard – generally, an area is what is being referred to in discussions of locational (dis)advantage. A location, region or place will be seen as disadvantaged if the 'bundle' of services and facilities it offers its residents is substandard. When used with reference to people or groups, the term acknowledges that by virtue of the opportunity a person has or doesn't have in his/her area to use facilities and services like schools, hospitals,

parks, libraries, public transport and so on, that person will be locationally disadvantaged or advantaged relative to others with different levels of opportunity. It may be that a person in a rural area is
isolated from apprenticeships or appropriate schooling; perhaps
a person living in the middle of a major city is close to a range of
educational and employment options.

Says one set of urban theorists:

> While not as fundamental as social and economic position, locational
> disadvantage is one element of broader social dysfunction ... Location
> becomes important because there are spatial constraints on the avail-
> ability and use of a range of resources which are not universally available
> but are located unevenly in space (Maher *et al.*, 1992, p. 10).

As is evident in this quotation, locational (dis)advantage refers
generally to the *physical* location of facilities – their placement as
a located group in a particular region, which is often an isolated
region if the area is disadvantaged. The term is about how hard or
easy it is for people to reach facilities because of their distance from
those facilities or the difficulty of travelling to them. Of course if
the facilities in question are absent from an area, the physical distance between the areas' residents and the facilities located elsewhere will be the disadvantaging factor. This emphasis on the
physical or spatial distancing between people and facilities may be
seen as narrow in that it discounts a notion of social distance, but
the emphasis on the physical effort needed to make use of facilities
is nevertheless a useful one. So, this way of thinking about space has
long concentrated on measuring distances to a range of facilities
within given areas. How far do most people live from a hospital or
school, or food shops, or how long does it take the average person
to get to one of these important facilities, given certain assumptions about their physical mobility? Indices can be developed for
particular areas, taking into account the sorts of facilities and the
levels of physical access thought to constitute a reasonable set of
resources. Then localities or regions can be compared one to the
other, seeing how the facilities and infrastructure available provide
for an average population or even how they provide for a population with particular characteristics (say, income groups, or particular age-groups or household types) (see Maher *et al.* (1992) for this

approach to the measurement of relative locational disadvantage of places).

Conversely, assessments of locational disadvantage might also measure the concentration of facilities or infrastructure perceived to be harmful to nearby residents. Living near particular facilities clearly provides opportunities or limits wellbeing. But, of course, this also depends on the nature of the facility in question and the person or group in question. There are also situations when facilities are physically located in places that neighbouring residents do not want them, giving rise to the expression of NIMBY (not-in-my-backyard) sentiments. A variety of urban facilities have been the target of 'NIMBY' complaints, from polluting waste disposal facilities, to electrical infrastructure and shelters and soup kitchens for the homeless. NIMBY complaints can result in facilities being removed or modified. Where such facilities are simply relocated to other areas, this can simultaneously improve the locational advantage of one area while increasing the locational disadvantage for another. Further, if the facility in question was of use to some residents (e.g. a homeless shelter), then its removal can increase a location's advantage for some but increase its disadvantage for others who may otherwise have used the facilities.

Now, one term used to describe this physical or material understanding of space has been 'firstspace'. Soja (1996, p. 10) has 'described ... a Firstspace perspective and epistemology, fixed mainly on the concrete materiality of spatial forms, on things that can be empirically mapped'. In interpretations of planning that emphasize its contribution to governmentality, to producing knowledge of citizens and places for governments to aid in their efforts at social control, such mappings of the characteristics of people and places can be read as sinister, especially when looking back over time rather than situating oneself in the complex present (Huxley, 2002, p. 144). Whilst it is certainly the case that the creation and presentation of data help to create problems to be solved, and are created in the interest of those in power, it is also the case that redistribution may be aided and even made possible by the gaps in provision revealed by the data displayed. In addition, if data are able to be formed and aired by those in government or in activist contest with it, who are committed to more progressive rather than conservative outcomes, then such data may aid positive change.

Now, one of the difficulties with the idea of a place as a bundle of sited facilities and services that we benefit from (usually – unless we live in an area in which polluting facilities are concentrated) and from which we derive relative locational advantage or disadvantage, is that it tends to portray a place as a container, a static and physically bounded area, with residents always looking inwards to this area in living out their lives. That is clearly an inadequate view of people's relations to place, and is a reason to think about people's *mobility* as a source of opportunities, rather than just to focus on an area as a static provider of opportunity to those located within it.

In summary, locational (dis)advantage is a term referring to the adequacy of the bundle of facilities and services available to those who need them in localities or regions. The most extreme cases of locational disadvantage include isolated communities; in Australia, for example, there are some isolated indigenous communities in the north where there are on the one hand inadequate services, and on the other hand people with insufficient mobility to have their needs met by travelling the long distances elsewhere to obtain the services they need. It is important to couple the matter of people's mobility with the matter of the facilities available in an area, for places do not contain people absolutely (though there are cases in which people are contained within areas more so than elsewhere). In cities and towns, there are sometimes NIMBY-based complaints that remove facilities from areas, if certain more influential groups within a population there wish for that political outcome. Assessing the degree of locational disadvantage or advantage of a population and an area is undoubtedly complex.

That complexity having been noted, planners in governments have long recognized the necessity of providing basic infrastructure (transport, water, electric power, communications technology, the means of waste disposal) to ensure that places are equitably treated at this basic level. This is the 'bottom line' for ensuring that locational (dis)advantage is not too pronounced between areas. For example, colonial and later state governments in Australia have long balanced the opportunities of city-dwellers directly through provision of transport, sewerage and water lines and later educational facilities (Gleeson and Low, 2000, p. 30). From the time of World War 2, in Australia, more generous spending on social provisions – on public housing, neighbourhood houses, local health clinics as well as centrally-located hospitals, kindergartens, schools and parks – occurred in some places, in the period of Keynesian thinking about the role of governments that we have noted. More recently, criticisms of the new patterns of private ownership and management of basic urban infrastructure, that cornerstone of preventing locational disadvantage, have begun to emerge (see Graham and Marvin (2001) referring to the 'splintering' of infrastructure provision in the current period, particularly in the United Kingdom, and its consequence of exacerbating social and spatial inequality). Strong controls need to be put in place by governments to ensure that this entry of for-profit management of basic infrastructure does not diminish this important part of the public realm of cities and regions.

Though planning to reduce disadvantage and inequality occurs on a range of scales, national to local, the efficient and equitable location of facilities and infrastructure may suffer if centralized and all-encompassing provision makes way entirely for localized provision undertaken through a range of different agencies and partnerships. Such localized planning may be more responsive to local needs, but in losing that central commitment to equity across population groups and places the differences between opportunities in places may be heightened. The question of whether or not redistribution to address locational disadvantage can be achieved through centralized regulation of market-based and localized provision, rather than through centralized provision, is currently a matter of dispute in a variety of national contexts.

Access and accessibility

Concepts of access and accessibility have tended to focus on the physical materiality of the distance between a person and the individual service or facility they might need. If one thinks about accessibility a bit more closely, however, it is clear that accessibility to services involves more than physical proximity to them – it also includes a sense of perceived closeness or ease of social access to facilities and services, for diverse social groups. Adequate access to services and facilities in a place requires perceived closeness to the services being provided, perception of a welcoming attitude in the services offered in a place, or a sense of belonging or entitlement to them. This is part of what Soja refers to as Secondspace (1996, p. 10) – our imagination about or perceptions of a place (or in this case a service

or facility), that influence our use of it and our feelings about how
appropriate it is for us. In a critique of studies of access which make
quantitative assessments only of the match between certain populations and the distribution of the facilities they need, Takahashi
(2001) argues that knowing the daily routines and social networks
of vulnerable groups dependent on particular medical and social
services indicates better the access they have to those services. She
observes, from her study of individuals living with HIV and AIDS
in American cities, that their access to care is affected by their own
individual behaviour, 'but also larger social relations (such as "race",
gender and sexual orientation) and institutional practices (such as
rules and procedures of the service delivery system)' (2001, p. 847).
Here, emphasis is given to the importance of recognizing group
differences in pursuit of redistribution. In another critique, this
time of a 'spatially-neutral' approach that sees planning to reduce
access to facilities implemented without taking due account of local
context, analysts have described a recent case in New Zealand in
which schools have been closed if actual and predicted student
numbers are too low. But the decision to close schools in some cases
has restricted the access to nearby facilities not only of the students
themselves, but also of the parents and families who relied on the
presence of the school for their sense of sociality and community
(Witten *et al.*, 2003b). Planners need to take these matters into
account in planning the form and location of services.

Adequate provision of accessible services means also that services
for 'the public' should not inadvertently exclude certain people or
groups. Place-based planning, in the services it provides as well as
in other ways, may exclude groups of people who don't fit in. The
more pronounced the processes for nominating an identity for a
place, which views certain groups or characteristics or actions of
people as its embodiment, the more there is the potential for exclusion of those unlike the ideal residents.

So, the idea of access clearly means more than the utopian aspi-
ration of making a spatially even distribution of facilities for people
across the metropolitan area. Any map of any city, as Smith (1994)
notes, will show a spatial clustering of advantaged and disadvantaged populations, with some spatial correlation of the locations
of poor people and poor services, and of wealthier people and better services. Such maps call for efforts to distribute facilities more
evenly, but force us to acknowledge that complete evenness is not

achievable. Obtaining a more equitable outcome in the distribution of facilities as opportunities for people in a place is, then, an ongoing project. Thinking of the distinction between planning for transformative planning outcomes, versus affirmative ones that make no challenge to the circumstances creating the inequalities in question, it seems clear that the more accessible a service can be for the individuals or groups requiring it, in the fullest sense of 'accessible', then the more likely it is that that facility may play a transforming role in the lives of users. But merely locating a facility or service closer, physically, is unlikely to have such potential. For contemporary thinking about accessibility, then, older ideas of spatial equity or justice that emphasized firstspace aims of achieving an even spatial spread of facilities are now to be combined with secondspace ideas of what service users will find appropriate and accessible. They are also to be combined with matters of procedural equity to ensure the involvement of local and relevant citizens in decision-making about the facilities and services. There will be different interpretations and practices of procedural equity and spatial equity, in different contexts of time and place. But in governance cultures in countries around the world in which rationalization and privatization of services and facilities is occurring that would in previous times have been government-controlled and owned, the importance of procedural equity in the delivery of accessible facilities and services is of increasing importance.

Decision rules and discourses: ways of crafting a just diversity through redistribution

The question of what decision rules to use in delivering services equitably across spaces and to people in places causes reflection about what is meant precisely by redistribution in a particular context, and how decisions taken might lead to particular patterns of advantage and disadvantage. There is also the question of the unpredictable outcomes that might result. In addition, the nature of the discursive justification of policy actions and the explanation of policy intentions is very important. We consider now these two matters – decision rules for particular situations, and the discourses accompanying them that justify redistributive planning.

Consider first the question of what decision rules to use in conceptualizing how disadvantage-reducing access to services might look. Decision rules are statements of the form of specific planning measures. Decision rules for use in redistributive planning can be used to indicate the way resources will be allocated to reduce disadvantage or inequality. They envisage redistributional outcomes in a certain way – imagining that certain groups or places will benefit particularly, for example. Sometimes they use a quantitative target, for example to specify the percentage of resources to be directed, or the characteristics required of the population or areas which are to be particularly supported. As noted in Chapter 1, we know that decision rules will vary in different contexts, as they are worked through in community consultation processes. But such variation notwithstanding, it is important that they are articulated clearly in such processes – decision rules specify people's material entitlements, and when they are not clear, difficulties arise.

Two decision rules observable in the efforts of planning agencies to be redistributive are: *equity* in the allocation of expenditure on different local areas and populations; and *social mix*. In the first of these, equity in the allocation of resources to localities, we might expect to see efforts made by a senior government agency to make resources available to local agencies under its jurisdiction in such a way that some specified measure of equity will have been achieved for all the localities. In the second, social mix, an agency would seek to ensure that concentration of disadvantaged residents in a locality is no greater than a certain percentage of the population, so that this group of residents is placed in a socially mixed setting in which a range of income groups or households live in proximity to each other.

Take the first decision rule here, equity in allocations to localities. A famous proposal of how this type of decision rule might have worked in practice, but in the event did not, was made by Levy, Meltsner and Wildavsky (1974) in their assessment of the provision of education and library services and street infrastructure by local government agencies in a Californian city, Oakland. Allocation of resources in Oakland was influenced for each of the three services by the budgetary processes of the agencies, which would seek available funds from state and federal governments by complying with what those senior levels of government might require. Allocations were also influenced by the professional norms of decision-makers – the engineers making specifications for road funding in the area, and the librarians deciding what should be given priority in library funding, for example. To establish the extent to which the agencies' resource allocations complied with a decision rule of equity across localities and population groups, the study found the following.

In Oakland's 63 elementary schools, resources flowed most to schools in wealthy and very poor neighbourhoods, and least to schools in not-quite-so-poor areas. Schools ineligible for compensatory federal funds, and not benefiting from parent contributions and the transfer of the best teachers, were relatively disadvantaged. With streets, the large arterial road system of freeways and major streets received the bulk of funds. This resulted from the planning criteria of the engineers in charge who viewed improvement of streets in terms of what they saw as contribution to improved overall traffic circulation. Oakland's libraries had resources allocated so as to give priority to the central library rather than to its branches, with no extra resources spent on branches in low-income areas and the same sorts of books purchased for every community, regardless of the characteristics or preferences of the locals.

On what basis might we assess the degree to which cross-neighbourhood equity (a quite general decision rule) is served by these planned allocations of resources? To make such assessments, a further elaboration of the criterion of equity is required. 'Market equity', 'equal opportunity' and 'equal results' specify the general decision rule further (Levy, Meltsner and Wildavsky, 1974, p. 244). Market equity would prevail when expenditure on services per resident was in proportion to the taxes paid by their neighbourhood. Equal results would prevail when expenditure on services was such that every resident performed at the same level (in schools) or every facility in each area was of the same quality and usefulness (however that might be measured). Equal opportunity, the 'middle ground' between the other two, would prevail when effective expenditure on each citizen or neighbourhood was equal. Assessing the outcomes observed for the three services in Oakland, one might conclude for each that though equal opportunity may have been sought in the decision rules used, in fact market equity was almost the result, however unintended. The planners in Oakland would presumably have taken these data, using the data (and consultation with service recipients) to re-assess their strategies and re-specify their decision rules.

The second decision rule often used in planning that attempts to be redistributive is that of social mix. Decision rules about social mix target particularly the spatial and social place of people with fewer resources. (Spatial and social concentrations of people of wealth are never targeted.) The intention is to 'mix' people of different income groups, particularly precluding 'concentrations' of poor people. Sometimes these policies identify the poor as 'ethnic', as well as poor, singling them out from the 'mainstream' in this extra way. A recent discussion of strategic policies and decision rules to reduce inequality has occurred in the United Kingdom in debates about whether there are local 'place effects' exacerbating inequality. Are poorer people influenced by living close to others without good incomes, and therefore are 'area-based' policies particularly useful in alleviating poverty that is associated with such place-based groupings of poorer people? Should there be decision rules that direct resources to poorer areas, or should there be resources directed to dismantling poorer areas by moving people out? This discussion is particularly sharp in the context of the Labour Government's emphasis on place-based social exclusion as a primary generator of disadvantage, its recognition of the ways that processes of different scales are experienced in the local neighbourhood, and its implementation of policies of 'urban regeneration' as a response (Meegan and Mitchell, 2001; Tiesdell and Allmendinger, 2001). This is by no means a new discussion, however, nor one limited to British policy and academic circles, having been a focus for urban renewal policies for decades in different countries (see Chapter 3 for a more extended discussion of this matter). Meegan and Mitchell (2001) provide a useful summary of the century-long history of this topic in the UK, noting how recent British government thinking has been influenced by that of the Americans Wilson (1987) and Putnam (1993).

The broad issue of the significance of spatial co-location of poor people – whether it isolates them from mobility and opportunity and therefore should be countered by policies that either focus resources on the area in question or move people away from it into neighbourhoods of more mixed income groups – has also been the subject of recent comparisons about evidence and policies in Europe and North America (e.g. Briggs, 2003). This debate amongst urban planning analysts draws on the distinction raised in section 2.2 of this chapter between seeing local places (in cities) as containers of people, or seeing local places as sites from which mobility of the population occurs. Reviewing the European and United States evidence, Briggs finds that neighbourhoods of low-income households are 'typically quite heterogeneous. Only the most chronically poor and socially isolated individuals and families lead lives circumscribed distinctly by the poverty and spatial form of their immediate neighbourhoods' (2003, 924). Further, discussing the case of a court-ordered move to scatter public housing in New York, Briggs found that though movement away from areas of concentrated poverty and crime may indeed benefit households and neighbourhoods, those households are simultaneously part of 'larger regional and global dynamics ... [such as] immigration flows, dispersed networks, shifting economic patterns within and beyond the immediate city limits, and the spatial reach of institutions that focus on the needs of poor minorities' (Briggs, 2003, p. 923).

So, on the one hand, the message is clear that few under-resourced individuals and households are utterly immobilized within the neighbourhoods in which they live – there is mobility of different kinds available to them within the broader city. Focussing all policy resources on the neighbourhood as the root and source of poverty is therefore a limited strategy in this view, as is focusing resources on helping households move out of those neighbourhoods. Multiple strategies to expand 'place-opportunity links' are recommended. But on the other hand, one would not want to use this view that people are generally mobile to justify the uneven distribution of public facilities across localities, and to allow areas in which larger numbers of poorer people live to have fewer facilities and facilities of lower standard than areas in which clusters of richer people live.

Place or area-based initiatives are clearly needed to provide some equity in access to facilities and services across areas – in the firstspace sense – and to preclude unacceptable levels of locational disadvantage or advantage. In addition, the evidence indicates that these policies are not sufficient to offset disadvantage, and that a range of policies is required (not all of them planning policies) to achieve benefits for low-income people themselves. In the case of social mix initiatives, where governments and citizens outside areas of concentration of low-income groups are anxious about those concentrations, and seek reductions of them for reasons of social integration or reducing government expenditure, one may question whether it is sometimes the case that the policies are formed less in the interests of the low-income residents themselves than in the interests of governments and their major constituent groups.

In addition, policies of enforcing social mix between less-resourced social groups and more-resourced social groups will inevitably have consequences for encounter as well as distributional impacts. Are these urban policies implementing interactive living of the kind we extolled in Chapter 1? In Chapters 6 and 7 it will be clear that policies encouraging interaction and coming together in public space are not about compelling people where to live or with whom to interact. Rather they set up 'opportunities for enrolment' for people in such interactions, a policy action like in spirit to that of equal opportunity described by Levy, Meltsner and Wildavsky (1974) in their Oakland study. At the very least, a redistributive approach that is sensitive to matters of encounter ought to be concerned with the harmful effects of concentrations of advantage, as well as disadvantage. Gated communities, increasing in number in a range of countries along with varieties of guarded high-density residential buildings housing wealthier people (Webster, Glasze and Frantz, 2002), do prevent interaction utterly between those inside the walls and those outside. Even casual passers-by are prevented from encountering the residents inside (Blakely and Snyder, 1997, 153). There are certain advantages to 'affinity group clustering', which higher-income people claim by their self-segregation and harnessing of high quality services (Young, 2000, 207). There is locational advantage, as well as locational disadvantage, then, involved in the spatial concentration of like people. A redistributive approach aware of recognition and encounter would limit the opportunities for the establishment of privatized residential communities for the wealthy, knowing how such self-segregation harms the urban public realm as the wealthy opt out of contributing to the services, facilities and interactions of the city broadly. Advantages for those within having been noted, a redistributive planning approach sensitive to matters of recognition and encounter could not advocate or condone high levels of segregation of wealthy groups spatially.

However, the fact that there are certain advantages to 'affinity group clustering' could also be mobilized in support of planning for redistribution. In Australian cities, where levels of segregation identified as ethnically-based are not high, the debate over the advantages or disadvantages of clustering by immigrant groups has emphasized the advantages for the settlement process of this spatial co-location (Burnley, Murphy and Fagan, 1997). And in contrast to the fortified enclaves of affluence, concentrations of poor people do not prevent entry by those living outside such areas or buildings (though in some cases it is perhaps unlikely there will be many casual passers-by).

Going beyond the matter of the service outcomes to be delivered to people in places, via the decision rules that specify allocations to designated groups and areas, we come to the important matters of how these policy and planning actions are presented or characterized. What is the rationale for a planning action; how is redistributive planning described and justified? The discourse enveloping a redistributive planning effort, and its specific decision rules, will determine the way that citizens will understand the planning and the way they will interpret those people and places receiving benefits from the planning.

Discourse, for our purposes, is the story, or the logic, developed to justify the redistributive planning and its particular decision rules. It is the interpretation and rationale given by broad policy frameworks and public discussion, and by use of particular language, to make sense of the policy action for 'the public' and for the policy-making audience. Rather than being separate from redistributive planning – an elaboration of it – we see discourse as an important part of this planning to reduce inequality. In particular, because redistributive planning concerns a redirection of governmental resources towards people and places of need and away from people and places of plenty, the way in which the people and places of need are depicted is important to the success of the redistributive activity. If those in need are depicted discursively as unworthy, then the politics of the redistribution in question will be vexed, and one outcome of the redistributive planning effort may be to stigmatize those areas and people receiving benefits as less capable. Public resentment may appear because of feelings that those benefiting from redistributive planning are undeserving. This will be fanned by the media.

There is indeed evidence in major Western cities of increased resentment towards redistributive planning for those in need, on the part of those who are less needy. A growth in resentment has occurred in the last decade towards the homeless in gentrifying American cities, and towards policies improving their access to public space (Smith 1996). In a major study of service provision in the United States for homeless people and those living with AIDS, Takahashi (1998, p. 130) has shown how certain groups needing provision of services and facilities, are deemed more deserving of such help than others by residents of their neighbourhoods, and how this affects NIMBY sentiments directed towards services and facilities. She says:

> The intensification in community rejection of facilities that provide human services may be due in large part to the representation in the popular media and within the wider populace of service-dependent populations and how that representation affects popular consciousness ... there remains in public discourse a highly stigmatised understanding of such groups. For example, ... the term 'homeless person' continues to be associated with laziness, alcoholism, drug abuse, mental disability, criminalism, and even perversion (Takahashi, 1998, p. 130).

These two American examples are not about governmental discourses justifying planning interventions or decision rules, but rather are commentaries about the views of 'the public' about those less fortunate. Governments in their planning discourses may make concerted efforts to dislodge such public opinions, however.

The important point is that governmental rationales for redistributive policies do contribute to the formation of public views about the entitlements of less-resourced citizens to public support. The politics of these discourses are of major significance for their success. Nancy Fraser's well-known analysis of the politics of need interpretation (1989) in American welfare policy illustrates well the ways that discourses about entitlement surround the decision rules chosen for implementing certain welfare regimes.

Of longstanding interest is the question of why it is that certain urban realities become discursively labelled as 'problems' and pursued in urban policy and planning. Jacobs, Kemeny and Manzi (2003) have recently analysed this process in the context of 'housing problems' in the UK. Of course it is important for those in power to define a problem that can actually be portrayed as having a practical 'solution'. Even so, it is the case that certain population groups and certain resource allocation matters do seem to attract disproportionate attention as 'problems'. The 'problems' of single mothers gaining priority allocation to public housing, and of 'anti-social behaviour' on public housing estates are two examples from the UK. The context of the former is the demonizing of the single mother as a specific social group. The context of the latter is the blaming of communities and 'problem individuals' for the stresses on large public housing estates for which funding has been reduced, rather than blaming government policies. The development of these discursive positions saw the introduction of certain policy responses. In the case of the negative stereotyping of single mothers, The Housing Act 1996 gave two-parent families priority in the allocation of public housing (Jacobs *et al.*, 2003, 438); in the case of the identification of anti-social behaviour:

> Legislation has been passed that enables landlords to introduce a swathe of measures to address this 'problem'. Alongside the 1996 Housing Act there has been the 1996 Noise Act, Protection from Harassment Act and 1998 Crime and Disorder Act bringing into effect injunctions, youth curfews and anti-social behaviour orders to criminalise behaviour which had previously constituted civil offences. ... [Further] The term 'nightmare neighbours' is symptomatic of a discourse that has powerful resonance in the media (Jacobs *et al.*, 2003, pp. 440–1).

Not only are discourses persuasive aspects of redistributional planning in the case of groups of people, they are also influential in characterizing places. An excellent illustration is by Gibson and Cameron (2001). Policy (and also academic) discourses of economic restructuring have depicted certain towns and their communities in southeastern Australia as lacking in appropriate assets and resources. In this region, unemployment has risen over the past two decades as government-owned utilities companies have been sold and reduced in size. Many people oppose the ways in which discourses of economic restructuring attribute negative features, or 'lacks', to these areas and their citizens as an explanation for current economic difficulties. Concepts other than that of economic restructuring have been developed instead, in local discourses that try to identify existing community assets and the subjectivities consistent with these (Gibson and Cameron, 2001). Such discursively-positioned community development strategies, building on the usefulness of existing community assets for developing viable economic and social activities and businesses, contrast with community development strategies made in response to policy discourses of restructuring, which see these areas and communities as disadvantaged and requiring outside assistance before any worthwhile futures can be built.

So discourses define the 'problems' that planning strategies fix. In periods like the present in the capitalist democracies, in which governments (often termed neoliberal) are emphasizing efficiency in and targeting of expenditure so as to produce budget surpluses, there is less and less discursive emphasis of universal provision for the population, of the kind that underpinned the post World War 2 welfare state. Redistributive planning is less an overall policy philosophy that applies universally, now, than it is a sharp targeting of the least resourced for assistance. With this shift in understanding of redistributive allocations can come public resentment that such assistance needs to be given at all. Of course, there is variation between countries and governments in the degree to which redistributive planning is seen as 'abnormal' special assistance, as opposed to a ubiquitous policy requirement.

Conclusion

Is it possible to identify any possibilities for transformation, for altering the causes of maldistribution so as to move towards a just diversity, in the redistributive policies of planning we have discussed?

As mentioned at the start of this chapter, the redistributive logics of the post World War 2 period have changed in the succeeding years. The possibilities for those in governments seeking to plan cities redistributively have altered along with this broader shift in political-economic approaches and methodologies of governance. On the one hand, contemporary politics and methods of governing often constrain the decision rules and discourses that can be used to plan redistributively. On the other hand, redistribution is still present as a social logic of much urban planning, whether or not the governments implementing such plans are fiscally more conservative than their Keynesian counterparts of the mid-twentieth century are understood to have been. And with the critiques of top-down planning, since the 1970s, and the increase in consultative processes in planning, has come a politicization of decision rules and planning discourses that increases the possibilities for biases in these rules and discourses to be redressed.

The 'universal citizen' was the individual in question in redistributive planning of the mid twentieth century, based on the assumptions that redistribution is about everyone being entitled to, and even desiring, access to the same set of resources, the same 'city', and that some are denied access to it by constraints which need to be ameliorated. Locational disadvantage and accessibility were key principles of the planning that resulted. These principles remain important anchors for ideas of a better diversity – there persist constraints on people obtaining access to resources, even if the levels and forms of resources desired are not the same for everyone as is now recognized, and even if everyone does not want to live in the city in the same way.

Changes in governance cultures have perhaps made the task of redistribution in planning more complex, particularly in parliamentary democracies whose public sectors have taken an increased focus on efficiency and targeting of redistributive benefits, rather than universal provision. In addition, planning for purposes like urban redevelopment, which for decades have been redistributive in intent, may increasingly also be combined with purposes that seem to contradict that intent, like gentrification or replacing public-sector provision with market-based provision. Despite this, we wish to argue that there have been benefits in the broadening of understanding of the possible stigmatizing effects of planning policies directed to disadvantaged groups and areas. These enhanced understandings have followed the critiques of the modernist welfare state and its modes of planning for the universal citizen, and they hinge on the development of concepts of recognition, and of planning practice and activism associated with this. Before we move to consider, in Chapters 4 and 5, planning that takes recognition as its starting point, let us reflect on some ways that redistributive planning has been, and can be, transformative, despite its current context of neoliberal governance.

We have noted in Chapter 1 Lees' comment that: '[the] diversity of different "diversities" is often under-theorised as are the benefits of, and relationships among, social and cultural diversity, economic diversification, mixed use and multi-purpose zoning, political pluralism and democratic public space' (2003a, p. 613). A focus on redistribution in planning for cities that acknowledge diversity means that we will be reminded always to think analytically about which forms of diversity are acceptable to us, and which are not. Those which are not are those that disadvantage certain people and places and increase inequality between them, however this might come about. Redistributive planning, taking up the newer social logics of recognition and encounter, in fact is transforming conceptually because it gives us a new understanding of the 'public good', one that does not rely upon the homogeneous conception of the citizen that characterized Keynsian welfare states. Redistributive planning can be transformative through its insistence that although a politics of recognition calls for respect for diversity amongst people, there are some forms of diversity that are more accepted than others and there are some that are associated with disadvantage and stigma. Redistributive planning can be transformative in emphasizing that although a politics of encounter calls for city spaces that encourage interaction between individuals and groups, those city spaces will almost always exclude particular social groups nevertheless. A focus on the existence of diversity in places of encounter does not translate into that diversity being accepted by so-called 'mainstream' residents and workers in those places, or even by their leaders.

In planning practice there are also examples of the ways that redistributive planning has been transformative, accepting that transformation of any kind is a long process and that the consequences of any planning act alone are hard to identify. As we move to Chapter 3, where three examples of redistributive planning – urban renewal, child care planning and deinstitutionalization – will be considered, we claim that in each of these areas of planning for the social life of cities there are transformative elements. Perhaps these were unintended and unanticipated: for how the planning actions of one period and place will be influential in another period and place is unknowable. Nevertheless it is important to analyze successes where they have occurred, as well as criticizing what has occurred for its limitations.

3 Planning for Redistribution in Practice

Three examples of redistributive approaches to planning cities will be presented in this chapter. The first, urban renewal, has sought to increase the public good in cities by improving living conditions in areas of poor housing. Insofar as it envisages its beneficiaries as citizens of particular disadvantage, urban renewal policy and practice does not designate these citizens in other terms. So, it is treated here as redistribution *qua* redistribution. Issues of group recognition and encounter are raised from time to time in circumstances of urban renewal, but the connection of recognition and encounter to redistribution is explored more explicitly in the chapter's other examples. The second example, local child care planning, seeks to redistribute advantage towards those requiring an accessible service in order to return to the workforce. It is redistributive planning directed particularly at women, recognizing their need for accessible child care if they are to discharge their caring obligations effectively whilst working in the paid labour force. So this second example of redistributive planning is one that combines its redistributive aim with that of recognizing the needs of a particular group (women working in the paid labour force). The third example is deinstitutionalization of people with disabilities

Box 3.1: Case studies in Chapter 3		
Redistribution	*Redistribution and recognition*	*Redistribution and encounter*
Urban renewal	Local child care planning	Deinstitutionalization

(focusing particularly on mental illness), so that these individuals might live outside an institution and in 'the community'. Seeking to redress the disadvantage of those who have lived for long periods in institutions because of a disability, this planning has also sought to facilitate encounter for the deinstitutionalized, by creating more opportunities for interaction with other members of the public.

Two decision rules were identified in Chapter 2 as means used in planning for the redistribution of resources to benefit the disadvantaged. Both are evident in the examples presented in this chapter. The first decision rule, that of equity in the allocation of resources to localities, is present perhaps most visibly in planning for local child care provision, in certain periods. The second decision rule, social mix, reveals itself in planning for urban renewal, not always in ways that actually benefit the poor. In using the decision rule of social mix as a means to improve housing and therefore the public good in a city, urban renewal actions can in some circumstances advance the interests of higher-income individuals over lower-income ones, therefore contradicting those redistributive aims that seek to improve the lot of the poor primarily. This does not always occur in urban renewal planning, but can happen in situations in which low-income individuals or households are removed from their homes without their wishing it. The accounts we present of the process of deinstitutionalization, in which little attention has often been paid to the urban outcomes of this national social policy setting, demonstrate market equity as a *de facto* decision rule in the distribution of community residential and health facilities for the deinstitutionalized. Like urban renewal, deinstitutionalization is demonstrated to have been less successful than its broad redistributive intentions might have suggested it would be, because of the common reliance, in the implementation of deinstitutionalization, on the housing market to determine the living circumstances of deinstitutionalized people.

What will be clear in the examples to follow is that political and economic realities in the capitalist democracies make very difficult the implementation of planning policies that have major redistributive intentions. That is not to say that these important redistributive intentions should be abandoned. Nor is it to forget that some redistributive gains are made for some people and places in these situations, even if we criticize what happened as we look back in retrospect overall and regret what might have been.

Looking at the realities of what has happened in past examples of urban renewal provides important insights for those contemplating such planning, with redistributive intentions, today.

Redistribution: urban renewal

Planners and urban policy-makers have long worked with the question of whether spatial concentration of disadvantaged people increases the disadvantage experienced by those people. This is the long-debated question of social mix, as we have noted. An important part of redistributive urban planning, intended to counter the concentration of poverty in places and to improve the quality of housing and urban life for poor people in the public interest, has been urban renewal, now sometimes tagged as neighbourhood renewal. We consider whether planning for urban and neighbourhood renewal, in a number of contexts since the 1950s, has succeeded in its redistributive aims. The earlier examples described in the discussion to follow seem to have been less successful than the later ones – probably in part because those involved in the later cases were aware of the failings of earlier examples, and so avoided repeating those mistakes!

In 1962, sociologist and urban planner Herbert Gans's book, *The Urban Villagers*, reported on his study of the lives and society of low-income Italian-Americans resident in the West End of Boston. This neighbourhood and social group were subject to clearance and removal, respectively, in the late 1950s, so that '[b]y the summer of 1960, only rubble remained where two years ago had lived more than 7,000 people' (Gans, 1962, p. 285). This particular example of urban renewal in Boston remains one of the most famous cases of this form of redistributive urban planning as practised in the 1950s and 1960s in the cities of some Western nations. Gans's account raises many questions for urban planners which remain relevant when we examine initiatives in urban or neighbourhood redevelopment. His overall concern is whether these forms of redistributive planning are actually redistributive at all, in the sense of benefiting those of low-income and few resources who live in the areas being redeveloped. Or rather, how we can be sure we ask the right questions about urban renewal so as to ensure that the beneficiaries are those of a low-income rather than others?

Gans, identifying as a middle-class academic himself, observed a middle-class bias in both the city planners of Boston at the time and in what he called the 'caretaking agencies' in the West End – 'missionaries from the outside world' (p. 142) in institutions such as charities, welfare organizations and the public library which existed to provide advice and caring assistance to West End residents. Staff of these organizations saw the West End as a slum, and believed its residents would benefit if the buildings of the area were removed and they were relocated. In contrast to this 'official' view of the West End, and without condoning or romanticizing the lack of resources available to the West End's residents, Gans found that:

> West Enders did not think of their area as a slum and resented the city's description of the area because it cast aspersions on them as slum dwellers. They were not pleased that the apartment buildings were not well kept up outside, but, as long as the landlord kept the building clean, maintained the mechanical system, and did not bother his tenants, they were not seriously disturbed about it. People kept their apartments as up-to-date as they could afford to, and most of the ones I saw differed little from lower-middle-class ones in urban or suburban neighborhoods. (Gans, 1962, p. 20)

People who lived there liked the high density of the West End, being able to maintain the privacy they needed despite the close proximity of their neighbours. They did not see housing as evidence of their social status. They looked inward to the neighbourhood in their socializing, and had little interest in governments, bureaucracy or politics beyond the very local. Distaste was expressed in the West End for the consumerism and suburban tastes of the middle-class, and a resistance to moving away from the society of the neighbourhood (pp. 218–9). But by the mid-1950s 'all of Boston was convinced that the West End was a slum which ought to be torn down not only for the sake of the city but also for the good of its own residents. This belief was supported by the general appearance of the area, by studies that had been made in the West End by public and private agencies, and by stories that appeared in the press' (Gans, 1962, p. 287). As we noted in Chapter 2, such discourses can have powerful effects in both framing the nature of policy problems and setting the direction of policy responses.

Boston's redevelopment authority acquired the West End's buildings from their owners and set in motion a relocation plan for residents, who could move into public or private housing as they desired but had to move away from the West End. In a sense, the goal of social mix was to be achieved through enforcing (rather than enhancing) the mobility of the poor to other localities. Until the very end, the West End's residents did not believe the process would begin, so dismissive were they of what they saw as the time-wasting machinations of bureaucracies and governments. When the formal relocation process did begin, most residents moved without calling on the city's agencies to help them relocate, something that was common also in other urban renewal projects (Gans, 1962, p. 304). The area was levelled, with only a few buildings, including the Catholic church, spared. Shortly, high-rise apartment buildings, privately owned and for the wealthy, and sited along the Charles River, were built.

What are the lessons for the planning of urban redevelopment in cities drawn by Gans from his powerful analysis? He did feel that 'the redevelopment decision itself was not entirely justifiable, but also that the planning being done for the West End did not take into account the needs of the residents who, among others, were supposed to benefit from slum clearance' (Gans, 1962, p. 306). For the West Enders themselves, a better planning solution would have been to rehabilitate most buildings in the area and remove only those which were structurally unsound, and to re-house residents in the existing buildings. Small parks, playgrounds and parking areas could have been created where unsound buildings were cleared. The residents could have stayed in a physically improved neighbourhood.

But urban renewal is supposed to benefit more people than existing residents, in the 'public interest'. Evaluating the way this 'public interest' was conceived by the planners and caretakers of the city's agencies, Gans found (and was critical of) their assumption that 'high-income residents benefit the city, while low-income ones are only a burden and a source of public expense' (p. 319). The important role of low-income people in the city was ignored here – they hold down important service sector jobs; shop, and therefore support small businesses; and generate demand for low-income housing. In addition, communication between the relocating West End residents and the city's redevelopment agencies was poor, resulting in little assistance being given to the departing residents. Residents failed to understand the taking of properties

by eminent domain, for example, and were upset by this practice.
Gans developed a long list of decision rules about urban renewal
programs, based on the premise that urban renewal is a desirable
objective, but should be carried out largely and explicitly in the
interests of slum dwellers rather than in the interests of developers,
retailers and those wanting outcomes such as attracting the middle-
classes back to the city. Some were:

- 'Greater emphasis should be placed on the rehabilitation of
  low-rent housing, and less on its clearance' (p. 330);
- '[R]elocation should be minimized unless adequate relocation housing is available in the proper locations, and unless
  the relocation procedures can be shown to improve the living conditions of the people who are moved' (p. 330);
- 'The relocation plan should take priority over the renewal
  phases of the total plan, and no renewal plan should be
  approved by federal or local agencies until a proper relocation scheme has been developed' (pp. 330–1);
- 'This relocation plan should be based on a thorough knowledge of the project area residents, so that the plan fits their
  demands and needs and so that officials will have some understanding of the consequences of their actions before they
  put the plan into effect' (p. 331);
- '[When] residents' housing costs are raised sharply as a result of relocation, the federal and local agencies should set
  up a rent moratorium to allow relocatees to save for future
  rentals before moving' (p. 331).

These procedures (and the many others recommended) would
increase the cost of the renewal program, said Gans, but this is only
fair. It was his view that those being relocated or disadvantaged as
a result of renewal should not be required to subsidize the process
and its private sector beneficiaries. Though his study was of one
urban renewal project only, Gans held that his findings and his recommendations were relevant to many such projects of the time.

If we move to other times and other cities, do we find that
Gans's recommendations have been heeded? Have we learned to
conduct redistributive urban renewal better? Certainly in those
Western cities in which large-scale clearance of 'slums' occurred
in the 1950s and 1960s activist movements emerged to criticize

and modify what had happened, and indeed to alter the way urban planning was subsequently conceived and conducted. (See Miller (2003) examining this process in a Scottish locality and a French one.) Consider now the rehabilitation of a neighbourhood in the Old City of Beijing, analyzed by the eminent architect and urban planner Wu Liangyong (1999) who has since the 1950s been closely involved with the Chinese and Beijing governments, trying to guide urban conservation programs in central Beijing for traditional courtyard housing. Clearly the national and municipal governments in question here are socialist, and in the past can be assumed to have been more sympathetic to the needs of the poor for affordable housing than we might have expected in economies and cities controlled politically and economically in other ways. Central Beijing had poor housing conditions: a survey undertaken in 1990 found that 44 per cent of the one-storey housing in the eight central urban and nearby suburban districts of the city was derelict. In the Old City, 128 renewal areas were designated, most of them located along former city walls and most of them having been slums for long periods:

> [M]ost of the houses have no direct water supply, sewerage, proper kitchens, or other basic facilities of modern life. The road conditions in some of these areas remain extremely poor. The areas lack open space, and high population density results in serious overcrowding. In many families, three generations have to share one room. Countless young married people have no choice but to live separately from their spouses due to the lack of accommodation (Wu, 1999, p. 49).

The reasons for this situation in inner Beijing in the early 1990s were several (Wu, 1999, p. 49). Some residents were immigrants, or people who had been forced to leave the area during the Cultural Revolution and had now returned. They were waiting for better housing, but the waiting lists were very long. Many residents were employed by 'work units' in the district, which owned the housing and made it available to their employees but did not have the resources to upgrade the housing, nor to provide extra housing for the growing families of their workers who therefore crowded into what was available. Against this situation of dire need for affordable housing, Wu and his students held out for the conservation and upgrading of courtyard housing for use by contemporary families. He cites Jane Jacobs's (1961) critique of the widespread slum clearances (such as those described by Gans in Boston) in American cities in the mid-twentieth century, having found inspiration in her call for cautious rehabilitation of urban neighbourhoods rather than 'cataclysmic' investment in large-scale clearance (Wu, 1999, p. 64).

The Ju'er Hutong area of 8.2 hectares in the Old City of Beijing is the case study of Wu and his students, who designed a new courtyard housing prototype with local laneways, supporting this design effort with surveys of and consultations with residents in the area before and after the rehabilitation. Interestingly, most residents of the area were not poor, as they worked in district-owned work units; the problem was that their housing and its surrounds were of poor quality. So the matters of urban renewal in the area were of how to finance the upgrading of the areas' buildings and infrastructure, as well as how actually to design the buildings so as to conserve them and also make them useable for contemporary living. The matter of design is not one we will discuss here. But the matter of the financing of the development and its consequences for relocation and resettlement policy is of interest. What the district-owned work unit (which owned the housing) was persuaded to do was to establish a housing cooperative in the area both to manage the financing of the redevelopment and the needs of residents. This began in 1989–90.

Construction commenced in 1991. Post-occupancy surveys of residents once resettled back in the area generated a very positive response. But given the requirement that those resettling in the area buy their housing units, there were some who could not afford to do this and therefore moved away from the Old City. Though those relocating gained good quality housing, they were displeased at leaving the Old City. Says Wu (1999, p. 172), speaking now about renewal projects in Beijing more broadly, 'the relocation problems that have more recently emerged with other renewal projects stem from a lack of resettlement options and the great distances that relocated residents have had to move. The result has been a growing resentment towards a situation in which "the wealthy stay and the poor must go".' As was the case in Boston, the poor were typically the ones forced to move in renewal projects.

If the lessons Wu drew in the early 1990s from the Ju'er Hutong project were about the importance and possibility of ensuring that the price of the housing, once rehabilitated, was within reach of resettling residents, then by the late 1990s his views were less optimistic. On the one hand, the political climate in Beijing had changed, making the outlook for the forms of 'organic' urban renewal he had been advocating less promising (1999, p. 202). On the other hand, the growth of the private real estate sector in the city posed an even greater problem. Where, early in the 1990s, all urban renewal projects in Beijing 'stressed social benefits and aimed at immediate reconstruction or rehabilitation of the most dilapidated houses ... [and it] was a fundamental premise that the majority of the original residents should move back afterwards' (Wu, 1999, p. 202), by the late 1990s the interest of the growing real estate industry in inner city land and property had removed this earlier orientation. Obtaining the greatest profit from inner area land and housing is inconsistent with rehabilitating and conserving modest housing for lower-income residents. Conflicts between developers and residents were increasing, and the relocation of residents to far-away affordable housing on the city's outskirts created resentment on an ever larger scale. Developers were gaining redevelopment rights in the old city areas and yet failing to undertake the work they had agreed to do. And in the metropolis as a whole, urban renewal took the form of large-scale clearance and redevelopment projects.

Against this background of some disappointment, Wu (1999, p. 211) included the following as the decision rules that should be guiding urban renewal in Beijing, especially in the Old City:

- 'Reduce the speed and scale of urban renewal';
- 'Seek new ways to develop real estate in the Old City, including reinforcing the openness of the land development and oversight systems, curtailing quick profits in development ... (this will involve regulation)';
- 'Continue the original small-scale renewal policy; enhance the definition and safeguarding of historical and cultural districts';
- 'the land development rights to which developers are entitled should be re-examined'.

In Wu's case study of urban renewal in the Old City of Beijing, the agreement with Gans (1962) is clear in that the primary focus of urban renewal should be on obtaining benefits for the existing, not-wealthy residents of dilapidated urban neighbourhoods. The questions to be kept to the fore in the thinking of planners about these complex situations involve the improvement of living conditions for those existing residents. But the primary objectives of bettering the lives of existing residents have been pushed aside here in favour of other urban interest groups and of definitions of the broader 'public interest' that privilege those interest groups over the existing residents of the areas. In the event, an appropriate redistribution has not been the primary outcome of this urban renewal planning. In any situation of urban renewal, tensions will exist between existing residents and their requirements for continuing affordable housing preferably in the locations they have long occupied, and the interests of other groups like real estate developers in the profits that could be gained by transforming the area into housing for the wealthy. The role of governments in directing outcomes from this situation is clearly of immense importance.

Turn now to the contemporary United Kingdom, where urban policy and renewal has taken a prominent place in the efforts to reshape the nation's cities being carried out by the Labour government since 1997. Unlike the examples of urban renewal described already, in the current British case the reduction of inequality in cities through a focus on the neighbourhood or community scale is a matter of policy initiated actively at the national level. Over several years reports had been made of growing and geographically evident disparities between rich and poor in cities. Public housing estates were singled out as especially disadvantaged and disadvantaging. It was felt by the late 1990s that past policies had been inadequate, and the incoming Labour government established a Social Exclusion Unit to examine the possibilities of regenerating the inner cities, in particular, but also other deteriorated urban localities.

It is not possible here to summarize the many polices that resulted (but see Imrie and Raco, 2003). Importantly for our purposes, the Labour Government have implemented area-based programs to alleviate poverty and disadvantage in the poorest places and populations (in addition to a range of other government-wide approaches, such as the development of a form of citizenship in which communities and individuals work alongside government agencies to take responsibility for change and betterment). For example, following identification of 'food deserts' – local areas where nutritious food was unavailable because it was too expensive for under-resourced local residents and/or because it was not stocked in those shops that were physically accessible to residents – planners in local authorities were directed by the central government to use improvements in local shopping areas as a central feature of their applications for urban regeneration funding (Wrigley, Guy and Lowe, 2002, pp. 2103–4). In addition, efforts by the British government are being made to reduce financial services disparities, encouraging the banking sector to seek competition and enterprise in disadvantaged areas of cities and to move towards greater social responsibility (Marshall, 2004, p. 246).

Here, in these area-based programs, are measures similar in their local scale and focus to those observed in Boston and Beijing. But, in the British case, their principal target is very much broader and more ambitious than housing alone (though poor quality housing is indeed the subject of many local council endeavours, and planning for the provision of affordable housing in newly-built estates of homeowners is a priority). Different kinds of locational disadvantage are being tackled. Also, in the British case the question of large-scale clearance of an area's buildings and the total relocation of its residents is not an aim; that was a policy phase in the UK in the 1950s and 1960s, as it was in Boston, and has been widely criticized. What is different in the British case from the Boston and Beijing ones is that efforts are being made, it seems, to reform the people in urban communities themselves, rather than merely their built environments. So, much effort in new programs is being expended in trying to equip local citizens to work with municipal councils and other governmental and non-governmental agencies to effect change in their areas (Imrie and Raco, 2003 p. 21).

There are some stringent criticisms of this overall policy approach and its specifics by analysts who would rather these efforts at redistribution took a different form. For some analysts, it is a deficiency that the approach identifies as 'the problem' the lack of participation by people in processes of governance in some neighbourhoods, and those people's shortcomings in this regard, rather than focusing on their material poverty and disadvantage and why that should persist (Kearns, 2003; Morrison, 2003). A further criticism is provided in one case example about affordable housing. Imrie and Raco (2003, p. 28) note a local activist's resentment of a municipal government's interest in reducing the number and spatial concentration of public-housing tenants and units in an area, replacing them by owner-occupied housing. The activist felt that the municipal government was trying to reduce poverty in the locality by attracting middle-income people and owner-occupied housing, so limiting the possibilities for poorer people to live there in public housing. If the municipal strategies succeeded, local poverty would certainly be reduced, but low-income public-housing tenants would not be able to remain in the area to benefit from the regeneration going on there. This activist foreshadows the possible outcomes of social mix approaches.

The discursive strategies of British urban policy since the mid-twentieth century have also been subject to critical review (Lees, 2003b, p. 66). Until the 1970s, urban renewal and redevelopment was undertaken by the public sector and directed at redevelopment of large areas of inner city 'slums'; since the 1980s urban regeneration and 'renaissance' programs have used public investment to attract private sector partners to render urban areas attractive places to live, usually for higher-income people. Despite their words about reducing poverty and inequality, and improving the places in which poor people live, in essence these policies are viewed by their critics as seeking to make urban places and populations middle-class.

Here, then, we are back to Gans's observations that the planners for and caretakers of the poor and their living places view the subjects of their urban renewal policies with an anxious middle-class gaze. In every situation of urban renewal, as Lees (2003b) says, there is the likelihood of gentrification. But be that as it may, and no matter what the policy discourses suggest, the decision rules about urban renewal policies have been laid out clearly by past analysts of the phenomenon. If these policies are to redistribute resources towards those of lesser means, then the criteria provided by Gans and by Wu are the ones to keep in mind. The 'community assets' approach to place-based economic restructuring proposed by Gibson and Cameron (2001) and discussed in Chapter 2, where the focus of policy discussions starts from a position of identifying locational assets rather than 'lacks', is suggestive of how redistribution through urban renewal might be discursively framed more productively.

How can redistributive urban renewal policies, when they really are redistributive in benefiting low-income groups in their neighbourhoods, be transformative? As is indicated in the case studies of the West End of Boston and the Old City of Beijing, allowing redistribution to be informed by recognition and encounter may assist redistributive policies to serve the interests of the less-resourced more directly. If urban renewal policies and practices clearly identify the populations they serve, the redistribution can be designed to fit the precise needs and character of that social group. Gans saw this in capturing, through close analysis of its class characteristics, the society of Italian-Americans he observed in the West End. Wu understood this in his emphasis on detailed surveys to understand the ways of living of the residents of Ju'er Hutong in Beijing, before design or construction began in their area. Though these analysts do not use the term 'recognition' to conceptualize their attention to the characteristics of the groups served by urban renewal policies, in fact recognition of those social groups in their neighbourhood places is what they were doing. In addition, paying attention to forms of encounter likely to be undertaken by these groups is a feature of their Boston and Beijing work. In each case, the question of whether residents will continue to live in the area once renewed, and if not what they would face in the areas in which they resettled, were paramount in the planning of the redistributive measures being taken (or should have been, had the urban renewal schemes followed Gans's and Wu's thinking). In both cases, the forms of interaction habitually experienced by residents before urban renewal occurred were studied, because of a belief that justice would be served if these patterns of interaction were able to continue post-renewal. What can be concluded, then, is that a properly redistributive form of urban renewal, which in its redistributive outcomes could transform lives rather than marginalizing original residents, would benefit from close consideration of recognition and encounter as intrinsic parts of that redistribution. In the following two examples, then, we explore the relationship of redistributive policies to recognition and encounter in more detail.

Redistribution and recognition: local child care planning for working women

Providing child care services locally is a form of redistributive planning that seeks particularly to assist women to participate in the paid workforce, when they have small children of pre-school age.

It seeks to improve gender equity through enhanced access to child care, thereby making the possibilities for men and women to work in the paid labour force more equitable. It prevails in those societies and cities in which care of young and elderly dependants is removed from the extended family structures in which it might still be expected that women at home would care for these dependants. And it prevails in those societies and cities in which nuclear families are no longer uniformly characterized by a male breadwinner and a female domestic homeworker and carer. The governments of many Western countries have had to respond to the 'care crisis' resulting from the decline over the past several decades of the nuclear family form in which women served as unpaid carers (Mahon, 2005). Redistribution towards greater gender equity, which is gender equity taking the form of equal opportunity between localities, can be assisted through child care arrangements if child care facilities are universally available to the children of all parents, if that child care is affordable and if there is provision for the involvement of parents in the control and management of the facilities (Mahon, 2002, p. 5).

Major capital expenditure on child care centres, regulation of child care standards, and schemes of subsidy or taxation benefits to child care users by governments have generally been the responsibility of national or state governments. And, in addition to the discourses of gender equity that can support these policies, there have been supportive national discourses sourced in economic policy (for having adequate child care will influence the decision of women with children to stay in the paid labour force), or population policy (for the availability of child care may influence women's decisions to bear children, thus influencing the future demographic profile of the labour force and the nation, and thus the society's capacity to support through tax revenues such things as its pension schemes for the aged).

There are considerable variations in the child care arrangements of different countries, associated with varying distributional outcomes. Mahon (2002, pp. 6–7) proposes a typology of 'liberal', 'conservative' and 'social democratic' regimes of state provision of child care, for 13 countries. In 'liberal' settings, such as those found in Australia, Britain, Canada and the US, public support of child care is generally through tax deductions or payments directly to parents, with some extra benefits for those who are vulnerable or on very low-incomes. Non-parental care is the norm. There is dependence on the market for supply of child care services. This is resulting in growing inequality in access to care, with those able to pay obtaining high quality, well-regulated child care, and those unable to pay receiving unregulated or informal sector care that may be of poorer quality. Low wages for child care workers are the reality, in both formal and informal care. Increasingly, in nations that have moved towards the low-income or single-parent recipients of government benefits being obliged to enter the paid workforce (workfare), child care is linked to this compulsory workforce participation. In 'conservative' settings, like those of Belgium, France, Italy and Japan in Mahon's (2002) classification, there is still the assumption of a female, familial carer for young children in the home, though there may also be high quality, publicly-supplied, part-time, pre-school education. Other than this pre-school education, which would not permit a parent to work in the paid labour force without supplementary child care, child care services are undeveloped. In 'social democratic' settings, non-parental child care is offered universally, with services both provided and funded by government. Denmark and Sweden are countries with such arrangements, and in both places child care is an accepted form of social infrastructure, underpinning labour market prosperity as well as moves towards gender equity (Mahon, 2002, p. 7). Looking at European countries, the thinking underpinning shifts in child care provision since the mid-twentieth century has moved (to different degrees in different countries) from the 'postwar dream' of 'children at home with their mothers', to the acknowledgement of the importance of gender equality in the period post 1960 (Jenson and Sideau, 2001a, pp. 243–7). But accompanying these broad changes have been the growing concerns of governments as to how to reduce government spending on child care – to develop cheaper forms of provision, and (relatedly) to decentralize provision increasingly to local authorities (Jenson and Sideau, 2001a, p. 255). Going 'against the current' is the Canadian province of Quebec, which since 1997 has implemented a new family policy including universal access to 'educational' child care available to all at the flat rate of $5 per day (Jenson, 2002). Before this, Quebec, since the late 1970s, had a child care system of the 'liberal' and market-dependent kind, like the other Canadian provinces still do.

So, the overall supply of child care is a national concern, and a question for economic and population policy rather than for urban, regional or planning policy alone. But the provision of child care is also a profoundly local matter, requiring planning for service accessibility for women (as it is still primarily women) who have hectic, spatially and temporally circumscribed, lives juggling paid work and caring. Feminist geographers have detailed the characteristics of women's lives in Western cities since the last quarter of the twentieth century, to demonstrate this complexity and its rootedess in place and locality (see Rose, 1984). Indeed, even policy analysts focused on the scale of the nation or the state/province in their study of the provision of child care services recognize that 'it is precisely the details of services, the eligibility rules, the forms of delivery, and their potential consequences for fostering equality or entrenching inequalities that matter' (Jenson and Sideau, 2002b, p. 5). National policy regimes are understood to have significance through their implementation at sub-national scales. In some cases, the provision of child care in major cities takes a different direction from that specified nationally, and is more generous, though this situation is difficult to maintain (Mahon, 2005). Local caring 'cultures' also affect the way child care is provided and consumed locally (Aitken, 2000).

We take the view that what might be termed the 'local state', that assemblage of local government departments and elected officials, along with the activist and volunteer groups that influence them and work with them, is the place where child care provision is actually planned and implemented in cities. This is the site of everyday social praxis that Mountz (2003) draws our attention to, in her conceptualization of the state in action. It is where urban policy-makers and planners, seeking to improve gender equity on the ground, in places, will find themselves considering their policy and implementation options. Of course, the policy provisions of higher levels of government will be influential in what can be achieved locally. Nevertheless, there are options available locally that can make redistribution through child care more or less effective, in support of women (and also of men) in their attempts to combine caring and paid work.

The importance of local decision-making and planning is illustrated with reference to the different child care opportunities of selected suburbs in Melbourne, in the late 1980s (Fincher, 1991; 1996). By the late 1980s in Australia, the emphasis of the earlier part of that decade on expanding publicly funded child care centres, with federal/state sharing of the costs of building new centres and the federal government retaining the task of recurrent funding of centres, had subsided. The preferences of the federal government were now for expanding family day care, in which carers looked after children in their own homes. Thus, federal funds for the building of centres declined, and federal subsidies for the staff of child care centres, that had previously set high staffing standards by paying for qualified staff, had been replaced with general and limited subsidies to centres based on the number of places they provided for children. In the State of Victoria (of which Melbourne is the capital) the state government set building standards for child care centres, as it long had done, and in the late 1980s set staffing standards for privately-run centres which at the time did not receive federal subsidies and so were not required to comply with federal guidelines.

Though major responsibility for shaping the extent and form of child care provision in Australia in the 1980s rested (as it does now) with federal and state governments through their policy regimes, local governments responded in different ways to this national agenda and to pressures from their constituents. Accordingly, local government areas could have quite different levels of provision in the same period, and could also take a range of views on whether caring was rightly provided non-parentally, or whether it should be the responsibility, still, of women in the family. Their decision rules about what constituted equity for their locality could vary. It should be noted that in every urban municipality at this time, expanded child care provisions to cater for the needs of working parents, especially working women, were needed by those working parents. And most potential users of services seem to have preferred publicly-run child care centres. But different local governments recognized this 'need' more than others in their actions. How did they do this? Over the 1980s, when it was possible to obtain funds to build new centres, they either applied for funding from senior levels of government to establish child care centres, or they did not. They established large family day care schemes, or they did not. These actions determined the number of child care places on offer, and their distribution across the municipalities and within them. Local government child care planners (or community services planners as they are sometimes termed) also took decisions about the quality of the services provided locally. Within publicly funded child care centres, the quality of the service rested on decisions about how far the minimum standards were exceeded in matters such as the proportion of qualified staff amongst those employed, and the number of special-purpose staff like cooks, maintenance people and speakers of languages other than English who were employed in the locality's centres. In addition, municipal governments could retain a helpful role in the management of a centre after its establishment, or could choose only to facilitate its construction and then leave it to the centre's director and parent-based committee of management to run. For home-based child care, generous training and resources provided by the municipality to carers were ways quality could be assured. And home-based family child care workers could be council employees or private sub-contractors, with greater benefits to those working as council employees.

One could argue that only wealthy municipalities could consider the possibility of allocating funds to improving quality in their child care services beyond the minimum standards, and to maximize the extent of provision of such services. The counter argument is that this is a matter of priorities. Sometimes, as in the Australian case cited in most of the 1980s, poorer municipalities had a greater likelihood of obtaining funds for child care centres from the federal and state governments than did wealthy municipalities. The case of two Melbourne municipalities, described below, does provide one example of a wealthy municipality (Camberwell) being less committed to the provision of quality child care than a poorer municipality (Sunshine).

Under the federal government's 'planning' approach to allocation of funds for building child care centres, operating in the early to mid 1980s, both municipalities were designated 'high need', reflecting the lack of local initiative taken in Camberwell to obtain child care centres over the previous years, and the continuing need in Sunshine for assistance to build centres even though their local efforts had long been considerable. In Sunshine over 20 years from the early 1970s, 11 child care centres were established, six of these the result of submissions for funds by local government planners to the federal government, and five proposed by local community groups who were then assisted by local government planners to obtain federal government funds. In Camberwell, over the same period, only one child care centre was established before 1983, with three more appearing in the mid 1980s. Camberwell's municipal government failed to make submissions itself for centres in its needy zones, and the centres that were established were initiated by groups outside local government, often negotiating directly with the federal government and without assistance from the local government in Camberwell.

These different outcomes in the two municipalities reflect the social relations of the local state in those places. In Sunshine, elected councillors and municipal community services planners were responsive to the requirements of local residents, as expressed to them in rounds of consultation about child care and the circumstances of local working parents. In Camberwell, despite lobbying by local community groups and detailed findings from the council's own consultations that a range of local child care services was needed, these expressions of need, particularly from local working women, were largely ignored by 'women in the home'-oriented local politicians (Fincher, 1991, p. 369).

As the overarching interest by contemporary Australian governments in reducing government expenditure has become more widespread, it is likely that those localities with skilled, middle-class populations might be the ones to have better child care services. They are the localities containing volunteers more likely to have the capacity to negotiate with governments, oversee the construction of buildings or the ongoing financial operation and management of child care businesses. Similarly in Canada, in 1980s Montreal: 'while it would be a dangerous exaggeration to speak of the "gentrification of daycare", it must be admitted that the cost structure, the emphasis on "voluntarism" in the setting-up and maintaining of services and the locational bias this tends to bring with it, do generate tendencies in favour of white-collar workers and professionals' (Rose, 1993, p. 205). For the Canadian province of Ontario, spatial inequities have appeared from the early 1990s as the trend towards decentralization of responsibility for child care provision goes on, and local governments' own initiatives become very significant. There, access to child care centres is better in areas where there is a high proportion of the labour force in white-collar occupations, because these people have the administrative skills to establish and run the services in the manner required increasingly in a decentralized system. On the other hand, provision of child care centres has been negatively related overall to labour force participation, because parents do not have the time to organize the establishment and provision of the services under such decentralized governance arrangements (Skelton, 1996, p. 74).

Now, the existence of local variations in child care services provision within a country or region – even where stringent funding guidelines from senior levels of government that might suggest that municipalities would have the same service outcomes and delivery processes – is not important for its own sake. Our reason for pointing it out is to suggest that local policy-makers engaged in the planning of child care services have options in what they can provide and the social relations they can establish in association with that provision. Of course, these options are limited by local finances and politics: few municipalities are likely to be able to provide universal access to publicly funded child care centres of high standard, if that commitment runs counter to state and national policy aims for child care services. But it is possible to set priorities in recognition of working women's needs, and to work towards a local practice that will redistribute resources to support parents with young children by providing appropriate child care services. It is also possible to establish productive relationships between elected councillors, municipal workers involved in the design and provision of child care services, and members of the community – be they in lobby groups, in consultative forums, or volunteers. Recognition of the interests of local working women (and parents, and young children) involves hearing their views, as was apparently not the case in Camberwell in the 1980s. When arrangements for the provision of child care involve the increasing use of volunteers to deliver core services, the task of the local child care planner can become difficult, and the ethics of the situation scream out for attention by governments as volunteers may come to resent the reliance upon them (Fincher, 1996).

Local child care planners and policy-makers work in the midst of such difficult and complex situations. Child care policy and service delivery is redistributive – it works in the interests of certain groups rather than others, sometimes unintentionally, and it varies spatially in the benefits it brings, as well as socially. Awareness of which groups are benefiting from the services, in the form they are being delivered, is a question to be kept at the fore in any planning of these services, if redistributional questions are being kept in mind. This is true even if senior levels of government distribute funds to localities according to a decision rule of *locational equity*. Recognizing the special significance of these services for women, who remain the principal carers of children even as most work in the paid labour force as well, means that *gender equity* matters are bound up with child care provision in any situation. Having a specific concern for gender equity ensures that redistributional efforts towards locational equity can be planned and performed more skilfully, with child care provision, than they otherwise would be.

Moving closer to the present, the situation of child care provision in Australia has altered and decentralized. The federal government policy has, since the mid 1990s, been of fee relief to parents, rather than the direct subsidy of child care centres. Through the 1990s, the only sizeable growth in child care services was in the provision of after school-hours care, and privately-funded centres, principally for-profit child care centres (Brennan, 2002, p. 104). Under a conservative federal government where this trend to market-based provision has continued, in the context of broad family policies that emphasize the importance of women caring in the home and exhibit a declining government commitment to publicly funded child care as a movement towards greater gender equity, many lower-income families are unable to afford child care and the option of paid work for women in such households is reducing (Brennan, 2002). From time to time, announcements are made that efforts to reduce the still-growing dominance of for-profit centres will be made by community groups: in Melbourne, in mid 2006, for example, a new, non-profit organization was having discussions with ten local government councils, trying to provide assistance to them with project and regulatory management and advice that might result in the establishment of new non-profit, publicly-run, child care centres (Gough, 2006). But in the meantime, 'the world's largest child-care operator', ABC Learning, which aimed to own 930 child care centres in Australia and New Zealand by June 2006, and which is seeking to move into the US market, 'plans to spend $140 million buying the Kids Campus group, which has 106 child-care centres' (Farouque, 2006, p. 2). In the flourishing for-profit child care business, the discursive emphasis is firmly on the educational nature of these centres rather than the gender equity of their provision. Business has boomed because federal fee relief subsidies come to parents who use these private centres. In a situation when local governments find it difficult to build and maintain child care centres without direct federal or state subsidy, the private sector does the building instead, in the locations it favours. In some studies, the quality of care in for-profit centres has been criticized, principally because the quality and quantity of staffing can be low in an effort to cut costs. (See Doherty, Friendly and Forer (2002) for a recent Canadian study of this issue).

In another 'liberal' regime of child care provision, Canada, the contemporary situation is perhaps somewhat more varied. As already noted, the province of Quebec in 1997 began a family policy that includes a universally directed program of child care at a flat and very low daily cost to child care users. Other than this, though, one informed assessment of the situation nationally is that 'in spite of the rhetoric of a comprehensive strategy to improve the well-being of all Canadian children, the emerging reality is a system of income support and subsidies targeted at very poor families. [And] the majority of dual earner families are left to buy the child care they can afford, with a little help from the Child Care Expense Deduction' (Mahon and Phillips, 2002, p. 210). At the scale of the metropolis, some of the options available to localities, discussed earlier in the context of Melbourne municipalities, are evident in Toronto (Mahon, 2005). There, from the 1960s and 70s, elected officials and child care policy workers associated with the metropolitan government of Toronto, and later with the city government, combined with activists and a range of powerful non-governmental organizations to develop a social democratic model for child care, which became increasingly at odds with provincial and national preferences over the decades to follow:

> Toronto's alternative model did not emerge overnight. From the mid 1970s on, Toronto began to expand the supply of subsidized child-care spaces substantially, while maintaining higher quality standards than required by provincial legislation. Also constrained by the CAP [Canada Assistance Plan] and the Province to subsidize only those 'in need', Metro came to interpret these rules in a way that maximized the range of those eligible. Moreover, within these limits, access was based on a 'first come, first served' principle characteristic of a public service. The City of Toronto staked out an even more egalitarian profile. Thus, a clear bias in favour of non-profit provision had been established, due in no small part to the Toronto Board of Education. The City also pioneered the day care grant designed to make quality childcare affordable, but not at the expense of childcare providers' wages and working conditions (Mahon, 2005, p. 347).

By the late 1980s, both provincial and national governments were reducing child care funding levels, wanting Toronto to focus its child care provision on the needy and to abandon its 'first come, first served' priority. For a while, the metropolitan government persisted with its preferred approach, making up the shortfall in funding itself. But after economic crisis and recession in Toronto in the early 1990s, and provincial and national budget cuts along with other economic shifts, the local government was unable to continue with its self-subsidy. The conservative provincial government insisted that workfare clients get first priority in child care centres, and provided for this at rates that would only permit low child care wages and reduced working conditions. The Toronto child care system was compromised (Mahon, 2005, p. 349). As in the Australian case, the appearance of conservative governments provincially and nationally in Canada, associated with this shift in child care policy, was also associated with an ideological shift towards familism and caring by women in the home, and away from the concept of non-parental child care as a norm.

From the Melbourne and Toronto cases, what are the lessons to be drawn for local child care policy and planning? The first is that for public provision of child care centres of high quality, great reliance is required on senior levels of government more capable than local authorities of providing the level of funds required. When variations occur in national and state level policies, as they seem quite frequently to do around issues of women's rights (if child care is so cast), local child care planning involves negotiating with those senior levels of government, and with local supporters and residents, to ensure the best outcomes locally. The second lesson is that to extend child care publicly, a great deal of innovative proactive work is required. The cases of Sunshine and Toronto showed how successful that can be, while the case of Camberwell showed the outcomes of failing to be proactive.

The third lesson, which was important also in the urban renewal example, is that redistribution in child care planning requires one's planning values to be identified and fought for. All forms of child care, and all forms of providing funding for child care, are not the same. There is some evidence to show that for-profit child care centres may provide lesser quality care than those centres which are publicly-supported or auspiced by non-profit groups

(Doherty, Friendly and Forer, 2002). Such centres are less likely to identify one of their core values as gender equity, recognizing and respecting the importance of women to these centres, preferring as the Australian case of ABC Learning shows to use the discourse of 'learning' to sell their product. If a particular form of child care provision generates a better outcome for local parents and children, and for working women, than others, then this may be identified by planners and set as the local standard to be sought.

In addition, different forms of redistributive policy are evident from the brief histories of child care policy given above. In both Australian and Canadian examples, a commitment of senior and local levels of government to the aim of universal, publicly funded, child care, has been replaced in these 'liberal' child care regimes by a commitment to targeting child care benefits to those disadvantaged individuals enrolled in workfare schemes. Both are redistributive approaches, but the discourses which shape and support them are quite different, and so are their effects. The latter, targeted approach may be criticized because it separates out vulnerable individuals from the societal 'norm' in their child care receipt, and may also stigmatize the child care centres they use as only being for workfare recipients. (In the US, an unfortunate association between certain services and certain groups of particular disadvantage has been noted, with cleavages along lines of race and class, this the product of the lack of a universal constituency for child care (Michel, 1999, p. 237)). The universal services approach to redistributive social policy through child care will be criticized, by governments especially, as too expensive. Those involved in the planning of local child care services must make important choices about which approach is valued and to be fought for.

Between localities in Canada and Australia, as well as within them, current trends are leading to growing inequalities in access to quality child care. This is a redistributional matter of significance. Planning for child care requires us to know the reasons for this, as they are indicated above, in order to organize to offset these trends however this can be achieved. Recognition of the groups whose particular interests are being sacrificed here is important in designing redistributive strategies for change.

Redistribution and encounter: deinstitutionalization of people with a mental illness

Planning for better lives of people with a disability has been dominated in the past half century by governmental decisions, particularly in English-speaking developed countries, to close the institutions in which many people had been housed and found sheltered employment for most of their lives, and to facilitate the transfer of these institutional residents to 'the community' and into the hands of community care networks of varying kinds (Gleeson, 1999, p. 155). This is deinstitutionalization. Generally, the disability in question is mental illness, though sometimes it is intellectual disability; in many cities the people deinstitutionalized are ex-psychiatric patients. Deinstitutionalization is a policy of redistribution through social mix. Based on a rejection of institutions as providing inadequate care and support to a vulnerable group, it has aimed to improve lives and that requires directing resources towards particular means of achieving this. (Though, as will be clear in what follows, the resourcing of the aftermath of deinstitutionalization decisions has been, everywhere, inadequate). In addition, deinstitutionalization is set in a policy philosophy that has the value of 'encounter' at its core, for it is a statement that living amongst a variety of others is preferable to a constrained way of living amongst those deemed 'alike'.

A particular set of factors set deinstitutionalization in motion 50 years ago. Institutions, though they varied in their quality, had been increasingly criticized for the forms of treatment they offered and their spartan living conditions. New drug treatments had become available that would allow outpatient care of those with mental illnesses, while they lived outside a hospital or totally institutional environment. The human rights of people living with a disability were seen by activists to be improved if they lived outside institutions, in the community, and received the treatment and support they needed by visits to hospitals and community health centres rather than incarceration within institutions. At the same time, in the senior levels of government making decisions about the future of institutions and their inhabitants, there were cost factors emerging. Closure of institutions would save money, and if deinstitutionalized people lived in community settings, there was a possibility of their support being provided in part by volunteers in these local communities. Some decentralization of responsibility for the mentally disabled who would be deinstitutionalized to the local communities in which they would be living, was also welcomed by those senior levels of government. So, as Dear and Wolch (1987, p. 17) say, in their landmark analysis of this situation in the United States and Canada: 'an unstoppable coalition of libertarian concern, treatment philosophy, chemotherapeutic advances, and politics and money came together almost by coincidence'.

Importantly, the outcomes of the deinstitutionalization movement in places have been strongly influenced by the level of hospitality offered to people from institutions by particular local urban communities, and by the planning of housing and access to social services in cities and towns. Many institutions which closed had, when they were built, been in small towns away from major cities. Earlier treatment philosophies had been to offer institutional inmates seclusion and peace in the countryside. By the mid-twentieth century, the growth of cities had engulfed them, and most were then in suburbs. As they closed, their former residents relocated to areas of major cities in which there was access to low-cost housing and treatment facilities. Attempts to create community facilities for deinstitutionalized people – of groups of affordable housing units or facilities for service delivery on a day patient basis – have been met in many locations by hostility and community opposition. NIMBY sentiments have been expressed by residents of some localities, depending on the kinds of facilities proposed and the kinds of deinstitutionalized residents who might occupy local housing. As a lengthy literature on this topic attests (see in particular Dear and Taylor (1982)), local residents in potential host communities express a variety of anxieties about the possible impacts of particular service-dependent groups on their lifestyles and their property values. Mobilization of such community anxiety through local governments' planning decisions has been a major reason (along with broader governmental cost-cutting and jurisdiction-shifting) for the lack of success of community care as an alternative to institutional care in many places (Gleeson, 1999, p. 156 ff.). Deinstitutionalized people have, in this context, located in those run-down inner city locations which lack hostile community activists, taking advantage of the cheaper accommodation there; shopfront services have sprung up to support them in these places.

But as gentrification of inner cities has rendered housing expensive where once it was cheap, even these 'asylums without walls' (as Dear and Wolch (1987, p. 28) have famously termed them) are being rendered inaccessible.

There are a range of actors who have created these outcomes, enacting the processes listed above (Dear and Wolch, 1987). We list them to emphasize the important role of the urban policy and planning professions in determining that the outcomes of deinstitutionalization are redistributive, even though this matter often seems to be primarily about policy decisions in senior levels of government dealing with health care and the manner of its funding. (In the same way, child care planning for cities can seem non-local, as we saw in the previous section, but in fact is profoundly important local policy and local planning). Drawing directly on the work of Dear and Wolch (1987) one set of actors here is that set in the care-giving professions, who formulated, along with activists supporting those with a disability, a powerful argument that interaction with a range of people in a 'normal' life outside an institution was socially just. This was a prescription and an expression of hope for redistribution as encounter. A second group of actors in this context are of course those now outside institutions, clustering in locations where they can. The third group are community residents, who may choose to organize against the presence of people with a disability in their neighbourhood. And the fourth set of actors are land-use planners and the planners and operators of services for the deinstitutionalized, who must respond to this situation, hopefully in such a way as to advance socially just outcomes for the vulnerable group. These actors together formed deinstitutionalization outcomes in the Ontario (Canada) city of Hamilton in the 1980s where an inner city locale hosted a concentration of service-dependent people, and in the Californian (USA) city of San Jose where such a locale was being fragmented. Again, the definitive work of Dear and Wolch (1987) provides these examples.

In Hamilton, social services facilities have concentrated around city hospitals. An area of lodging homes developed near the central business district (CBD), in which large older houses have been converted by private, for-profit operators to house populations dependent on the nearby services. For the provincial government, housing service-dependent people in these privately owned and

run houses was cheaper than the cost of institutional care. After a
spate of community opposition in the 1970s to the concentration
(or 'saturation') of lodging homes in these locations close to
downtown, which also raised concerns about licensing procedures
and accommodation standards, a new city bylaw (taking effect in
1981) set out stricter definitions of a lodging house as opposed to a
residential care facility, and imposed spacing requirements on such
facilities. Importantly, these facilities:

> were classified as 'permitted uses' in all residential and commercial
> zones of the city. This condition was introduced because it was the spe-
> cific intent of the legislation that lodging homes be accepted through-
> out the city (even though 'fair share' provisions did not appear as such).
> Previously the absence of the 'permitted use' designation had frequently
> caused an application for zoning variance to be made; this application
> tended to be a significant factor in alerting community opposition (Dear
> and Wolch, 1987, p. 121).

The growth of this location as a ghetto for the service-dependent
(a majority of whom had previously lived in institutions) continued in Hamilton, with lodging home operators siting their facilities
there because of proximity to clients and their support services.
The new bylaw seemingly allayed community opposition through
the 1980s. The availability of affordable (private) housing, and the
designation in planning law of these facilities as a 'permitted use' had
a great deal to do with the emergence of this particular situation.

In contrast, the Californian city of San Jose was the site in the
1980s of a dismantling ghetto of the service-dependent. The
seedy downtown area of the city had been home to many from
institutions, following the closure of a major hospital in 1971:
'[b]oard-and-care facilities for ex-convicts, ex-drug addicts and
alcoholics, Jobs Corps workers and juvenile wards of the court
existed alongside over 1,000 discharged mental patients and their
programs in the downtown area near San Jose State University'
(Dear and Wolch, 1987, p. 143). As in Hamilton, Ontario, suitable
housing for conversion by private operators to lodging homes
existed in this part of the city, and operators received payments
to house their clients there, often finding this more reliable
rental money than that paid by university students (p. 145). At the
same time, suburban municipalities surrounding this core area
resisted any provision of residences either public or private for

'the elderly, handicapped and mentally ill via zoning ordinances that prohibited these uses or required them to obtain permits in order to operate' (p. 145). Through the 1970s, as the inner city ghetto of the service-dependent grew, complaints developed that the area was a dumping ground for those unwanted elsewhere; by the early 1980s economic development in the region gave rise to gentrification of the inner city housing stock and the appearance of urban renewal plans for the city. Further facilities for the service-dependent were prohibited and in a short time increasing housing values saw the disappearance of both board-and-care facilities and their residents (p. 149). Such residents dispersed, community-based services for them declined and reassignment of them to less appropriate institutions like prisons became common. Local government actions were significant in the outcomes observed, and in fact 'land-use planners may play a role in fostering ghetto decline and the development of more deleterious service patterns for service-dependent groups' (Dear and Wolch, 1987, p. 168).

In the New Zealand city of Auckland, the importance of the intersection of changes in health and welfare policies, with changes to housing markets and planning regulations, have also been noted, as the 1990s have seen the fragmentation of the concentration of service-dependent people previously built up in the inner city (Kearns and Joseph, 2000). In health policy, through the later 1990s, spending on mental health declined dramatically as a proportion of health care expenditure overall, with governments having used the opportunity presented by the growth of community care and deinstitutionalization (which came late to New Zealand) to direct funds elsewhere. In planning policy, community housing has been classified in Auckland as a discretionary use, requiring permission. This (as noted in the Hamilton, Ontario case) is a situation that alerts community residents to the opportunity to make an objection to proposed facilities for service-dependent groups. Public rental housing is now administered by a market-oriented (though state-owned) company. Private housing prices have escalated in Auckland, including in the inner city where people using psychiatric services have clustered (Kearns and Joseph, 2000, p. 162), though the government's housing allocation to the service-dependent takes no account of this fact. In this context, dispersal of those in this cluster has begun, as service users seek cheaper housing in the suburbs, at the expense of proximity to support services. Suppliers of services cannot cope with servicing the number of sites to which their clients have gone. Community objections to the presence of this group from certain suburban communities have increased (Kearns and Joseph, 2000, p. 166).

In this context of inadequate support for community care of the deinstitutionalized and indeed for other service-dependent populations, due both to restricted government spending and to the anxieties of suburban populations faced with hosting community facilities and their needy clients, several trends have been observed. These are present, of course, in different forms and degrees in different cities and countries.

First, tensions associated with concentration of service-dependent populations, and the high costs of housing in gentrifying locations, have in some places (as in Auckland and San Jose) led to dispersal of these individuals to suburbs and to places of non-concentration of services and facilities. While in an hospitable world, as envisaged by the caring professionals advocating deinstitutionalization in the mid-twentieth century, this deconcentration would result in positive and redistributional experiences of 'normal' encounter across urban landscapes, in practice that experience is probably not the norm. Second, many mentally ill people, once deinstitutionalized, have become homeless. Third, re-institutionalization has been occurring in a number of settings as an emerging policy option. Twenty years ago Dear and Wolch (1987, p. 190) observed that re-institutionalization might overtake community care as a dominant policy option, particularly in the United States, citing the growing role of prisons as places of custodial care for the mentally ill and the construction of huge shelters for the homeless in rural areas outside major cities in some American states. In the United Kingdom, a decade or so later, there are reports that 'confinement' is becoming a respectable plank of mental health policy once more, due to the perceived failure of community care and the risks to communities and populations of violent offences carried out by the non-confined mentally ill (Moon, 2000). Central to this situation is that encounter, the visibility of the deinstitutionalized and the mentally ill and their quite frequent interactions with everyone else in major cities, which the original advocates of deinstitutionalization saw as a good health outcome, is in fact 'the problem' that community care cannot 'solve'. Visibility and encounter will of course be reduced by confinement. And fourth, even for those service-dependent people who remain within central city areas in which there are concentrations of relatively supportive services, their lives are a constant 'churn' between those services and between other, somewhat hospitable, urban sites like fast food restaurants or drop-in centres. The fast food restaurants of the Canadian city of Montreal, for example, are described as more significant in the daily lives of the deinstitutionalized mentally ill, along with drop-in centres run by church-based charities, than what one might think of as 'formal' community care facilities (Knowles, 2000). In the United States, individuals do still find themselves in institutions when there is no alternative or when their behaviour results in their being removed from public view and spaces according to the current rules governing those spaces. But these institutional placements are for short periods, are merely strategies of 'poverty management' and do not involve provision of therapies for residents (DeVerteuil, 2003).

Attempts have been made, mostly in discussions about the design of policy approaches that could be pursued in future, to tackle this current, deeply unsatisfactory, situation. Twenty years ago, Dear and Wolch (1987) proposed in detail, in the American context, a set of planning principles that would produce a 'fair share' approach to the siting of community care facilities and housing in urban localities. This was a decision rule about the equitable distribution of resources between localities. Accepting that the concentration of service-dependent people in inner city 'ghettoes' might have provided informal as well as formal support for these people, as well as an economically efficient way to provide services, they nevertheless found the dispersal everywhere of service-dependent people to be more equitable that an 'asylum without walls'. So, in their view there was need to develop planning strategies to make local environments able to be more welcoming, and for facilities to be less stigmatized. Their strategies included establishing 'of right' zoning ordinances for community care facilities, along with community services departments and architectural review services to integrate these facilities well, socially and design-wise. Community education would involve local residents as volunteers to get to know the users of the facilities. Importantly, regional-scale planning would allocate services and service-dependent clients across jurisdictions, and allow a forum for communication about these matters (p. 229). Of course this would require planners and a sufficiently large number of community members to be advocates for this 'landscape of caring' (p.255), and for funds to be available to provide facilities and services in dispersed locations to the appropriate level and standard. It would also require regional planning institutions powerful enough to be heeded locally.

More recently, Gleeson and Kearns (2001) have argued that the 'moral binary' present in discourses which present institutional care as wholly bad and community care as wholly good needs to be reshaped. In certain situations, combinations of different kinds of care could be arranged, and a progressive social and urban policy should be able to comprehend and organize this. Narrow views of what constitutes appropriate lives for vulnerable people and appropriate care modalities should be avoided. The power of the discursive 'moral binary' has been such that a range of groups have felt unable to propose alternatives of care. If they wanted some form of institutional support to remain, they were derided by those who saw deinstitutionalization as the only 'good' form of care, having identified the institutions of the past as quite inappropriate. If they wanted community care they were unable to argue for any centralization of facilities or services to that community because this seemed to have the attributes of the old centralized institutional forms. So, 'alternative moral landscapes – notably the "reformed institutions", service hubs, and the "village" – suffered political erasure because they were demoralised' (Gleeson and Kearns, 2001, p. 72). Avoiding narrowness, and rejecting a one-size-fits-all approach that sees individualized assistance to people with intellectual disabilities by government and other agencies as the only proper approach to the facilitation of their independent living, is advocated in a Toronto case study (Lemon and Lemon, 2003). Rather, the benefits of government support for a variety of innovative programs that are led by a range of community and inter-familial organizations are demonstrated. These programs, often led and organized by parents working with governments and community organizations, are suggested as better at recognizing disabled individuals' characteristics, preferences and entitlements. There is no suggestion here of a return to institutional care of the kind so criticized by health care professionals in the 1950s. Rather, there is a view that redistributive planning has to encourage a range of forms of encounter, depending on the service-dependent individuals and the urban contexts in question.

Like child care, the matter of providing appropriate care for the mentally ill and deinstitutionalized poses major, current, policy dilemmas for local (as well as national and regional) governance. In Australia, following a report by the Senate in late March 2006 recommending substantial expansion of government funds on mental health after years of neglect, the federal government has announced that expenditure of $1.8 billion will be made over the next five years, in areas of community support which will include overnight and daily respite care for people with a mental illness and their carers, rebates for the costs of patients seeing psychologists, and an extra 900 'personal helpers' to assist people living with mental illness 'in the community' (Prime Minister's Press Release, reported in *The Age*, April 5, 2006). State governments have been named as responsible for the matter of accommodation for the mentally ill. No mention has yet been made of the fact that this is a local, urban question as well as one to be tackled at larger scales; the matter is still being defined as a question of health care policy. This discursive presentation of the matter will probably draw resources from government. But as the relative failure of community care so far tells us, the intersection of this social and health care matter with the regulation of urban landscapes is a crucial one, if encounter in places is going to occur in people's daily lives.

Conclusion

In the three examples of redistributive planning presented in this chapter, urban renewal, child care provision and community care for the deinstitutionalized mentally ill, we have observed how recognition and encounter were present in various ways in strategies of improving redistribution in cities. Recognizing the claims and needs of particular social groups occurs in those efforts to plan child care locally which see the need for women in the paid labour force to have support in their caring roles, through local and high quality child care provision. In the case of urban renewal, recognition of the particular characteristics of the residents of the Old City of Beijing – their ways of living in a community, and the forms of privacy and publicity they thought important – enabled better planning in the interests of some (though the suggestions of researchers were not fully heeded on this by municipal authorities). Encounter as a value in planning for recognized and vulnerable groups is clear in the decision to close institutions for those with mental disability, at least as this was understood by the health and caring professions of the time if not always by local urban planners.

These questions of social welfare are profoundly local and urban matters. Though each of the matters discussed here, particularly child care and the appropriate care of the mentally ill and service-dependent, is usually framed discursively as a matter of primarily national concern – with child care as a matter of education or national fertility or sometimes gender equity, and care of the service-dependent as a matter of health – these are urban planning and policy questions of some consequence as well. What is clear in each of these cases is that the values of redistribution, together with recognition and encounter, are not necessarily shared equally or interpreted similarly by those effecting policy change. Negotiation by planners with governments of a variety of levels on these matters is required, on the basis of values planners hold that are clearly stipulated in the political contexts in which their actions will always be embedded. Only this will result in resources being available to fund the desired local outcomes. Here, we have seen in each of our examples that the discursive shaping of policy 'problems' and their potential 'solutions' is crucial.

In some cases redistributive planning that has an eye to recognition and encounter has been transforming, and planning for diversity in these cases has improved the circumstances of relatively disadvantaged groups or communities in sustainable ways. With child care, the Melbourne municipality of Sunshine used the resources of its local community planners to leverage funds for widespread provision of publicly-owned and controlled child care centres, that supported the working women of the municipality years before some other municipalities in their planning strategies were doing so. The initiative was taken by local planners, using their political context to advantage. In the Canadian example described by Lemon and Lemon (2003), of how supportive accommodation was provided for individuals with disabilities who in previous times would have been accommodated institutionally, the transforming effects on those people's lives of the programs and accommodation designed for them is most evident. In this case, volunteer supporters of the individuals, often parents, planned this outcome using their own personal skills to tap available government funds and subsidies. These examples are local and small. It is at such scales, perhaps, that transformation is most readily observable when it is the product of planning that presents plainly its redistributional values of supporting a just diversity, which recognizes precisely the particular groups to whom resources should be directed, and which acknowledges the beneficial role that encounter can play in their situations. In the contemporary and past examples discussed of urban renewal, however, encounter in the form of social mix seems to be muddying the outcomes of avowedly redistributional policies.

4 Conceptualizing Recognition in Planning

As we noted in Chapter 1, cities are characterized by different kinds of diversities. In Chapters 2 and 3, we argued that working towards 'rights to the city' should involve redistributive policies which work to reduce some forms of diversity – the diversity of rich and poor. But not all forms of diversity in cities are to be reduced through redistribution. Indeed, the devaluing and stigmatization of some urban identities and ways of life is one of the principal forms of injustice in cities. In the following two chapters, then, we develop a case for the *recognition* of some forms of diversity as a guiding principle for efforts to shape cities. Here, we are concerned both with identifying those forms of diversity that warrant recognition and with outlining some of the urban political and institutional mechanisms through which that recognition can be achieved. In this chapter, we build our case for recognition as an important social logic of urban planning by examining the nature of inter-subjective relationships among urban inhabitants, exploring in particular how modes of social ordering constrain and enable different ways of being in the city. Our aim is to develop a framework that can be applied to evaluate critically a range of remedies that seek to address the systematic deprecation of categories of people and their ways of inhabiting urban space.

Planning and the politics of difference

The field of urban politics is populated by a wide range of actors whose claims are constructed with reference to their uniqueness and specificity. Disputes over all sorts of urban issues are instigated by groups who argue that their *particular* values and needs ought to be taken into account in the shaping of cities. Women have mobilized to 'take back the night' and to establish adequate facilities and support for victims of domestic violence; faith groups have mobilized to challenge zoning regulations which are perceived to block their forms of worship; youth groups have mobilized to contest policing strategies which are perceived to unfairly target youthful occupations of public space; groups of sexual dissidents have campaigned for the provision of 'safe places' and other strategies to combat homophobic violence; ethnic minority associations have mobilized for government services to become more accessible to the populations they represent through the publication of information in community languages and 'cultural awareness' training for service providers; sports groups have campaigned for the provision of lighting to enable parks to be used for evening training sessions; the list could go on and on.

Political claims of this nature, based as they are on the needs and values of particular 'communities' or 'identity' groups (such as 'women', 'young people', 'British Asians', etc.), have come to be known as 'identity politics'. The rise of identity politics is particularly associated with the emergence of 'new social movements' during the latter half of the twentieth century. The new social movements did not mobilize exclusively (or even at all) around questions of class, distribution and the relations of production. Rather, these movements tended to challenge the experiences of discrimination and disadvantage that were associated with the devaluation and stigmatization of their particular identities. Feminists challenged the patriarchal ordering of societies, anti-racist movements emerged to contest discrimination against indigenous and migrant groups, youth movements emerged to challenge the draft of young people into military service and to explore 'alternative lifestyles'. Perhaps most importantly for our purposes here, many of these new social movements in fact took the form of 'urban social movements'. In his influential 1983 book *The City and the Grassroots*, Manuel Castells argued that these urban social movements challenged existing 'urban meaning', by which he meant that they challenged taken-for-granted assumptions about how city life ought to be properly conducted that were inscribed in urban form, urban design and urban planning. According to some observers, processes of economic and cultural globalization have given rise to a surge of identity-based political claim-making in contemporary cities (see for example Castells, 2003; Sandercock, 2003). The global movement of different people, ideas, cultural forms, commodities and technologies is said to have produced new and significant forms of urban diversity which sustain identity politics.

Of course, the general notion that cities bring together people with diverse identities and values is by no means novel – indeed, diversity has long been a primary concern for observers of urbanization. Writing at the beginning of the twentieth century, sociologist Georg Simmel argued that life in the metropolis inevitably involved a kind of *estrangement* – as cities continued to grow, they brought people together as strangers to whom they were 'not organically connected, through established ties of kinship, locality, and occupation' (Simmel, 1950, p. 404). While the question of how urban inhabitants, and indeed urban planners and policy makers, ought to deal with their particularity may have achieved a new urgency, it is a question that has been at the very core of urban studies for at least a century. The answers offered to this question have been fiercely debated by thinkers coming from quite different schools of thought.

Throughout the twentieth century, many observers of urban life have treated cultural diversity as a condition that needed to be *overcome* through the (re)formation of closer-knit communities with shared values. The influential Chicago School sociologists argued that the 'differentiation' characteristic of urban life contrasted unfavourably with the intimate sociability of earlier small-scale village and town life, which aided individuals to be properly 'socialised'. Without these socialization mechanisms, cities tended to be home to differentiated individuals, some of whom were likely to engage in 'anti-social' behaviour and even petty or violent crime, making cities threatening to the majority of the community (Katznelson, 1992; Brain, 1997). This view of particularity and the associated differentiation among the urban population remains very influential. As Katznelson (1992, pp. 22–3) notes, for most of the last century:

> The portrait of differentiation versus order has provided the stock imagery of urban life. ... [T]he analytical tradition of differentiation and its depictions of cities and their spatial patterns have continued to prove immensely appealing, in part because they seem so readily to make sense of social reality.

So, for example, urban parks and squares were promoted by some planners on the grounds that they would instil an appreciation for publicly acceptable forms of sociability and behaviour, by providing a space in which common norms could be promoted and small-scale community life replicated. Frederik Law Olmsted, the designer of New York's Central Park, declared that:

> No one who has closely observed the conduct of people who visit [Central] Park can doubt that it exercises a distinctly harmonizing and refining influence upon the most unfortunate and most lawless classes of the city – an influence favourable to courtesy, self-control, and temperance (quoted in Kasson, 1978, p. 15).

More recently, the so-called 'New Urbanist' design movement has sought to mobilize urban design and architecture in the service of building 'shared values' and 'community' in order to overcome differentiation. Their advocacy of the 'urban village' is premised (in part) on the belief that more multi-functional and dense forms of urban development can best promote vigorous forms of community solidarity and sociability. Through the sociability of the urban village it is hoped that urban dwellers can retrieve the shared community values that have allegedly broken down in cities. This is reflected in the title of Katz's (1994) influential book – *The New Urbanism: Towards an Architecture of Community*.

But this perspective is not without its critics. Since the 1960s and 1970s, a range of scholars influenced by the new social movements have advocated new perspectives on city life which do not consider particularity and difference as a condition which needs to be 'overcome'. In particular, the notion that the goal of urban policy and politics should be the formation of shared values and community has come into question. As Marshall Berman (1986, p. 481) has asked:

> Why should [we] accept an ideology that stigmatizes difference as 'deviance', and that considers it normal to flee from anybody different from ourselves? After all, any idea of normality is a norm, and as such necessitates a choice of values.

For these critics, the claims of identity groups and communities should draw our attention to cultural modes of social ordering which establish hierarchies between different identity groups and the qualities and lifestyles with which they are associated. The very

notion that 'community' should be the positive goal of urban policy
and planning is in fact a mode of ordering which inevitably works
to privilege the values of some groups over others. A model of the
good city informed by this normative outlook will invariably result
in attempts to exclude those who, by being 'different', cannot or
choose not to 'belong':

> If community is a positive norm, that is, if existing together with others
> in relations of mutual understanding and reciprocity is the goal, then it
> is understandable that we exclude or avoid those with whom we do not
> or cannot identify (Young, 1990, p. 235).

Of course, these modes of social ordering have a fundamentally
spatial dimension. For example, groups of people might be marked
out because of their *behaviour in* a particular place. Here, laws or
social norms relating to the use of particular places impose limits on behaviour which are experienced by some groups as unjust
constraints on their uses of the city. For example, gay and lesbian
activists have pointed to the ways in which hegemonic heterosexual
norms in most public places make the simple act of holding hands
or kissing in the street a risky proposition for homosexual couples. While such acts by heterosexual couples go almost unnoticed
because they appear to be 'normal', displays of homosexual affection in public often result in harassment and violence (Duncan,
1996). Alternatively, people might be marked out as different
because of their *associations with* a particular place. For example, a
range of studies have demonstrated the negative stereotypes which
are frequently associated with people who live in particular parts
of the city – be it the western surburbs of Sydney (Powell, 1993)
or the *banlieues* of Paris (Body-Gendrot, 2000). Such stereotypes
can have harmful consequences for people's experience of the city,
including their job prospects, their ability to access urban public
facilities and commercial spaces, their treatment by police and the
like. The heightened visibility which comes with being marked out
as 'different' from a 'norm' in these ways is often associated with
a kind of invisibility, as the actual values and aspirations of these
groups are excluded from the realm of political discussion and
debate (Fraser, 1997b, p. 198).

In order to overcome the harmful consequences of these
modes of social ordering in the city, we must devise a new way of

conceptualizing the particularities of the different groups who share the city. The sheer variety of urban populations militates against any notion that urban policy and politics can work on behalf of 'community' or a universal 'public' that shares values and visions of the good city. Instead, what is required is a *politics of difference* where identity groups with different values and visions of the good city can participate in a sometimes conflictual dialogue as equals in status. Here, equality is not a matter of all people being treated equally because their differences are ignored or put aside (in the sense of women being treated 'the same as' men, for example). Rather, as Young put it in her influential *Justice and the Politics of Difference* (1990, p. 47):

> social justice … requires not the melting away of group differences, but institutions that promote reproduction of and respect for group differences without oppression.

A vision of the city as a 'heterogeneous public' is the centrepiece of attempts to develop a new conception of social justice that is informed by, and can inform, contemporary struggles against various kinds of group-based oppression. This vision takes as its starting point the existence of a variety of social groups or publics in the city. These are not the 'interest groups' or 'associations' of conventional pluralist political theory, founded by private individuals with common interests. Rather, they are 'identity groups' whose members 'have a special affinity with one another because of their similar experience or way of life' (Young, 1990, p. 43). Individuals are not prior to such groups, but rather, individual identities are shaped by belonging to a group:

> A person's particular sense of history, affinity, and separateness, even the person's mode of reasoning, evaluating, and expressing feeling, are constituted partly by his or her group affinities (Young, 1990, p. 45; and see also Phillips (1993, p. 17) who makes the same point).

These groups exist in relationship to one another, and can only be distinguished as groups because of their differences. Some of them are 'defined by a common experience of exclusion or oppression' (Phillips, 1993, p. 17). When such exclusion or oppression exists, interactions among groups are likely to be characterized by a mutual hostility concerning the association of 'specific attributes, stereotypes and norms' (Young, 1990, p. 46) with particular groups – certain identities might be devalued or suppressed, while the potential for the exploration of other identities may be truncated. This hostility between groups, then, is not simply a contest over competing *preferences*, but a contest over the very *construction* of group identity and difference itself.

So, at their heart, the contests associated with urban identity politics pose the question: what kinds of identity qualify one to participate as a peer in the life of the city? On one level, this question is fundamentally a question of establishing equality between different identity groups. And as we have already argued, this equality importantly requires the equal distribution of economic resources among these groups. But the form of equality at stake in identity politics also has another dimension. When some groups feel that their very identities and ways of being in the city are unfairly denigrated or stigmatized, justice is fundamentally a matter of *status* and has an inter-subjective dimension: the pursuit of equality involves working against 'cultural patterns that systematically deprecate some categories of people and the qualities associated with them' (Fraser, 1998, p. 31).

Important concepts: affirmative and relational models of recognition

How, then, can urban planning and policy work against the hierarchical framing of some groups relative to others? What kinds of remedies exist to address the injustices produced by such status hierarchies? The notion that justice involves the *recognition* of cultural differences has been the most widely articulated and debated response to the claims of identity politics. But the proper model of recognition remains a contentious matter in social and political theory. Important questions are posed by the notion of recognition: what is the nature of the 'identity' to be recognized? And who or what does the recognizing? In this section, we distinguish between two ways of framing models of recognition: an affirmative model of recognition, and a relational model of recognition. As we shall see, these two models are premised on quite distinct understandings of both identity and recognition.

Affirmative models of recognition

As we noted at the beginning of this chapter, claims for the recognition of particularity are often mobilized on behalf of a given category of people – so, for instance, rules or normalizing spatial arrangements might be criticized on the grounds that they have failed to take into account the needs of 'gays and lesbians', the needs of 'women', the needs of 'young people' or 'the elderly', 'the disabled' or some other group. But what precisely are the needs of such groups? Do members of identity groups share a common set of needs or interests? Is there an authentic or essential gay or youth experience, for example, which can be better recognized in urban policy and politics? A so-called essentialist or authenticity model of identity would suggest that there are boundaries between these different groups, who do have a shared set of interests and experiences. This understanding of identity lends itself towards what we might call an *affirmative* model of political recognition. Where different identities are considered to be the product of pre-existing differences between those who belong to distinct groups, then recognition becomes a matter of defining, acknowledging and/or protecting group distinctiveness. Recognition, in this form, establishes and maintains boundaries between groups in order to protect their members from any social norms or institutional arrangements which prevent them from 'being themselves'. Here, the capacity of group members to 'be themselves' is measured with reference to a model of self-hood derived from a set of characteristics and orientations considered to be essential and unique to the group in question.

We share with many social and political theorists of identity a suspicion of essentialist and affirmative forms of identity politics, where recognition is claimed on behalf of groups which are understood to be homogenous or self-contained. It is relatively easy to show that different identity groups are in fact internally differentiated, that they have unstable rather than immutable boundaries. Any individual is likely to 'belong' to many such groups, and the meaning of belonging is always far from settled. As Calhoun (1994, p. 27) has argued, 'every collective identity is open to both internal subdivision and calls for its incorporation into some larger category of primary identity'. So, for example, the identity category 'woman' may in fact be internally differentiated, cross-cut by differences of ethnicity, age or sexuality. Where claims made on behalf of 'women' ignore these internal differences, they may privilege some groups of women over others, thereby producing their own forms of exclusion by presuming (or worse still, enforcing) a kind of conformity within the group. Responding to this problem is not simply a matter of refining some list of identity groups to make it more accurate (such as 'white women', 'women of colour', 'young women', 'lesbians', 'bisexual women', etc.). As Anne Phillips (1996, p. 146) notes:

> the critiques of essentialism deprive us of any simple mechanism for achieving the appropriate balance, and remind us that diversity is too great to be captured in any categorical list.

An inclusive list would always be beyond the horizon, each category always open to new claims of closure and exclusion.

Relational model of recognition

In response to these critiques of essentialist understandings of identity and their associated affirmative model of recognition, some social and political theorists have attempted to develop new understandings of identity which suggest a different model of political recognition. Here, identity is re-conceived as a kind of *relation*, 'based on *difference* from others but not on *separation* from others' (Rose, 1997). Identity groups are understood to be *formed through* the politics of identity, rather than existing prior to politics. That is, collective attachments to particular identity groups are formed precisely through attempts to mobilize that identity for a particular purpose. In specific circumstances, collectives of individuals who may be quite different in some ways nonetheless adopt a common frame of reference. In particular, 'where a particular category of identity has been repressed, delegitimated or devalued in dominant discourses, a vital response may be to claim value for all those labelled by that category' (Calhoun, 1994, p. 17). This 'where' (and its associated 'when') are particularly important. The politics of identity and difference is always a geographically and historically located politics (Fincher and Jacobs, 1998). In an urban context, for example, calls for group recognition are likely to emerge in relation to specific political issues where the allocation of resources and opportunities, and the regulation of spatial practices, are at stake. That is, collective identifications (both ascribed and elective) emerge in relation to other identifications in particular circumstances. A social group in this sense 'is defined not primarily by a set of shared attributes, but by a sense of identity' (Young, 1990, p. 44) and by 'the relations in which they stand to others' (Young, 2000, p. 90). So, as Isin (2002, p. 26) puts it, 'social groups are not things but relations.'

But without some essentialist concept of an 'authentic' identity, how can such claims for the recognition of group needs and interests be adjudicated? As Jacobs and Fincher (1998, p. 9) have argued:

> to conceive of difference as constituted through a more fluid and nonessentialist performativity of identity at once dispenses with some of the more persistent problems associated with identity politics and poses new problems in terms of the pragmatics of politics and governmentality.

In response to such dilemmas, a range of critical theorists have argued that a relational understanding of identity lends itself to what we might call a *relational* (rather than affirmative) model of cultural politics and recognition. While the dimensions of this relational model of recognition are still a matter of vigorous debate among political theorists, there are nonetheless some features on which there is general agreement. Those who believe that cultural differences are not total or essential argue that claims for recognition of cultural difference should not be made with reference to a fixed or stable conception of group identity based on some vision of an 'authentic' self. Rather, for advocates of a relational form of identity politics, claims for recognition should instead be based on appeals to justice which are open to public discussion and debate among all members of a polity. That is, advocates of a relational model of recognition share a commitment to 'a normative ideal of *public justification*' (Benhabib, 2004, p. 295, original emphasis; see also Young, 2000, Fraser, 1998). Once claimants are engaged in a process of public discussion and debate, the characteristics and interests associated with group identities are themselves open to change and transformation. As Young (2000, p. 26) puts it:

> this model conceptualizes the process of democratic discussion as not merely expressing and registering, but as transforming the preferences,

interests, beliefs and judgements of participants. Through the process of public discussion with a plurality of differently positioned and situated others, people often gain new information, learn of different experiences of their collective problems, or find that their own initial opinions are founded on prejudice or ignorance, or that they have misunderstood the relation of their own interests to others.

From this position, critical theorists have argued that competing claims for the recognition of difference can be assessed with reference to 'the logic of public claim-making' which they deploy, rather than with reference to some vision of natural/essential/authentic group needs and interests (Benhabib, 2004, p. 296). Here, however, the general agreement among critical theorists begins to break down, as different theorists posit different bases for public claim-making from which to distinguish between warranted and unwarranted claims for recognition. Some theorists – for instance, Seyla Benhabib (2002) and Axel Honneth (1995) – argue that public claims for recognition are warranted to the extent that they establish conditions for a process of identity formation which is free from oppressive interference and distortion. Benhabib (2002, p. 80) argues in favour of 'a model of public life in which narratives of self-identification would be more determinant of one's status in public life than would designators and indices imposed on one by others'. Honneth (1995) suggests we should support claims for reciprocal recognition which seek to sustain three forms of relation-to-self: self-confidence, self-respect and self-esteem. Here, both Benhabib and Honneth have sought to rescue the concepts of 'self' and 'identity' from a theory of 'natural kinds', replacing essentialism with a more fluid concept which can nonetheless still ground a universal normative political theory.

In opposition to these frameworks for assessing different recognition claims, Nancy Fraser has recently argued that *status* should form the basis of public justifications for recognition rather than *identity* and self-realization. For Fraser, recognition is important insofar as it addresses institutionalized patterns of cultural value which deny some groups the status of full partners in social interaction. She is less interested, then, in relations-to-self than she is in the relative status of social actors:

> On the status model, misrecognition is neither a psychical deformation nor an impediment to ethical self-realization. Rather, it constitutes an

institutionalized relation of subordination and a violation of justice. To be misrecognized, accordingly, is not to suffer distorted identity or impaired subjectivity as a result of being deprecated by others. It is rather to be constituted by *institutionalized patterns of cultural value* in ways that prevent one from participating as a peer in social life (Fraser, 2003, p. 29, original emphasis).

The implication here is that 'only by forswearing recourse to the prevailing identity model can theorists make normatively important distinctions between warranted and unwarranted claims for recognition' (Zurn, 2003, p. 520). By supplanting identity with *status*, Fraser seeks to assess claims for recognition from one another by criteria derived from social-scientific observations of whether or not particular groups are subject to institutionalized social relations of status subordination (Fraser, 2003; Zurn, 2003, p. 519–20).

Decision rules and discourses: ways of crafting a just diversity through recognition

These debates about the different modes of recognition are of more than theoretical interest. Whatever model of a politics of recognition one adopts in principle, the question remains: what can critical theories of recognition offer beyond social-scientific critiques of actually existing political conditions? Indeed, as Benhabib notes (2004, p. 299), critical theorists who claim to make normative distinctions between different models of recognition must take an interest in questions of institutional design and decision rules. It is one thing to prefer one form of claim-making over another, but critical theorists have also sought to reflect on the institutional arrangements and decision rules for the conduct of cultural politics which might actually work to 'transform discourse from self-regard to appeals to justice' (Young, 2000, p. 115). Here, there has been a particular concern in recent critical theory to (a) identify and reject institutional arrangements and decision rules which are said to support essentialist/separatist/affirmative claims for recognition, and (b) identify and encourage those institutional arrangements which might support relational claims for recognition. Structures of urban governance and planning have emerged as a key site in these debates. When the activities of state agencies classify populations through the identification and recognition of particular groups, these structures of identification and recognition have effects. As such, these state structures of recognition are often conceptualized as the impediments to, or the incentives for, the institutionalization of a relational model of recognition. In what follows here, we distinguish between a *group checklist* form of decision rules associated with the affirmative model of recognition, and a *cross-group* form of decision rules designed to foster a relational model of recognition.

One common kind of decision rule designed to recognize the needs and interests of different groups in the city might be described as a *group checklist* approach to recognition. By this, we mean a rule that requires a planner or agency to establish and then consult with a list of different groups before coming to a decision on a given planning issue. Sometimes the group checklist approach might be implemented in the form of a quota system, in which a given agency or decision-making body is required to include representatives from different groups (such as women, or African-Americans, etc.). Or, the group checklist approach might be implemented in the form of state funding for representative organizations for particular groups, who are then consulted about significant decisions or included in decision-making forums. Such mechanisms have been established in order to pluralize the perspectives that are taken into account in decision-making, based on an acknowledgement that some points of view have been systematically marginalized and are in need of inclusion. As such, they clearly represent an advance over structures for planning which are premised on the notion that there is a universal 'public interest' which planners are able to represent.

But the checklist approach is informed by an affirmative model of recognition. As such, group checklist decision rules for recognition have been increasingly subject to critique – not only from conservatives who are suspicious of *any* forms of recognition, but (and most importantly from our perspective) also from advocates of relational models of recognition who are concerned about the potentially pernicious effects of such rules. These latter critics are concerned that 'checklist'-style decision rules might actually work to *entrench* some forms of marginalization and misrecognition, by imposing bureaucratic categories and distinctions on top of more fluid forms of urban diversity. In devising checklists of groups who are to be recognized, planners may inadvertently (or indeed deliberately) over-emphasize differences between groups and underplay differences within groups (Uitermark *et al.*, 2005, p. 624). Further, the checklist approach relies on the notion that group interests are stable enough that they can be adequately recognized in policy through consultation with a small group of leaders or representatives, and this may work to encourage group elites (often pejoratively referred to as 'the usual suspects' by planners engaged in checklist-style consultations).

To illustrate the notion that group checklist decision rules might promote harmful essentialist and affirmative forms of recognition politics, consider Amin's analysis of the civil unrest which occurred in the northern English mill towns of Bradford, Burnley and Oldham in the summer of 2001. In these towns, inter-ethnic tensions had historically been addressed through the inclusion of representatives from ethnic minority communities. Community 'elders' and 'leaders' were identified, resourced and consulted by local authorities on a variety of matters of urban and neighbourhood policy, based on the assumption that ethnic minority communities had essential characteristics and interests. As a consequence, these community leaders often framed their demands in terms of ethnic recognition and ethnic cultural preservation – a typical example of the affirmative model of recognition in action. However, in making these claims they tended to obscure the different demands welling up in other parts of 'their community', as well as generating resentment from other communities. According to Amin (2002, p. 7):

> The new politics ... bottled up difficult problems such as gender inequality and the growing drug problem within the Asian community, it fragmented the Asian community by forcing different groups to compete with each other for grants, and it allowed the White communities to see themselves as victims, based on rumours of special deals for Asians. But, above all, it suppressed the voice of young Asians, one mixing tradition and modernity, diaspora and English language. We see this in the desire of young women for better and longer education and some choice over marriage partners, but within a frame of commitment to Islam and kinship ties, ... and in the desire of young men to mix consumer cultures and meet racist insult with attitude, but also not to question existing gender inequalities and diaspora beliefs.

For Amin, then, existing institutional structures designed to recognize and include particular minority ethnicities in the mainstream planning process had a series of harmful effects. First, the affirmative structure of recognition in place here was premised on the assumption that minority ethnic communities could speak with one voice. As such, they marginalized some voices within those communities – in this case, the voices of young second generation migrants, who felt that their concerns were not adequately represented by the community grounds and leaders consulted by local governments. Second, these structures of recognition did not facilitate inter-community dialogue and instead encouraged different groups to pursue their interests in isolation from others. This, according to Amin, 'bottled up' a series of issues which eventually came to a head as these young people became the target of resentment from both their own community leaders and racist organizations. Paradoxically, then, a checklist form of recognition sustained a form of misrecognition which eventually exploded into violence.

But in light of the potential limitations of checklist-style decision rules, what are the alternatives? Anne Phillips (1996, p.149) draws attention to the dilemma:

> does this mean that nothing can be done – that given the risks, on the one hand, of an imposed and misleading uniformity, and the absurdities, on the other, of an endless search for sufficiently pluralized categories, we have to abandon the quest for specifically political mechanisms?

What are the prospects for establishing institutional arrangements which might work to foster and sustain a relational model of recognition that can address the limitations of affirmative, 'checklist' approaches? What kinds of decision rules might be established which can enable people to 'articulate group difference without thereby "disciplining" group members into a single authentic identity' (Phillips, 1996, p. 145)?

According to Benhabib (2002), a set of decision rules devised by Amsterdam City Council to address questions of recognition and just diversity provide us with an example of institutional arrangements which encourage relational rather than affirmative kinds of recognition claims. There, the council sought to overcome the limitations of 'group checklist' recognition politics by reorganizing their funding and consultation structures to establish a set of decision rules which were explicitly dialogic and cross-group. During the 1980s, the city had institutionalized an affirmative form of recognition by funding organizations to represent the interests of different minority groups, as in the English case. However, in the 1980s and 1990s, both members of the funded groups and the city council began to express concerns with this approach. Precisely because of the differences within the migrant and religious communities who were funded to establish consultative bodies, these bodies sometimes found it difficult to formulate positions and political agendas. As a result, government agencies were also not convinced that the advice they received from these consultative bodies was either representative or useful. So, as Uitermark *et al.* put it (2005, p. 627):

> Self-organizations could, on the one hand, not put pressure on the government and, on the other hand, the government could not use the self-organizations to reach all or even most of the members of the newly construed target groups.

In response, the city devised new structures of funding and consultation designed to establish cross-group dialogue about diversity in the city, thus breaking down rigid distinctions and categorizations based on fixed concepts of identity. In shifting from 'minority policy' to 'diversity policy', the council moved from funding consultative organizations for specified groups to funding collaborative projects which involved a range of groups. The new decision rules explicitly stated that community-based projects were more likely to be funded if their supporters could demonstrate that they involved collaboration across a variety of groups and organizations. The city's approach was premised on the argument that 'Amsterdammers cannot be captured in one group. They are part of many groups' (quoted in Uitermark, *et al.*, 2005, p. 629). As Uitermark *et al.* (2005, p. 630) note:

> The stress on projects chimes with some central assumptions and recommendations in post-multiculturalist literature, notably the idea that individuals move in and out of different contexts and thereby gain a hybrid or polyvalent identity that negates any categorization of these individuals into ethnic, seemingly homogenous groups.

Here, the authors refer to the Amsterdam approach as deriving from a 'post-multicultural' approach to the politics of diversity, which they distinguish from those forms of 'multiculturalism' which tended to privilege affirmative or essentialist forms of identity politics. The policy is neither 'assimilationist' nor 'multiculturalist' (in the affirmative sense of that term). Rather, the aim of the new institutional arrangements was to 'create new forums where participants from various backgrounds debate ideals and practices of diversity' (Uitermark, *et al.*, 2005, p. 630).

For Benhabib (2002, p. 79), the Amsterdam policies suggest the grounds for a new set of institutional arrangements and decision rules that can address the limitations of group checklist rules. She argues that the cross-group decision rules developed in Amsterdam:

> encourage the integration of foreigners into Dutch society through more fluid, egalitarian, and democratic means, all the while acknowledging the complexity of the constitution of collective identities.

She supports these new institutional arrangements because they do not start from the premise that groups are homogeneous and that their identities are fixed. Instead of dictating an administrative 'checklist' of which identities are legitimate and which are not, the council has established a set of decision rules designed to open the question of group identity and identification to a more fluid process of dialogue and debate. As such, Benhabib (2002, p. 80) argues that the Amsterdam experience is illustrative of the kind of institutional arrangements and decision rules which might 'move a democratic society toward a model of public life in which narratives of self-identification would be more determinant of one's status in public life than would designators and indices imposed upon one by others'.

But the Amsterdam approach has certainly not solved all of the dilemmas associated with the politics of recognition. Indeed, in their close analysis of the operation of Amsterdam's diversity policy in its first few years, Uitermark *et al.* (2005, p. 632) argue that it has produced new forms of exclusion and marginalization:

> Since the diversity policy denies the validity of identities like 'Moroccans', 'Turks' or 'Muslims', the organizations that strive to represent the interests of those who are categorized as such are themselves marginalized. The ambivalence here is that the local government feels too much importance is granted to these categories and therefore seeks to select

organizations that are not based on ethnic identities. [...] The result of
this policy is to deny the identities that are of importance to many members of ethnic minorities.

This is particularly significant in circumstances where those particular ethnic identities are explicitly denigrated and stigmatized
in the wider public sphere. For instance, issues of crime and anti-
social behaviour in Amsterdam are frequently and explicitly associated with Moroccan young people. Journalists and politicians
routinely call upon 'the Moroccan community' to do something
about the issue. But how is the Moroccan community to respond,
given that Moroccan organizations have been delegitimized in the
new diversity policy? The cross-group decision rules for recognition
therefore have some paradoxical effects:

> The official policy line is not to support homogenous organizations and
> to de-politicize local problems (such as youth crime). However, indi-
> vidual politicians as well as the general public associate certain groups
> with problems, thus raising the political profile of the issues. It is no
> surprise, therefore, than in practice ethnically homogeneous organi-
> zations are called upon to provide services and to cooperate with the
> municipality. ... Exactly the kinds of organizations that are rejected as
> part of the philosophy of diversity are taken back on board when problems
> proliferate. The fact that such counter-publics are valued in difficult
> circumstances whilst they are excluded in ordinary situations reveals some
> of the ambivalences that underlie the diversity policy (Uitermark et al.,
> 2005, p. 635).

Indeed, it could perhaps be argued that the council has simply
replaced one form of 'checklist' (based on fixed identity categories)
with another (based on cross-group collaboration and 'fluid' identifications). For those people whose 'narratives of self-identification'
are primarily ethnic, the council's new administrative arrangements
seek to impose new forms of self-identification through a denial of
funding and recognition. For Uitermark *et al.* (2005, p. 635), then,
the city council's new approach to urban governance has produced
new 'dynamics of selectiveness' which continue 'to produce and
discipline subjectivities'.

These reflections on the Amsterdam experience alert us to
the difficulties of translating socio-theoretical observations about

different models of recognition into principles for institutional design and planning decision rules. Indeed, perhaps one of the lessons we can draw from this brief survey of debates over different structures of recognition in England and the Netherlands is that this process of translation warrants further analysis. The position of the planner in establishing decision rules for recognition is a key issue here. In much of the socio-theoretical writing on questions of recognition, theorists are explicitly concerned to develop an approach to adjudicating various kinds of recognition claims from 'an observer's point of view'. For example, Seyla Benhabib (2004, p. 294) asserts that in *The Claims of Culture* she is seeking to develop a set of principles which can act as 'normative guidelines to help us navigate the validity of identity/difference claims from an observer's point of view'. Likewise, Nancy Fraser explicitly proceeds first by considering different kinds of recognition claims 'from the external perspective of a sociological observer' (Zurn, 2003, p. 522). However, the question of turning observations from an 'observer's point of view' into practical measures that can be implemented from a 'planner's point of view' is highly fraught, to say the least. Planners are not neutral observers, but active players in urban politics. And yet this issue seems to have been of less theoretical interest in the existing literature on recognition. Certainly, the state (and by extension, urban planning) looms large in many accounts as 'both a player in the injustices and a potential player in the remedies' (Feldman, 2002, p. 418). But while the state is treated as a central player, it remains 'severely underthematized as a site of power, and an arena of contestation' (Feldman, 2002, p. 418), as we have already noted. That is, the state tends to be implicitly and rather unproblematically viewed as the agent responsible for determining the regime of recognition and for adjudicating recognition claims. Of particular concern here is the positioning of citizens as passive recipients of recognition – as though 'recognition' is a matter of the state recognizing different groups in the way that the chair of a meeting might recognize a speaker (see Markell, 2000). So, while advocates of a 'relational' model of recognition such as Benhabib might argue that the cross-group rules established by the City of Amsterdam are preferable to the more 'affirmative' structures established in the north of England, they leave the capacity of the state to 'do the recognising' untroubled.

Conclusion

In this final section, then, let us sketch out the implications of our analysis for efforts to transform unjust structures of recognition and status hierarchies through planning. The first conclusion we want to draw might at first seem pessimistic. Our analysis suggests that the state and planners are far from 'neutral observers' in the politics of difference. Any set of decision rules established by planners and state agencies will reward some kinds of recognition claims while discouraging others. As such, these rules inevitably act as technologies of power and control. As Margo Huxley (2002, p. 146) reminds us, 'any form of classification and regulation and any reform or policy, no matter how progressive, is inescapably enmeshed in control and normalisation.' This would certainly seem to be borne out by Uitermark *et al.*'s analysis of the Amsterdam experience. But to acknowledge the normalizing effects of planning is not a reason to give up on urban planning and action through the state as a progressive force. Rather, it forces us to rethink the ways in which planning structures might be mobilized in support of equality and the 'right to the city' through recognition.

This leads us to our second conclusion. The task for planners, we would argue, is precisely *not* to act as though they were neutral observers who are in a position to adjudicate between 'valid' and 'invalid' forms of recognition claims. As such, the task for planning for recognition is not to devise and implement a fixed and permanent model of recognition (either 'affirmative' or 'relational') as though this single model could address every status harm. As we have seen, both 'group checklist' and 'cross group' decision rules potentially have positive and harmful effects. Anne Phillips (1996, p. 146) puts it neatly:

> We have become sufficiently attuned to the politics of presence to distrust the notion that anyone can 'stand in' for anyone else, and sufficiently alert to the coercive powers of homogeneity to want to reflect diversity.

The task, rather, is to identify and support the form of claim ('affirmative' or 'relational') which best remedies the particular harm which is to be addressed. In other words, the shaping of decision rules should be guided by an appreciation of the different uses and effects of 'affirmative' or 'relational' models of recognition and their associated rules. So, we are suggesting that planners can best advance a transformative politics of recognition by taking a *pragmatic* and *contextual* approach to the question of recognition. There is no 'one size fits all' solution to the problems of identity, recognition and rights to the city that can be easily derived from the 'observer's point of view'. The choice between group checklist and cross-group decision rules for recognition, as with the choice between decision rules for redistribution based on addressing locational disadvantage and accessibility, is not one that can be made in advance of planning. Both approaches have their uses in addressing particular forms of harm. Such pragmatic and contextual calculations can only be made on the understanding that planners are in fact active participants in the politics of difference rather than neutral observers. When planners are responsible for existing structures of recognition in urban politics and when they advocate for new structures of recognition, they must remain focused on the nature of the status harm to be addressed and the most appropriate decision rules.

In the next chapter, then, we seek to flesh out the contours of the pragmatic and contextual approach to recognition which we have advanced here.

5 Planning for Recognition in Practice

In Chapter 4 we emphasized how decision rules for planning that recognize difference cannot be straightforwardly devised from theoretical discussions, ready-made for application to any number of real-world settings. Rather, in awareness of the range of options that have been tried in certain contexts, decision rules may be selected, pragmatically, for use in the context at hand.

In this chapter we consider the ways in which planning for recognition has been practiced in a range of settings. We organize the chapter in a manner that seems, at first glance, grounded in the affirmative model identified in Chapter 4 – that is, in each example we start by identifying 'groups' of people often recognized, or labelled, in planning and policy thought. The groups we begin our discussion around, however, are not groups that necessarily attract pejorative labels, though they may lack status in that their requirements and characteristics are not particularly known or supported by existing institutional arrangements. Rather, these groups are broad starting points for us – and within these groups will be designations of sub-groups that may be negative in some situations.

Box 5.1: Case studies in Chapter 5		
Recognition	*Recognition and redistribution*	*Recognition and encounter*
Child friendly cities	Planning for immigrants	Contesting hetero-normativity through planning

Our first example of planning for recognition is that of planning for child friendly cities, with the discussion here about Italian efforts to inscribe the presence of the young into the shaping of urban areas. This we consider from the perspective of recognition alone, backgrounding efforts to redistribute resources to this population segment, or to facilitate encounter between its members. We focus in particular on efforts to foster children's development through their interactions with cities – turning planning to the task of enhancing their urban experiences by recognizing and acknowledging their special requirements but not by segregating them. Second, planning for the presence of immigrants is discussed, with examples primarily from Canada and Australia, countries in which multiculturalism has been a national policy framework for some decades now. Planning for immigrants is considered as planning for recognition that also seeks to redistribute societal resources to new citizens, many of whom are disadvantaged upon arrival in the country and, importantly, are not known about or recognized for their cultural roots and practices. Thus, they are a 'group' lacking status. This is in part because their presence is not known about by the host society; their presence requires acknowledgement. The third example of planning practice in the chapter considers planning for recognition that particularly facilitates encounter. Here, we draw on recent UK and Canadian efforts to plan for sexual diversity, recognizing particularly the presence in the city of same-sex groups whose forms of interaction are not acknowledged as widely in public policy and planning frameworks as those of the heterosexual norm. As such, we consider the ways in which recognition of these groups may also require attention to the nature of encounters among strangers in the city.

Recognition: planning for child friendly cities

The place of children and young people in city life is increasingly fraught with anxiety and tension. From panics about the vulnerability of children in a world of dangerous strangers to panics in which groups of young people are labelled as dangerous or 'anti-social' strangers, concerns about the dangers and risks posed to and/or by children and young people seem to dominate considerations of children and the city. As Sophie Watson (2006, p. 124) and others have pointed out, the more such discourses of fear, risk and danger circulate, the more they work to produce the circumstances of which they speak. So, for example, 'parent's anxiety and fear limits children's movement and freedom. ... Yet as children are withdrawn from public space, through its emptiness and lack of use it becomes more threatening.'

In much urban planning, the response to these concerns about risks to and from young people often involves the provision of child- or youth-specific facilities. As Watson (2006, p. 125) notes, 'In this climate of fear of and withdrawal from outdoor public space, there has been a marked increase in the provision of formal spaces for play – such as indoor activity centres, climbing areas and so on – provided by local councils on the one hand, and on the other, by a growing commercial play sector.' Concerns about children's safety in the urban public realm, for example, often result in the provision of fenced playgrounds which afford adult surveillance. Or, a skatepark is offered as a 'solution' to the 'problem' of boisterous teenagers using car parks and gutters as props for skateboarding manoeuvres. But in his groundbreaking 1978 book *The Child in the City*, Colin Ward suggested we should be suspicious of these conventional planning responses. He approvingly cites Hermann Mattern's observation that 'the failure of an urban environment can be measured in direct proportion to the number of "playgrounds"' (Ward, 1978, p. 87). While we have nothing in particular against playgrounds and skateparks *per se*, we think Ward and Mattern have a point. Certainly, we do want to argue that planning must address – must recognize – the particular identities and interests of children and young people. But we want to suggest that this recognition should not (always) take the form of providing child-specific facilities which address adult concerns about child and/or community safety by *segregating* children and young people from the wider urban context. Here, the child's city becomes rather an archipelago of 'safe' spaces in a sea of adult-centric space. Rather, we want to demonstrate another approach to planning for children and young people which proceeds from a *recognition of children's and young people's capacities and interests* – a form of planning which recognizes children and young people as urban citizens, not as citizens-in-waiting or citizens-in-training.

So, we will proceed in this example by thinking first about the place of children and young people in the city. First, we will articulate our understanding of the political lack-of-citizenship which structures the lives of children and young people, and how it can be addressed through recognition of their capacities and interests. We then move on to consider ways in which planning can address the misrecognition of children and young people, by looking into the growing global planning movement dedicated to the creation of 'Child Friendly Cities'. After considering the forms of recognition that underpin the child friendly city concept, we move on to explore how the concept has been mobilized in practice, by looking at how planners, local politicians and activists have worked together with children and young people across a range of Italian towns and cities over the last decade. This example of planning for child friendly cities is focused on those planning activities based on recognition alone, without explicit attention to the ways in which the objective of recognition might be complicated by concerns with redistribution or encounter (although, as we shall see, it is clear that elements of redistribution and encounter are present in the activities that result from this planning).

Contemporary Western societies are fundamentally structured by a form of inequality based on age which marginalizes children and young people. As Colin Ward (1978, p. iv) noted some years ago, 'a whole series of laws, or rather a random accumulation of laws, grants rights or imposes duties at different ages, which in very general terms define the status of childhood'. These laws ensure that while children might have some of the formal rights of citizenship, they are generally denied the rights associated with full membership in a political community:

> Children in democratic polities inhabit an uncertain space between alienage and full citizenship. Children are simultaneously assumed to be citizens – they hold passports and except in the rarest of cases receive at least one nationality at birth – and judged to be incapable of citizenship in that they cannot make the rational and informed decisions that characterise self-governance. In place of democratic citizenship, children hold an ill-defined partial membership (Cohen, 2005, p. 221).

The permanent exclusion of children and young people from the status of full citizens is typically assumed to be quite natural – as Cohen (2005, p. 223) goes on to note, this exclusion has typically been 'seen as a justifiable and somewhat uninteresting exception to the rules of democracy', so taken-for-granted are the assumptions upon which this exclusion is premised. Children, by virtue of the very fact that they are not adults, are simply assumed to be incapable of dealing with the rights and responsibilities of citizenship. Indeed, the very capacities ascribed to autonomous citizens are, to a significant extent, defined *in opposition to childhood* – in much political theory and practice, a 'view of autonomy has been defined in opposition to the cultural meaning of childhood. Children are cultural symbols for the opposite of autonomy' (Kulynych, 2001, p. 257).

To the extent that children figure in public policy deliberations about citizenship, then, such deliberations tend to be overwhelmingly structured by a dual emphasis on *protecting* children from threats which may impede their transition to adulthood, and *preparing* them for their future as adult citizens through education and normative guidance. (Of course, in making such an argument we are conscious that there are significant differences in the construction of childhood across national contexts – indeed, such national differences are explicitly thematized later in this discussion.) Children and young people, then, are constructed as citizens-in-waiting. And where the transition goes wrong, through a failure of protection and when preparation breaks down, children and young people are constructed as anti-citizens, threatening the community of citizens with their anti-social behaviour. Here, it is the community which is said to require protection from children and young people, not the other way around (Iveson, 2006a, pp. 53–4).

This construction of children as lacking a set of capacities which they will (hopefully) acquire later as they reach adulthood has profound consequences for the ways in which children experience urban life. Fundamentally, this construction of childhood has served to restrict the spatial ranges of children and young people. Independent access to the urban public realm is assumed to require the capacities associated with adulthood, which children and young people are assumed to lack by definition. As we have already noted, for example, children are frequently considered to be at risk from menacing strangers and dangerous machines, thus requiring adult supervision. Or else, they are assumed to lack the shared values (such as 'respect' and 'responsibility') which are required for full participation in adult society, thus again requiring adult guidance and supervision. While, of course, we must not assume that all children experience the city in the same way (Watson, 2006), we can nonetheless identify a range of techniques that are deployed to limit children's and young people's access to the city – from parental controls through to school rules and new anti-social behaviour regulations and curfews which are growing ever more prevalent in English-speaking cities around the world. As one of us has argued elsewhere (Iveson, 2006a), we can usefully divide such techniques for limiting children's spatial ranges between those which create 'circuits of inclusion' – that is, a set of 'safe' and supervised spaces for children – and those which create 'circuits of exclusion' – that is, a set of spaces which are made off-limits for children and young people without adult supervision (see also Rose, 2000).

Urban planning is one of the technologies through which these circuits of inclusion and exclusion for children and young people have been established. As Claire Freeman notes, urban planners have tended to act on the basis of the negative assumptions about childhood discussed above, such that their efforts to 'act on behalf of the public and plan for the "public good" ... often inhibit and frustrate children's and young people's lives' (Freeman, 2006, pp. 69–70). This is not simply a case of urban planners ignoring the needs of children and young people – although this has often been the case. It is, more significantly, a matter of urban planners acting on the basis of a construction of childhood and youth which works to privilege adult concerns and marginalize the concerns of children and young people. As such, planners' efforts have often tended to be focused on protection and preparation.

We share the concerns of a growing number of observers who suggest that this trend towards the marginalization of children and young people from the life of the city is unjust and must be reversed. Fundamentally, we want to argue, reversing this trend requires a form of urban planning which *recognizes* the particular interests and the capacities of children and young people. This will require a significant shift in the way that urban planning approaches the needs of children and young people. Let us make it very clear that we are not suggesting that children and young people should simply be treated 'like adults' – far from it. Rather, we want to argue for a kind of urban planning which is premised on a different concept of childhood – one which recognizes the capacities and interests of children and young people *as* children and young people in the here and now, rather than reducing the needs of children and young people to the kinds of protection and preparation that are geared towards their future adult selves. To put this more plainly, we are arguing for a form of urban policy and planning which recognizes the things that children and young people *can* do, rather than one which is premised on a series of assumptions about what they can not do (defined from an 'adult' perspective). In particular, we are arguing that children are competent to evaluate their own urban environments and experiences, and to make a substantial contribution to urban governance on the basis of their evaluations (see Malone, 2006). As Jans (2004) puts it, we need a form of urban policy and planning which incorporates a 'child-sized concept of citizenship', where participation is not premised on a concept of 'autonomy' and 'capacity' which is defined in opposition to childhood.

So, exactly what would it mean to 'recognize' children and young people in urban policy and planning? What specific forms might this recognition take? In keeping with the framework set out in Chapter 4, we suggest that such questions should be answered with reference to the specific harms that need to be addressed. In the case of children and young people, it seems to us that both 'checklist' and 'cross-group' forms of recognition might be usefully deployed to address the lack of citizenship they experience. 'Checklist' recognition can be useful in at least raising the profile of children's and young people's issues in urban policy and planning where they have been ignored altogether. But alongside this, there is a need to transform dominant constructions of childhood and youth, so that children's and young people's needs are not defined exclusively with reference to adult concerns about protection and preparation. This can only be achieved through forms of planning which encourage 'cross-group recognition', by encouraging new forms of engagement between adults and children and young people of different backgrounds, based on an acknowledgement that children and young people have a range of capacities which could be of value in reshaping the city.

This cross-group recognition is probably the most challenging for currently-dominant frameworks of urban policy and planning in most contemporary Western societies. Peter Moss and Pat Petrie (2002) describe the necessary shift in public provisions for children as a shift from 'children's services' to 'children's spaces'. It is worth quoting their definition of these concepts at length, as it usefully

encapsulates the kind of shift in approach which might result from
the recognition of children's and young people's capacities and
interests:

> The concept of children's services, so it seems to us, is bound up
> in a particular understanding of public provisions for children: a
> very instrumental and atomising notion, in which provisions are
> technologies for acting upon children, or parts of children, to produce
> specific, predetermined and adult-defined outcomes. The concept of
> 'children's spaces' understands provisions as environments of many
> possibilities – some predetermined, others not, some initiated by
> adults, others by children: it presumes unknown resources, possibilities
> and potentials. These environments are understood as more public
> places for children to live their childhoods, alongside the more private
> domain of the home (Moss and Petrie, 2002, p. 9).

Importantly, as Moss and Petrie go on to note, the concept of a
'children's space' as a more 'public place' does not just imply a set
of physical spaces. Rather, the concept of 'children's space' implies
the cultural, social and discursive spaces through which children
and adults can engage with one another, 'where there is room
for dialogue, confrontation (in the sense of exchanging differing
experience and views), deliberation and critical thinking, where
children and others can speak and be heard' (Moss and Petrie,
2002, p. 9). Their framework echoes the work of Colin Ward, who
noted the need for children's and young people's advocates to
shift their thinking beyond a concern for playgrounds and other
physical spaces:

> It is hard, no doubt, for those who have devoted themselves to
> campaigning for physical space for the young in the city ... to accustom
> themselves to the idea that, very early in life, another more urgent and
> more difficultly-met demand arises, for *social* space; the demand of the
> city's children to be part of the city's life (Ward, 1978, p. 31).

This is not to deny the importance of play to children and young
people – on the contrary, it is to think of the city and the urban
public realm in particular as a space of play rather than restricting
play to designated spaces:

> children *will* play everywhere and with anything. The provision that
> is made for their needs operates on one plane, but children operate

on another. ... A city that is really concerned with the needs of its young will make the whole environment accessible to them, because, whether invited or not, they are going to use the whole environment (Ward, 1978, p. 86).

In demonstrating how the recognition of children and young people might be pursued through new forms of urban policy and planning, we now consider the recent efforts of the international 'Child Friendly Cities' movement, in particular exploring how this concept has been developed in Italian towns and cities. Here, we again see action across a variety of scales, this time as local action is shaped with reference to national and global policy frameworks which are all concerned with the nature of urban life for children and young people.

The last two decades have witnessed a growing international movement for the creation of 'Child Friendly Cities'. This movement has its antecedents in the United Nations 1989 Convention on the Rights of the Child (CRC), the principles of which have formed the basis of UNICEF's *Child Friendly Cities Initiative*, which was formally launched at the UN's Habitat II Conference in Istanbul in 1996 (Malone, 2006). The *Child Friendly Cities Initiative* can usefully be understood as an attempt to operationalize the more general principles articulated in the CRC concerning citizenship, rights and participation by children, by suggesting a framework through which those principles could be incorporated into urban policy and planning frameworks. UNICEF's efforts with respect to Child Friendly Cities are not so much geared towards projecting a standard model of 'child-friendliness' – rather, the *Child Friendly Cities Initiative* advocates a set of nine 'building blocks' designed to facilitate implementation of the CRC in a local governance setting. These building blocks are: children's participation; a child friendly legal framework; a city-wide child rights strategy; a children's rights unit or coordinating mechanism; child impact assessment and evaluation; a children's budget; a regular State of the City's Children report; making children's rights known; and independent advocacy for children (UNICEF, 2004).

UNICEF's *Child Friendly Cities Initiative* has been strongly influenced by activities in a number of nation-states where new forms of recognition for children and young people have been pursued in public policy. Italy has been one of the key influences here, and is frequently held up as an exemplary (if not wholly successful) model for national and local efforts to build Child Friendly Cities (eg Malone, 2006; UNICEF, 2005). UNICEF's 2005 review of progress towards Child Friendly Cities in Italy provides a very useful discussion of Italian policies designed to recognize children and young people in urban governance, and much of our account of planning efforts in Italy is drawn from this report. Two key policy interventions set Italy on its current path. First, in 1997, the Italian government produced a *National Plan of Action for Children and Adolescents*, which was the product of several years of negotiation among government and non-government agencies at both local and national levels concerning the implementation of the CRC. This plan of action 'marked the passage of the child from being an object of protection to being a citizen, with the recognized right to express needs, potentials and expectations that should be taken into account in decision-making processes affecting local communities and the country as a whole' (UNICEF, 2005, p. 12). At the same time, the government also established the *Sustainable Cities for Girls and Boys* project, which was driven by the Ministry of the Environment's efforts to develop a framework for the implementation of Agenda 21 in Italian towns and cities. This policy aimed to promote a new culture of urban governance, linking sustainability to democratic participation by all citizens including children and young people. Importantly, both these national policy initiatives were supported by the introduction of a number of institutional incentives and legal instruments. So, for instance, both policies came with a series of grant programs and financial incentives designed to encourage regional and local governments to shift their practices. Law 285/97 (Provisions to Promote Rights and Opportunities for Children), attached to the *National Plan of Action*, established a series of legal requirements for municipal and regional governments to develop local plans of action.

Recognition of children's capacities and interests has been at the heart of these national policy interventions in Italy. The three agreed pillars of the policies have been:

- affirmation of a new culture of childhood that recognizes the child as an active subject from his/her own young age and promotes innovative policies which encourage empowering education and participation processes;
- emergence of a new sustainable and participatory culture of the city;

• emphasis on a new relationship between the child and the city, constituting the synthesis of the first two and standing at the core of the Italian CFCs (UNICEF, 2005, p. 9).

In Moss and Petrie's (2002) terms discussed earlier, these pillars signal an intent to work towards 'children's spaces' rather than 'children's services'. As UNICEF's 2005 report on the Italian experience puts it, 'this model does not propose the improvement of specific services for children but rather a general change to the city, which should be designed to take account of children's needs' (UNICEF, 2005, p. 17). Significantly, the policies are designed to foster children and young people's access to the physical, social and political spaces of the city. At the national level, then, we can discern a combination of the two forms of recognition discussed in Chapter 4 – the legal measures designed to force localities to take children's needs into account take the form of 'checklist' recognition politics, while efforts to use these measures to produce a 'new culture of childhood' clearly aspire to a more transformative form of 'cross-group' recognition which seeks to unsettle essentialized conceptions of the child (as a 'future citizen' needing protection and preparation for adulthood).

By their very nature, the Italian Child Friendly City frameworks deliberately leave plenty of room for local actors to interpret their requirements in quite different ways. Not surprisingly, then, there have been experiments with a wide range of activities in different localities. Local activities have tended to be focused on six main areas of action: encouraging participation in city life by children; reforming urban governance; encouraging services and facilities for play and socializing; encouraging socializing within the community; raising awareness in the city; and pursuing new environmental policies. Within each of these areas, there has also been a diversity of measures. So, for instance, with respect to children's participation in city life, local measures have included children's councils, participatory planning workshops with children and mobility projects designed to enhance children's independent access to physical spaces such as safe school routes and child friendly shopkeeper networks.

It is fair to say that efforts to marry the checklist and transformative forms of recognition have not always been a success. There is plenty of evidence to suggest that much of what has been done in Italy in the name of Child Friendly Cities fits comfortably within a 'checklist' approach to the recognition of children and young people that does not really affirm the 'new culture of childhood' that is fundamental to a more transformative politics of recognition. Consider efforts to include children and young people in planning and decision-making. While the number of local Children's and Young People's Town Councils in Italy has grown spectacularly from around 30 in 1995 to 580 in 2004, not all of these councils reflect a significant shift in dominant assumptions about children and childhood. In some cases, participation is largely organized through schools, with some involving teacher selection, and the efforts of the council are largely tokenistic and designed to educate children about how decision-making works rather than actually encouraging them to participate in meaningful decision-making. Similarly, participatory planning workshops conducted under Child Friendly Cities auspices are often shaped by adult-defined educational objectives rather than children's own interests.

Nonetheless, in other cases these same measures have incorporated more transformative approaches to the recognition of children and young people in urban policy and planning. For instance, in some Children's and Young People's Town Councils, participants are drawn by lot, and facilitators actively work to involve children and young people in efforts to transform city life in collaboration with other residents and officials (UNICEF, 2005, pp. 19, 37). Similarly, many participatory workshops are run by planners and architects with expertise in participatory planning rather than school teachers, and have a stronger focus on allowing children to pursue their own interests in collaboration with adults rather than learning outcomes which form part of the school syllabus (although, of course, some learning does take place in these workshops!). In their own evaluations of participatory planning activities, children and young people:

> observed one notable difference in these activities compared with work normally done in school: there was greater attention to their points of view and a more interesting and entertaining way of working, especially in participatory planning (UNICEF, 2005, pp. 39–40).

Nonetheless, these transformative approaches face a range of difficulties, not least of which is the fact that even when the workshops are genuinely participative and seek to involve children and young people in decision-making, there is no guarantee that their recommendations will be implemented – a feature of all efforts to encourage citizen participation in planning deliberations, not just those targeted at children and young people. Thus, there can be an understandable tendency to prepare children for this reality by not:

> guaranteeing the children that their projects can actually be carried out and lead to any real change in the city. Caution like this, however, amplifies the educational and scholastic aspect of the activities at the expense of children's participation, which ends up seeming useless or superfluous (UNICEF, 2005, p. 35).

Nor should it be assumed that the 'new culture of childhood' requires a complete break with past practice. For example, in some Italian towns, child- and youth-specific facilities and services which found their initial justification from a 'children's services' approach to public policy have been re-oriented to a more 'children's spaces' approach. Play centres, games libraries and youth centres have all been mobilized as key spaces for facilitating children's and young people's engagement with city life, by facilitating socializing among children and between children and adults which is not instrumentally geared towards (adult-defined) educational ends. The more radical of these facilities also take a participatory and democratic approach to management which moves away from traditional adult-run facilities. Further, these child- and youth-specific services have sometimes acted as the launching pad for forays into the city, rather than acting as containment spaces to keep children and young people 'off the streets'. For instance, some of these services have established 'playbuses', which are temporarily parked in different neighbourhoods, closing off the street to other car traffic in order to facilitate play situations. The playbus acts to 'suspend, even if only momentarily, the rules governing the urban space, encouraging the presence of children within the community' (UNICEF, 2005, p. 29).

So, the Italian experience is at least suggestive of how an approach to urban policy and planning premised on the recognition of children and young people might take shape. Certainly, the Italian experience suggests that co-ordinated action at a variety of scales will be crucial to these efforts. With international and national policy frameworks in place, there have been significant intellectual, political and financial resources available to local planners, children's advocates and children who wish to recognize children and young people's capacity to participate in urban governance. As such, actors in other contexts might need to pursue action across these different scales – networking internationally for intellectual resources and examples of best practice, working through their regional and national associations to secure political and resource commitments for child friendly policies, and working at the local scale to raise awareness and foster new forms of participation and urban form in collaboration with children and young people themselves. As we mentioned in Chapter 1, and as is clear in this example, the benefits of international networking for innovative planning practice are considerable.

Now, as will no doubt have become apparent, there are also interesting questions of redistribution of resources, and encounter, that might have been addressed in relation to Child Friendly Cities. For example, the resourcing of recommendations made by Children's Councils raise related questions about the redistribution of public resources to address the needs and aspirations of children. The playbus concept also involves questions of encounter, and whether or not children will have access to spaces and events 'in the community' as well as spaces and events segregated from the rest of the city. Our next two examples take up the relationship of recognition to redistribution and encounter more explicitly.

Recognition and redistribution: planning for immigrants

The extent and form of immigration in many wealthy countries since the middle of the twentieth century has had profound consequences for cities and city life. Current forms and levels of immigration in highly-developed countries are resulting in a more varied ethnic presence within the nation. Just as the national health policies concerning deinstitutionalization we discussed in Chapter 3 are also urban policies, so too national immigration policies are also urban policies. As is generally acknowledged, immigrants tend to travel primarily to major metropolitan areas. So, while the consequences of immigration are often debated with reference to their impact on the nation-state and national cultures, cities and neigh-bourhoods within them are usually the site of lived experiences of inter-ethnic relations. As such, immigration poses a set of impor-tant questions and challenges for urban planning.

In this example, we consider ways in which planning might work to recognize the particular needs and values of immigrant groups. We begin by thinking about the relationship between immigration policies and city life in more detail, expanding upon the ways in which national immigration policies affect urban life and describing the kinds of challenges that immigration has posed to pre-existing planning frameworks. We then move on to explore the ways in which planning frameworks in Canada and Australia have responded to these challenges. In our discussion of local planning responses to immigration in these two countries, we are particularly interested in how planning frameworks have responded to claims for recognition of new, group-specific uses of spaces which challenge the assumptions of existing user groups about the 'proper' uses of those spaces. And as we shall see, planning efforts to address the forms of inequality experienced by many recently arrived migrants often combine a concern for recognition with a concern for redistribution of resources towards immigrants.

In cities with substantial immigrant populations, urban planning and governance mechanisms play a key role in shaping the terms on which inter-ethnic relations are organized and conducted. Questions of recognition inevitably confront planning frameworks in the presence of ethnic diversity. As immigrants settle in metropolitan areas, they often find their ways of inhabiting the city stifled, as 'host' populations object to practices and land uses which do not conform to their expectations about what is 'proper' and 'improper' in different parts of the city. For example, proposals for the location of non-Christian places of worship in the suburbs of London have engendered protests about loss of 'amenity' in those suburbs (Naylor and Ryan, 2002). Proposals for the location of shopping malls containing many restaurants in the suburbs of Toronto, directed at a local Chinese population whose habit it is to eat out more often than is perhaps the norm of the Anglo suburbs, have been criticized in comments suggesting that it is inappropriate to socialize outside the home so much in the suburbs, for this reduces the quiet of those suburbs (Preston and Lo, 2000, p. 188). This latter example presents a moral view about the social practices appropriate to suburbs which are supposed to be quiet and internally-focused on the domestic home, and also hints that immigrants should adhere to this view when they come to live in such a place.

Indeed, frequently the expectations of host populations about how city spaces and services ought to be organized are naturalized in the planning system and urban policy more generally – the 'hosts' assume that their way of doing things is *the* way of doing things. In addition, the adversarial nature of local planning processes based on the gathering of local residents' objections to proposed actions can give rise to racist or at the very least NIMBY-type comments from long-established residents of a place, about culturally varying uses requested by immigrant groups for local built environments (Sandercock, 2000). In this context, recognition is crucial as a means to challenge injustice by de-naturalizing assumptions about 'proper' forms of urban conduct and urban form which underpin planning and governance, making them open to debate and political determination by diverse publics.

Furthermore, these same questions of recognition are also fundamentally connected to policies concerned with the redistribution of resources to immigrant groups who may be experiencing relative disadvantage associated with their recent arrival in a country. For instance, the provision of resources such as public housing for recently arrived immigrants can be premised on a range of assumptions about family structure and size which are particular to the 'host' culture. The provision of housing and other forms of public assistance might also take for granted language capacities and legal understandings which are not shared by recently arrived immigrants from countries with different languages and legal systems.

In considering how planning might work to address the kinds of inequality experienced by immigrants described above through recognition of ethnic differences, it is important to acknowledge that national immigration policies will establish the context for localized structures of recognition. Precisely because these national frameworks vary considerably, so too localized efforts towards recognition will also vary considerably across different national contexts. There can be no 'one size fits all' approach to recognition which will apply across every national context. Planning for recognition in relation to immigrants will inevitably need to negotiate the particular ways in which national policy frameworks informed by concepts such as 'multiculturalism', 'social cohesion', 'human rights' and 'anti-discrimination' shape both the localized experience of ethnic diversity and the possibilities for local action (Sandercock, 2000; Qadeer, 1994; Reeves, 2005, p. 68 lists such 'primary equality legislation' for a number of countries). So, any formal 'overhaul' of urban planning frameworks to rectify their cultural biases would need to be made with reference to these national policies (Sandercock, 2000, p. 17).

Now, let us consider the ways in which urban planning and policy have responded to immigration in Canada and Australia. These two countries are useful to consider here because the planning issues are remarkably similar, as are the composition and extent of immigration flows and the national policies of multiculturalism. These are, of course, not the only two countries whose cities have a substantial immigrant presence, and our discussion would take quite a different direction were we to focus on other contexts. For examples with rather different inflections and outcomes, consider Diken's (1998) interesting discussion of planning responses to Turkish migration to Aarhus in Denmark, and Yiftachel's (1995) work on the planning of an Arab village in the Galilee under the Israeli planning system.

The major cities of Canada and Australia have been the destinations for large flows of immigrants since the Second World War. Not only have these immigrant flows been very large in size, but they have been extraordinarily diverse both in their origins (that is, the places from which immigrants have come) and the kinds of immigrants they have contained (including economic or business migrants, refugees and family-reunion migrants). In both countries, immigrants in the middle of the twentieth century were primarily from Europe but in the last two decades have been mainly from Asia and non-European countries. In both countries there has been a shift in immigration policy towards favouring economic migrants. Burnley *et al.* (1997) provide discussion of these trends in the Australian context, and Ley (1999) in the Canadian one.

What has planning for immigrants actually meant in these places of large-scale immigrant settlement? Planning has typically followed the lead of the national multicultural policies in treating immigrants from particular countries and regions as ethnic 'groups'. These groups have been defined primarily with regards to ethnicity, rather than (say) to gender or age or sexuality (though those aspects of personhood may be encompassed within an imagined ethnic group). The particular differences that immigration is seen to bring, and that the group-oriented planning and other policy strategies therefore identify, are differences of birthplace, language and cultural (including religious) practices, where the latter often include spatial practices and ways of using the built environment. Often an ethnic identity that crosses birthplaces and cultural groups is used by governments and host society groups to designate what seem to them to be visibly different people and practices – for example in a White settler society like Australia or Canada an 'Asian' designation might be used, or an 'African' one, despite great variations between immigrants from those regions.

Since the 1970s, when this form of multiculturalism took effect in Canada and Australia as a national policy framework, social planners have organized the provision of ethno-specific services for those identified immigrant groups. These services have been provided by government agencies and by non-government organizations, largely using federal funding. First, access has been provided to public housing in both countries. Immigrants have gained access to government-owned public housing (or at least to its waiting lists), if they have met the income criteria for such housing. But the form of housing provision has not particularly been amended to take into account the different family configurations of particular immigrant households. In Australia, suburban housing estates and the inner city high-rise housing that form much public housing stock have provided little choice in the form of housing available, being two and three-bedroom units for the most part. Though one local government in western Sydney, Fairfield, has tried to facilitate the accommodation of larger family groups by making 'granny flats' available for the suburban backyards of its public housing estates, and by allowing houses to be expanded by extensions or additions (Watson and McGillivray, 1995, pp. 171–2). In Canada, the emphasis in public housing provision has been on the use of access and equity criteria for allocations that emphasize household income, as in Australia. Housing standards in Ontario, for example, have not been responsive to questions like: what is a household, and how extended can a 'family' forming that household be; what levels of privacy between family members and between families have to be provided for (Qadeer, 1994, pp. 194–5)? In the Canadian case, where discrimination is outlawed in federal law, Mohammad Qadeer (1994, p. 195) finds it particularly inappropriate that biases like this in housing standards have not been considered more closely.

Second, there have been a range of services provided to 'ethnic communities' under federally-prescribed multiculturalism, whose form has been more sensitive to the cultural practices of those groups. Local governments have provided some of such services, though not evenly – in Australia it has been remarked that those urban areas in which immigrants have settled most densely and over long periods are the areas whose local governments, not surprisingly, adopt social and land use planning, and other, practices that most readily recognize immigrants' requirements (Thompson and Dunn, 2002). A major study of the way 'the family' was understood and provided for in 'settlement services' in Australia in the two decades of the 1970s and 1980s gives insights into the way multicultural planning has operated around issues of recognition and redistribution (Morrissey, Mitchell and Rutherford, 1991). These services and approaches were envisaged by the federal government, and then echoed at the state and local levels of government and in funding provided to non-government organizations. The study was properly critical of the limited form in which 'cultural relevance' was understood in policy-making:

> One of the main points of debate has been the question of 'mainstreaming' services to immigrants as opposed to providing 'ethnically-specific' facilities. ... a significant part of the Federal Government's Ethnic Affairs Program has been concerned with community development in various ways, including funding of community development workers attached to ethnic organisations. All of this rests on many often unvoiced theoretical beliefs: that ethnicity, culture and community are, to an extent, interchangeable – or at least complementary – categories, and that the ethnic group or 'community' is a legitimate object of social policy and in many cases an appropriate policy instrument. A critical examination of this model is required (Morrissey, Mitchell and Rutherford, 1991, p. 11).

(This comment, of course, echoes our discussion in Chapter 4 about criticisms of what we dubbed the 'group checklist' approach to planning for and with 'ethnic communities' in certain British cities in the 1990s – that the approach papers over differences within so-called communities, in favour of viewing them as homogeneous, and thus fails to recognize some important sources of diversity (see Amin, 2002)).

Having acknowledged this criticism, the study elaborates the ways 'equity' was understood in federal policy-making for the 'settlement' of immigrants in Australia as the 1980s unfolded, by the selection of particular services to fund and emphasize. The strategies to obtain 'equity' for immigrants included:

- Equipment of immigrants with access to survival resources including accommodation, English-language proficiency, usable occupational skills, income, information and support networks.
- Institutional change in which access and equity plans would be the primary step towards improved service arrangements.
- Improved community relations through the establishment of legally enforceable rights to non-discriminatory treatment and through community education.
- Cultural support so that immigrants may 'enjoy and develop' their culture and pass it on to their children unhindered (Morrissey, Mitchell and Rutherford, 1991, p. 29).

It was accepted in federal policy that the need to target resources to areas of greatest need would limit the achievement of all these aims in all the places they should be implemented. In local areas, these broad, federally-articulated goals were of course achieved through the implementation of the policies of lower levels of government. In a survey of local governments and their development of access and equity plans recognizing the presence of culturally-diverse immigrant groups in their municipalities, it was found that staff in the community services branches of local government (in which we note that social planners often work) have responded better than have land use planning, health and engineering branches (Thompson and Dunn, 2002). Land use planning officers were working through different consultative practices to try and engage different cultural groups in responding to planning proposals, but few local authorities procured regular community input from these groups, and ever fewer used their ideas to initiate planning proposals rather than to react to them.

In both Australia and Canada, the definition of services to be provided to immigrants, and a considerable amount of the funding to provide them, has been dominated by the federal governments whose policies attract immigrants to these two countries. Lower levels of government, state or provincial and local, have long complained that to them falls a burden of service provision for which they are not adequately funded, from an immigration program on which they are not consulted. For proper planning of service delivery for immigrants in cities, as in the case of the child care provision we discussed in Chapter 3, it has for many years been suggested that intergovernmental cooperation rather than federal domination is needed (Lanphier and Lukomskyj, 1994).

Mitchell's (2001) study of the arrival in Vancouver of large numbers of business migrants from Hong Kong illustrates one consequence of the last two decades' ongoing cut-backs to the federal and provincial funding of social services in Canada. As provision of services by governments has declined in Vancouver, including services for new immigrants, wealthy donors and volunteers from amongst the Hong Kong immigrants have stepped in, making contributions in particular to the non-profit social services organization SUCCESS (the United Chinese Community Enrichment Services Society). As a result, SUCCESS is now the largest provider in Vancouver's Chinatown of services like family and youth counselling, language training and a range of settlement services for immigrants of Chinese origin. It has established strong relationships with government as a key provider of settlement services, receiving government funds but also providing much in funding and volunteering so that those services remain of high standard. Its existence, claims Mitchell (2001), has muted complaints about the decline in service provision by governments, at least for this particular segment of the new immigrant population.

It is in the mediation of disputes over land use that local planning has had perhaps its most visible engagement with recognizing diversity, whilst simultaneously trying to provide access and equity as a redistributional aim. These engagements have occurred over the use of public space, particularly in suburban locations where, as we have noted, objectors to the changes proposed to local public spaces have sometimes used stereotypical notions about the desirable and unchanging uniformity of the suburbs to sustain their points of view. The building of non-Christian places of worship has been one frequent planning issue over which the mediation of planning has been required. In the suburbs of Melbourne, issues to do with religious buildings have generated heated discussion, with numerous examples of planning permission being denied for applications to build mosques or Buddhist temples in suburban areas. Rather, planners have directed applicants to build in industrial zones, citing probable noise and parking problems for the suburbs as reasons for this determination (Sandercock and Kliger, 1998, p. 130). In one municipality, an exception was made for very small Buddhist temples which could be located within suburban housing – these facilities could locate in the suburbs 'as of right'. Similarly in Sydney the location of religious buildings and the traffic they might and do generate have been the subject of planning controversies (Watson and McGillivray, 1995). The situation typically occurs thus:

> In several local government areas Muslim or Hindu communities have either established in existing residential areas, or submitted a development application for, a mosque or temple. In some cases, a number of individuals have come together to acquire a site on which a residential dwelling or warehouse is currently located. In the instances examined, the course of events is as follows: the local Muslim or Hindu community begins to use the building/s as a place of worship. As time goes on more and more people visit the site until, on certain festival days like Ramadan, very large numbers of people arrive. This causes traffic and noise problems for the local residents who alert the local council. The planning officers visit the site and inform the group that it can no longer be used as a mosque or temple unless certain regulations are complied with. In many cases, either at the end of the above stage or in initial applications, site selection for places of worship causes conflicts. The architectural forms proposed are distinct and the patterns of usage are different from the Christian norm. Parking becomes an issue because of regional drawing power and poor public transport. It is also argued that the noise impact is greater because mosques and temples are used as social meeting places as well as places of worship (Watson and McGillivray, 1995, p. 168).

From his Ontario study, Qadeer (1994) notes the issues that arise for planners at each stage of the development of a new religious building, relaying findings for Toronto similar to those about Sydney and Melbourne. Because the zoning and other planning regulations there for religious buildings are based on the characteristics of churches, standards and by-laws must be altered in order for the building in question to be a mosque, with its minarets and domes differing from a church's clock tower and spire. Over quite a long time, in Ontario, mosques have been added to the 'planning repertoire', as have Buddhist temples and Sikh gurdwaras, in a gradual process Qadeer calls 'institutional learning' (1994, pp. 195–6) which relies on an ongoing synthesis of individual cases into applied planning knowledge.

From the outer suburbs of Toronto comes another celebrated case of the interface of local planning practice with the diversity of a changing immigrant population. This is the case of Chinese shopping malls. Planning controversies about the introduction of these malls raise questions about the degree to which so-called 'neutral' or 'uniform' planning standards about retail development actually are not so 'neutral' and 'uniform'.

Wang Shuguang (1999) describes what has happened in some detail. Over the last 20 years, while the three Chinatowns of the metropolitan area of Toronto have remained important retail and services centres for the local Chinese-Canadian population, major new Chinese-identified and owned retail businesses have appeared in the suburbs. These new businesses have been targeted at the affluent immigrants from Hong Kong, who have taken up suburban locations, unlike other immigrant groups who have generally settled in inner cities. (As we have remarked already, immigrants of Chinese ethnicity make up a major proportion of immigrants to Canada over these two decades; 40 per cent of these Chinese immigrants live in Toronto.) The new businesses are in enclosed shopping malls or plazas, as opposed to the strip shopping streetfronts of the Chinatown businesses. The malls include the grocery stores and restaurants usually found in Chinese business precincts, but also many business and consumer services targeted at the immigrant Chinese market. They are located primarily in the four outer suburbs of Toronto in which the recent Chinese immigrant population has a strong presence, and are concentrated within these suburbs in addition. Wang's figures show that in 1996 there were 52 such Chinese shopping centres ranging in size from 15–200 units, in the Toronto municipality, and 22 more were proposed or being built. One of the real differences between these malls and other shopping malls is that retail ownership of units within the malls is on a condominium basis – individual businesspeople purchase the shops in the mall, rather than leasing them from the mall owner as has been common practice in the past.

The difficulties posed for municipal planning policies and practices by these new retail and business centres have been these (Wang, 1999):

● The changes have been rapid, with developers wanting to establish new malls in anticipation of an increase in the immigrant population in the localities, as well as in response to existing demand. The speed of the change has been difficult for the planning system to cope with.

● In those municipalities planning for a 3-level hierarchy of shopping centres in their areas (local, regional, specialist), these new Chinese centres do not fit into the categories. Because of their targeting of Chinese consumers, some local residents have complained these are 'specialty' centres, and that therefore there are too many of them built and proposed for the municipality to support. The centres, these arguments go, are drawing people in from other areas and therefore do not fit into local planning policy. (A similar argument is made sometimes about large mosques).

● Planning regulations about condominium retailing had not been developed. Issues like the number of units that should be permitted in such developments, and their size, had been unclear. Often in such malls the units are small and there are many of them, and so pedestrian and automobile traffic is maximized.

● The nature of the stores or businesses in the malls has been questioned. Chinese malls tend not to have department stores as 'anchor tenants', as other malls do, and contain more restaurants. The stance of planning policy on this matter has not been evident.

The response of local governments to this situation has varied, and Wang (1999) contrasts the suburban Toronto municipalities of Scarborough, Markham and Richmond Hill for the way they have applied their planning policies to the growing presence of Chinese shopping malls. Scarborough has been 'neutral' in the application of its planning policies, emphasizing only zoning, building design and site layout for the Chinese shopping centres in the same way that it does for other major buildings. But Markham and Richmond Hill have been less neutral. They have required that the Chinese-targeted

centres have department stores as anchors, like non-Chinese shopping malls do, and that the focus on restaurants and grocery stores in
the malls be reduced. This, finds Wang (1999), means that the malls
would be bound to fail, as department stores would not be interested
in anchoring a mall targeted at a population less than interested in
its goods. Restaurants and grocery stores are what guarantee the success of the Chinese malls, attracting their customers. The speed with
which Richmond Hill adjusted its by-laws to curb the development of
Chinese shopping malls has also 'hardened views prematurely, sharp-
ening the boundary between developers and concerned residents'
(Preston and Lo, 2000, p. 189).

Another local manifestation of the recognition of an immigrant
presence by planning is the facilitation of special 'ethnic settlements'
within cities, usually developed as tourist precincts and often
Chinatowns. This planning engagement differs from the examples
given above, in that the planning work required is often facilitating
or coordinating development opportunities for businesspeople to
develop the precinct. Often these are businesspeople other than
those from the ethnic group whose presence is being marked in
the local area. So it is an interesting question why Chinatowns can
be developed in this way, as business and entertainment precincts,
but not when proposed for the suburbs by Chinese businesspeople
themselves. (The fact of the location of proposed new developments
in the suburbs, and the rapid appearance of the new Chinese
malls, is no doubt a factor here.) Kay Anderson has examined
the production of Chinatowns in Canadian and Australian cities
in great detail (1990, 1991, 1998), including the role of planners
and planning in their emergence in their contemporary form. Of
course in those countries to which there was Chinese migration
in the nineteenth century, including Australia and Canada,
Chinatowns were long the locations of poverty, stigmatization and
segregation of the resident population. Until the 1970s, when
multiculturalism as a national policy perhaps suggested there were
commercial opportunities in the consumption of ethnic difference,
the major planning response to the presence of Chinatowns was to
want to do away with them. In post World War 2 Vancouver, for
example, 'urban surgery' (government-directed urban renewal)
was suggested for the longstanding Chinatown area by government
agencies which had labelled it a slum (Anderson 1991, p. 186).
(Recall from Chapter 3 this same circumstance occurring in Boston

in the 1950s, though in that case in an Italian-American residential area.) A freeway was proposed by planners for Vancouver, which would have marginalized Chinatown even further. Alliances of protesters formed, Chinese and non-Chinese. Anderson remarks:

> It was only when a new image of Chinatown was forged by a non-Chinese reform lobby in Vancouver sympathetic in outlook to the Trudeau government [proposing multiculturalism] that appeals to the district's 'difference' began to subvert the influential post-war ideology of progress (1991, p. 210).

Chinatowns do not only form because Chinese immigrants live in them and develop their businesses there, Anderson finds. In addition, Chinatowns form in Western cities, and are identified as such, because members of the host societies come to see them as representing something quintessentially 'Chinese'. The individuals in cities who shape the built environment, including business investors, developers and planners, have been significant players in this societal process of imposing a view of what is 'Chinese' on a local area then identified and marketed as Chinatown. Not only has Anderson described this process in Vancouver, but also in the Australian cities of Melbourne and Sydney (1990) and in New York City (1998). In the Australian cities, a teaming-up of Chinese entrepreneurs and non-Chinese developers and planners has resulted in the revitalization of the Chinatown tourist precincts of the inner cities, and the generation of economic benefit through increased consumption in that urban built environment. In New York City, different forms of economic benefit have been derived from the responses of government to their own and others' views of what is 'Chinese'. There, Anderson finds (1998, p. 209), the State Labour Department has allowed exploitative working conditions to exist, in the belief that the resulting 'Dickensian conditions' are what happens in Chinatowns. So economic benefit is derived in this Chinatown from the exploitation of working people, including that by Chinese entrepreneurs, but with the knowledge of government. Though the engagement of recent Chinese immigrants in the activities, workplaces and housing of Chinatowns varies from place to place, what is common to these much marketed and planned local areas is the investment in them of belief by the host society that they are appropriate representations of what is 'Chinese'. There are differences between this situation and that of attempts by entrepreneurs to establish large Chinese shopping malls in the outer suburbs. The role of planning in the situations differs too. From the cases of the suburban shopping malls described for outer Toronto, it is clear that the 'host society' of those suburbs has some doubts about the placement of something 'essentially Chinese' in a location that is 'essentially suburban'.

So what could be considered good planning practice in the situations we have described, of recognizing the diversity that immigrants bring to cities, and acknowledging that the status and well-being of newly-arrived immigrants depends on appropriate recognition? As we noted at the end of Chapter 4, there is no easy planning formula here; the various approaches available all have their limitations and benefits and must be judged as to their 'fit' in the contexts in which planning is required. Two things seem clear, however. The first is that grand planning gestures – like the encouragement of Chinatowns quite well-provided for materially but segregated from the full range of urban sites in the city in question – are less likely to result in positive outcomes than are the smaller planning gestures of fitting the recognition of immigrants' buildings and spatial practices into a range of public spaces and sites around the city. This is a message that can be gained also from claims that the 'success' of multicultural living in inner city Toronto is due in part to the visibility of diverse practices of everyday life there (Wood and Gilbert, 2005, 686). The 'institutional learning', in relatively small steps, (alongside plenty of mistakes) identified by Qadeer (1994) to be occurring in Ontario, as planners learn to cope with proposals by new immigrant groups within the planning schemes they have available to them, is producing growing numbers of more adequate outcomes. It seems unlikely that the amendment of major planning schemes by governments, to have them include the sorts of responses that should be made to immigrants' diversity in Western cities, will occur with speed, especially with the current withdrawal from multicultural advocacy of many Western governments (Mitchell, 2004). This having been said, the value in guiding planning practice that would accrue from this amendment occurring would be incalculable. The profound effect of a stated national policy of multiculturalism in Australia and Canada from the 1970s, as its implications trickled down to various areas of more local public policy, demonstrates this point.

Second, alongside a willingness to be on the lookout always for ways that the 'fit' of immigrants' diversity in local public spaces can be achieved in the full range of urban contexts, leadership should be provided by planning practice. Planning leadership should demonstrate that immigrant diversity can be accommodated and encouraged in urban landscapes, and that this is not to be feared, even if the resulting urban landscape is somewhat different from what it was some time previously, according to Preston, Kobayashi and Siemiatycki (2006). This team of Canadian urbanists, writing after the planning conflicts associated with Chinese shopping malls in the outer Toronto suburbs, makes a further vital point. They argue that a true multicultural city accepts changes that will be transforming, rather than changes which merely separate 'different' parts of the population from each other. To enable this, our norms about acceptable ways of living in the city and acceptable ways of forming the built environment need to be re-examined (Preston, Kobayashi and Siemiatycki, 2006).

Recognition and encounter: contesting hetero-normativity through planning

Our example of planning for recognition that has a concern also for encounter is of cities in which attempts have been made to accommodate diverse sexualities, rather than merely assuming heterosexuality. Recognizing the significance of same-sex relationships is rare in urban planning – the consequences of a dominant heterosexuality or 'hetero-normativity' for city life are widely unappreciated.

In this example, we consider the ways in which planning might work to recognize rather than repress alternative sexualities in the city. We begin by considering the relationship between the politics of sexuality and urban space, noting how both the normalization of heterosexuality and the construction of alternative sexual cultures are bound up with the city. We then move on to consider two examples of forms of urban governance which have worked to recognize alternative sexual cultures, looking at the formation of the Gay Village in Manchester, and the spatiality of lesbian sociability and communality in Montreal. In these examples, we demonstrate the ways in which planning might seek to combine a concern for recognition with a concern for encounter in addressing the forms of inequality associated with hetero-normativity.

Since at least the 1960s, organized social movements of gay men and lesbians have vigorously contested the normalization and privileging of heterosexuality in Western societies. These movements have drawn attention to the ways in which societies are fundamentally structured by sexualized hierarchies, which work to oppress those people whose sexuality does not fit a heterosexual norm. As these movements have shown, heterosexuality is taken for granted and therefore privileged by a constellation of institutional arrangements and moral codes. This is not only a question of whether more obviously sexualized social institutions such as marriage are restricted to heterosexual couples, or whether displays of homosexual affection and desire are subjected to violence and repression. As Lauren Berlant and Michael Warner (1998, p. 555) argue, hetero-normativity is also 'supported and extended by acts less commonly recognized as part of sexual culture'. It is:

> produced in almost every aspect of the forms and arrangements of social life: nationality, the state, and the law; commerce; medicine; and education; as well as in the conventions and affects of narrativity, romance, and other protected spaces of culture (Berlant and Warner, 1998, pp. 554–5).

In contrast, alternative sexualities are poorly represented in institutional frameworks (Berlant and Warner, 1998, p. 562). Some sexualities are not accepted or even listed, for example, in citizenship rules and welfare entitlements. Public acceptance of non-heterosexual intimacy cannot be relied upon. Simple acts of affection like kissing and holding hands, which are unremarked when heterosexual couples engage in them, can attract abuse and even violence when performed by gays and lesbians (Mason and Tomsen, 1997; Valentine, 1993).

The design and regulation of urban space contributes to making heterosexuality seem normal and natural. In cities of the contemporary West, heterosexuality has been both presumed and reproduced 'in the designs of neighbourhoods, homes, workplaces, commercial and leisure spaces' (Knopp, 1995, p. 154). Displays of sex are everywhere in public space (Valentine, 1993), from family photos on office desks to holding hands in a park. Even though sexuality would appear to belong in 'private space' rather than 'public space', in fact displays of heterosexuality across a range of apparently 'public spaces' are so ubiquitous that they are 'nearly invisible to the straight population' (Duncan, 1996, p. 137).

While complicit in the normalization of heterosexuality, cities have also provided supportive spaces in which non-normative sexual practices have been able to be established. This has occurred both through the market and local political channels. Both residential and retail capital has been used to create urban zones which are identified with gay and lesbian 'communities' – here, we might think of places such as the Castro District in San Francisco (Castells, 1983), Oxford Street in Sydney (Wotherspoon, 1991), or the Gay Village in Manchester (a place to which we will return later in this example). In such places, non-heterosexual practices and identities may become normalized, and are certainly common and visible. Furthermore, political actions by queer activists have frequently sought to contest the taken-for-grantedness of heterosexuality in the city by staging overtly non-heterosexual actions in public spaces across the city (e.g. ACT UP's 'kiss-ins' (Sommella and Wolfe, 1997)).

The emergence of identifiable 'gay spaces' in cities and insurgent protest activities have, of course, not always been welcomed by urban authorities. Indeed, in some cities such spaces and actions continue to be actively repressed. Urban planning tools are frequently mobilized in these efforts, thus working against the recognition of sexual alternatives to heterosexuality. Michael Warner's (2000) account of the impact of changes to zoning laws in New York City during the late 1990s provides a stark example of the ways in which urban policy and planning measures continue to be used to suppress alternative sexual cultures. Under the rubric of Mayor Giuliani's 'quality of life' initiative in the city, a series of planning measures were introduced which were designed to break up existing spatial concentrations of sexual countercultural activity, and to prevent the formation of new spatial concentrations. New zoning restrictions divided up the city into zones which were off-limits for 'adult businesses', and those in which adult businesses could still legally operate. Within those zones in which adult businesses were still legal, further zoning restrictions were applied to ensure that adult businesses could not be located with 500 feet of another adult business, a place of worship, a school or a day care centre. Signage and display restrictions were also introduced for adult businesses. These zoning laws were further bolstered by health ordinances which were applied to shut down commercial sex-on-premises venues, the targeted application of licensing laws to close down gay and lesbian bars and clubs, and police raids on these bars and clubs justified as drug raids. As Warner notes, the new zoning laws and other measures were designed with three principles in mind – to shift alternative sexual communities from concentration to dispersal, from conspicuousness to discretion, and from residential/commercial sites to remote sites. These measures were justified on the grounds that they would both improve 'quality of life' (which, as others (e.g. Smith, 1998) have noted, tended to be defined in very narrow terms during Giuliani's term of office), that they would reduce the 'secondary effects' associated with adult businesses (such as stifling growth in the value of nearby properties), and that they would address public health concerns (about the transmission of HIV/AIDS in particular).

But the application of dispersal, discretion and remoteness to adult businesses through urban planning has also had quite profound and harmful consequences for same-sex-based encounter in New York City. In particular, the measures have constituted an attack on the queer scene which had taken shape around Christopher St in the West Village. The small street, which had been the scene of the Stonewall Riots of 1969 which are often credited with kicking off the contemporary movement for Gay Liberation in the United States, concentrated a number of gay- and lesbian-friendly social and economic spaces. Since the introduction of Giuliani's measures, the street has been transformed. As Warner (2000, p. 169) wrote shortly after their introduction:

> Since the Stonewall Riots of 1969, queers have come to take for granted the availability of explicit sexual materials, theatres and clubs. That is how we have learned to find one another, to construct a sense of a shared world, to carve out spaces of our own in a homophobic world, and, since 1983, to cultivate a collective ethos of safer sex. All that is now about to change. Now those who want sexual materials or men who want to meet other men for sex will have to travel to small, inaccessible, little-trafficked, badly lit areas, mostly on the waterfront, where heterosexual porn users will also be relocated, where risk of violence will consequently be higher and the sense of a collective world more tenuous. The nascent lesbian culture is threatened as well, including the only video rental club catering to lesbians. The impact of the sexual purification of New York will fall unequally on those who already have fewest publicly accessible resources.

Warner's important point here is that while the measures may be impartially applied, their effects are far from impartial and will be felt more strongly by some groups. In particular, while the measures are not explicitly justified as an attack on gays and lesbians, they nonetheless work to privilege particular forms of heterosexuality at the expense of alternative forms of sexuality. Christopher St had assumed a role as a safe space for gays and lesbians due in large part to the concentration of adult businesses there:

> Not all of the thousands who migrate or make pilgrimages to Christopher St use porn shops, but all benefit from the fact that some do. After a certain point, a quantitative change is a qualitative change. A critical mass develops. A street becomes queer. It develops a dense, publicly accessible sexual culture (Warner, 2000, p. 187).

The queerness of the street has been threatened by hetero-normative zoning and planning measures. Some businesses have managed to get around the new laws by exploiting the so-called '60–40' rule. An 'adult business' is defined in the laws as one which has more than 40 per cent of its floor space devoted to 'adult material'. Shops can therefore avoid the application of the new measures by diversifying their content, to ensure that adult material constitutes less than 40 per cent of their floor space.

So, in the rest of this chapter, we ask about the alternatives for urban governance: how might urban policy and planning work to *recognize*, rather than repress, the production and expression of diverse sexualities in the city? Such a question is by no means simple to answer. In particular, debates within gay and lesbian politics and social theory more generally about the nature of sexual identities and identity politics tend to suggest different kinds of planning responses. These debates have focused on the question of whether homophobia is best addressed by recognizing the particular needs and interests of 'the gay and lesbian community', or whether it is best addressed by 'queering' society more generally so that a diversity of sexual orientations might co-exist in non-hierarchical relation to one another? In some ways, this debate maps quite neatly onto the 'check-list' versus 'cross-group' forms of recognition discussed in Chapter 4. As we shall see, planning for the recognition of diverse sexualities is not only a matter of supporting the development of so-called 'gay spaces' in the city. While such spaces are significant, as Warner and others suggest, it is important that planning for the recognition of diverse sexualities also works to challenge and transform the ambient heterosexuality of the rest of the city. In order to achieve this, we want to suggest that planning measures which take account of the importance of encounter alongside recognition can help to address some of the conditions which work to privilege particular forms of heterosexuality in the city more generally. Indeed, as we shall see in Chapter 6, sexuality theorists such as Samuel Delany have been at the forefront of work on the significance of 'encounter' for everyday life.

In order to consider the different forms that recognition of sexual diversity might take in urban governance, we want briefly to present two examples. First, we consider the production of 'gay spaces' by looking into the history of Manchester's Gay Village. Then, we move on to consider the production of what we might call a 'queer space', drawing on Julie Podmore's research on Montreal's Boulevard St Laurent.

The efforts of local activists, politicians and planners in Manchester, UK, during the 1990s to develop the 'Gay Village' present a striking contrast to the situation in New York City under Giuliani described above. The Gay Village – a relatively compact area centred on Bloom and Canal Streets in Central Manchester – is now officially recognized by the city's planning authorities and codes. While such recognition is still occasionally politically contentious (Binnie and Skeggs, 2006, p. 232), political support for the Gay Village is so strong that it regularly appears as a featured attraction in state and commercial efforts to market Manchester to tourists from the UK and further abroad:

> Maps of the Village produced by the City Council's tourist office not only formalize its boundaries and plot its entertainment institutions but also produce it as a desirable local, national and global tourist space (Moran *et al.*, 2001; see also Binnie and Skeggs, 2006; Quilley, 1997).

While Manchester had a gay and lesbian scene through the twentieth century, the growth of an identifiable Gay Village since the 1980s marked a significant shift in the spatial patterns of that scene. As Stephen Quilley (1997, p. 280) notes:

> The uniqueness of the Village lies in the fact these patterns have moved out of discrete basement bars, onto the street, and into the public

space between the bars – creating a bubble in which different rules and conventions are accepted.

The initial development of an identifiable Gay Village in Manchester can be understood to have resulted from a range of political, economic and cultural factors (Quilley, 1997, pp. 278–82). During the 1980s, Manchester's Left Labour City Council developed strong alliances with gay and lesbian activists in the city. The administration was sympathetic to gay and lesbian demands for affirmation and anti-discrimination, and materially supported community facilities and media servicing the gay and lesbian communities in the area as well as challenging homophobic attitudes in other state agencies such as the police force. At the same time, commercial operators targeting the gay and lesbian market began to take advantage of gentrifiable building stock, culminating in the construction of bars such as Manto – a spectacular piece of architecture fronted by 30-foot glass windows which was 'a brick, glass and mortar refusal to hide any more, to remain underground and invisible' (Binnie and Skeggs, 2006). Culturally, Manchester was also the centre of a significant youth subcultural movement which had taken shape in part around the gay-run and gay-friendly nightclubs and warehouse parties in the area.

By the early 1990s, the Gay Village had established a visible presence in Manchester's urban and social landscape. This visibility came to be mobilized as a resource by the city administration as the 1990s progressed, as it became increasingly concerned to make Manchester economically competitive through a combination of place-marketing efforts and property-led urban regeneration (Quilley, 1997, pp. 284–6). In this context, the Gay Village was identified as a cultural-economic asset that could be 'harnessed as an exotic proof of the city's cosmopolitan and progressive credentials' (Quilley, 1997, p. 285). As Binnie and Skeggs (2006) note, such a policy in some ways reflected Manchester's position at the vanguard of cultural-economic strategies for urban regeneration which have subsequently become more widespread. Richard Florida's (2002) widely cited work on culture-led urban development strategies makes an explicit link between the 'Gay Index' (a measure designed to capture a city's gay friendliness) and the presence of the 'Creative Class' which is required to drive development.

Now, the consolidation of the Gay Village represents a significant victory for Manchester's gay and lesbian communities. The recognition of gay and lesbian attachment to this part of the city has helped to construct a concentration of community and commercial facilities which sustain, rather than repress, the formation of communities which seek to explore alternative forms of affection and desire. Further, the official recognition of, and support for, the Gay Village has helped to make these sexual alternatives more visible in the wider public sphere, rather than forcing them into the shadows in order to survive. However, as with other 'gay spaces' around the world, the Gay Village has also produced its own set of contradictions and difficulties.

First, the nature of the Gay Village as a predominantly (and increasingly) commercial space has produced its own forms of inequality and inaccessibility. With its gentrification and incorporation into Manchester's economic strategy, the Gay Village has been explicitly marked as a 'cosmopolitan' quarter of the city. The more 'cosmopolitan' bars, cafés and clubs that have opened up since the gentrification of the area in the 1990s tend to be targeted towards young, relatively wealthy and male clientele. Due to their relative economic position, both working class gays and lesbians have a much less visible presence in, and connection to, the forms of sociability privileged in the Village (Moran *et al.*, 2001, p. 410). So, as Moran *et al.* (2001, p. 410) put it, 'The Village is thus predominantly represented as gay = gay men'.

Second, for some gays and lesbians, the safety associated with being in 'their' Village is bound up with a fear of incursion. Precisely because the Gay Village is a bounded 'gay space' within a wider urban context, anxieties over the boundaries of this space and their effectiveness have emerged. On the one hand, the very visibility of the Village has made it an obvious target for homophobic violence (and, indeed, ongoing police repression). On the other hand, the 'gayness' of the space has also drawn large groups of straight women, hoping to escape the unwanted attentions of straight men which are characteristic of other nightlife spaces in the city. As a consequence, interviews with gay men and lesbian women in Manchester conducted by Leslie Moran and her colleagues (2001) revealed a widely-shared fear of 'heterosexual invasion'. The very notion that the Village was 'gay space' or property, in other words, helped to sustain both feelings of security *and* violation, such that when the gay and lesbian community acquired a territorial status in the Village, this worked to 'produce simultaneously a property relation and an experience of a violation of a claim to property' (p. 408).

So, the experience in Manchester suggests that when recognition takes the form of official affirmation of 'gay spaces' which are effectively islands in a surrounding sea of heterosexuality, this outcome works to address some forms of inequality and harm while not necessarily addressing others. Gay spaces both enable the critical mass required for the formation of alternative sexual communities, while also potentially containing those alternative communities and their norms to bounded and identified parts of the city.

Perhaps the experience of lesbians in Montreal points to alternative forms of recognition which might be pursued simultaneously with the affirmative forms of recognition described above. Montreal, like Manchester, has its own identifiable 'gay village'. And, like in Manchester, this gay village has tended to be overwhelmingly gay *male* space (Podmore, 2006). Julie Podmore's (2001; 2006) investigations into the territorial dimensions of lesbian sociality in the city suggest that other spaces have acquired an important role for lesbians alongside the gay village. In particular, her informants spoke of the significance of another space – 'the Main', a section of Boulevard St-Laurent. 'The Main' is not, as Podmore points out, a 'gay' or 'lesbian' or indeed 'queer' space. It is, rather, a street which is shared by a remarkable diversity of uses and users:

> The heterogeneity involves the mixing of class, age and ethnic groups, as well as an assortment of land uses, including commerce, residence, industry and cultural production. ... While strolling 'the Main' on an afternoon, one encounters the clientele of some of the most expensive and fashionable restaurants in the city, suburban shoppers in search of European foods and newspapers, tourists disembarking from buses for a lunchtime stroll, new immigrants and neighbourhood residents shopping for inexpensive household goods, and, occupying the street itself, are a wide array of interrelated youth subcultures (squeegee punks, students, artists, musicians, and gays and lesbians). At night, many different populations find their niche in the bars and restaurants, but the majority cater to heterosexual populations from outside the area, especially suburban youths and/or young professionals (Podmore, 2001, p. 338).

Podmore (2001, p. 338) refers to Boulevard St-Laurent as a 'space of difference', but in our terms here, we might also refer to this street as a 'space of encounter'. Interestingly, for our purposes, the vibrancy of this street as a space of encounter:

> facilitates [lesbian] patterns of sociability and communality, place-making strategies and even the expression of desire – despite the fact that it is not a 'lesbian territory' (Podmore, 2001, p. 351).

This occurs, according to the women interviewed by Podmore, because on 'the Main' they feel able to 'blend into the crowd'. Precisely because the street is not 'owned' by any one group, there seems to be a 'greater possibility for a lesbian presence' (Podmore, 2001, p. 342). And precisely because the street is felt by those who share it to be an 'alternative' space, sexual alternatives become just one alternative among many. As one of her informants put it:

> You see it all, the whole gamut. In that aspect, I find that people tend not to look or stare or tend not to be shocked by [homosexuality] as much as they would in other areas that tend to be a little more conservative (quoted on p. 343).

Or, as another put it, 'on St-Laurent it's just so full of freaks that you're never the weirdest one there' (quoted on p. 342). The lesbian women of colour interviewed by Podmore also drew favourable comparisons between St-Laurent and Montreal's gay village. As one put it:

> You escape the ghetto of being in the Village where everybody assumes that you're a lesbian and nothing else. You can go to St-Laurent Street and be a lesbian and be so much more, it seems to me, than just a lesbian. It's where I feel the most comfortable with all the things that I am (quoted p. 343).

Such descriptions of how it feels to use the Main fit nicely with the 'cross-group' forms of recognition we described in Chapter 4, which emphasize the need for decision-rules to move beyond the 'affirmation' of essentialized identities in favour of a more transformative politics of identity. The notion that one can 'be lesbian and be so much more' is a lovely description of a transformative politics of identity. To put this in more abstract terms, on Boulevard St-Laurent one can be both a 'lesbian' and a 'stranger' among others strangers – and as such, a transformative politics of recognition is associated with the capacity of the street to sustain encounters among strangers.

This second example from Montreal, then, suggests that an acknowledgement of the importance of encounter in urban policy and planning can itself work to address inequalities associated with misrecognition, by facilitating the recognition of alternative sexual cultures as one alternative among many. In this instance, we see the repression of lesbians in Montreal being addressed by their capacity to 'blend into the crowd' as strangers rather than being negatively marked as 'deviant' with reference to a heterosexual norm. Now, it may appear that 'planning' does not have much to do with this outcome. However, as we shall argue in the next chapter, spaces of encounter such as Blvd St-Laurent do require planning, even if that planning involves a 'light touch' (Shaw, 2005).

Finally, we would emphasize that such a strategy for recognition also has its limitations. In this case, the integration of lesbians into heterogeneous spaces does not necessarily facilitate the 'critical mass' of commercial and community facilities that are possible in more territorialized community formations, thus potentially reducing lesbian visibility in the city. As we noted in Chapter 4, while 'transformative' or 'cross-group' forms of recognition do mitigate some of the problems associated with 'affirmative' or 'checklist' forms of recognition (such as the affirmation of 'gay villages' through planning), they bring with them their own tensions and difficulties.

Conclusion

This chapter has presented three cases of planning for recognition: planning for child friendly cities, planning for immigrants and planning for sexual diversity. In each example, our concern has been to discuss ways in which planning for recognition can address 'taken-for-granted' spatial norms which privilege some groups and their uses of the city over others.

In the examples, it is evident how concerns for redistribution and for encounter have accompanied the attempts we have described to plan for recognition of group characteristics and needs. With planning for Child Friendly Cities, the identification of children as a 'group' lacking adequate citizenship and representation in the city has been presented here as a case of recognition alone. But it also has elements of concern for encounter (of bringing children together in a range of non-segregated settings), and of redistribution (if one interprets the extending of citizenship rights to the city as a redistribution of access entitlements). Planning for the presence of immigrants has a redistributional interest as well as an interest in recognizing immigrants' diverse cultures and ways of living in the city, for this planning understands the need to direct special governmental services to often-disadvantaged new arrivals in cities. We could, of course, also see an interest in encounter in planning for immigrants, for the facilitating of public buildings desired by immigrant groups is all about encouraging those groups to gather together. Planning that recognizes a more diverse range of sexualities is about facilitating encounter and sociality within and between sexually-identified groups. To the extent that it goes beyond enhancing the interests of well-resourced gay men, and extends to consider the social needs of economically less-advantaged same-sex groups, this planning may also make a strong contribution to redistribution.

Of importance in all three case examples is the tension between providing separate and possibly segregated services or urban spaces for an identified group, as a form of recognition of that group, and integrating services and spaces for that group within the 'mainstream' public culture and its spatial expression (however this 'public' might be defined – a political question in itself). Of course this is the longstanding policy and political issue of whether 'mainstreaming' is better than 'separating' provisions for groups. (Reeves (2005) has some discussion of this). This tension also maps on to the decision rules for planning for recognition that we described in Chapter 4 – the checklist and cross-group approaches to resource allocation in planning – in which mainstreaming is perhaps an intention of cross-group approaches, and making separate provisions is perhaps an intention of checklist approaches (though we do not wish align the ways of proceeding too closely). As we have argued through the book, there is no one easy answer as to which is the best way forward, for all situations. In a perfect world, one transformed so that the interests and needs of many groups were routinely recognized and imaginatively and progressively planned for, the cross-group strategy would be preferred. It has the benefit of allowing people to have a range of identities, as one of Podmore's (2001) respondents appreciated about Montreal's Boulevard St-Laurent, a heterogeneous and inclusive space. In the absence of suitably transformed urban settings, however, both checklist and cross-group decision rules, and indeed mainstreaming and particularistic policy approaches, must be available to be used as a context demands.

6 Conceptualizing Encounter in Planning

So far, we have considered both redistribution and recognition as goals for planning which seek to promote just diversity by fostering rights to the city. As we have seen, the logics of redistribution and recognition are designed to deal with different kinds of diversity. The former seeks to eradicate the diversity of 'rich' and 'poor', by reducing or eliminating those forms of urban inequality which are a product of the maldistribution of resources. The latter seeks to accommodate the diversity of group distinctiveness, by attacking those forms of inequality which are a product of failures to recognize the existence of different needs and values. However, the forms of diversity which we have discussed in relation to redistribution and recognition do not exhaust the forms of diversity experienced in city life. Indeed, while these two strategies are concerned with the diverse *identities* of urban inhabitants (as citizens and group members, respectively), we should not reduce urban inhabitants to these rather fixed identity categories. To do so is both to miss the individual urban inhabitant's own potential for multiplicity, and to neglect the role of planning in enhancing their opportunities for 'becoming someone else' as well as 'being themselves'. In this chapter, we argue that such matters are appropriately the object of urban planning and policy, alongside those discussed in previous sections. For city life can both constrain and enable our capacity to explore different sides of ourselves and to craft new identifications through encounters with others as strangers. As such, the right to the city is also a right to *encounter*. In the following two chapters, then, we develop a case for encounter as a goal of planning. In this chapter, we build our case for encounter as an important social logic of urban planning by examining the unpredictability and complexity of urban life, exploring in particular the ways in which planning might foster the kinds of conviviality which can sustain encounters among the strangers who share (and pass through) cities. As with previous sections, our aim in this first chapter on encounter is to develop a framework that can be applied to develop a set of 'rules of thumb' which might inform planning efforts to promote encounter, which are then illustrated with examples in our next chapter.

Planning for disorder?

In contemporary planning commentary about the social complexity of the city, it is often claimed that we need (perhaps paradoxically) to plan for greater experimentation in cities, and to accept variety and unpredictability in outcomes. Consider, for example, Iris Marion Young's (1990, pp. 238–41) call for urban policy and planning to promote four virtues of urban life: social differentiation without exclusion; variety; eroticism; and publicity. Each of these virtues is clearly related to the inherent disorder at the heart of urban life in cities. Social differentiation without exclusion is a matter of groups overlapping and intermingling across neighbourhood borders which are 'open and undecidable' (1990, p. 239). Variety of land use in neighbourhoods is important because it will draw people to 'go out and encounter one another on the streets' (1990, p. 239). Eroticism concerns the 'pleasure and excitement of being drawn out of one's secure routine to encounter the novel, the strange, the surprising' (1990, p. 239). And in public spaces, an urban inhabitant 'always risks encounter with those who are different, those who identify with other groups and have different opinions or different forms of life' (1990, p. 240). Here, a new logic for planning is being enunciated: the need to facilitate *encounters* between people, like and unlike, through a planning practice which does not seek to eradicate all forms of disorder in urban life.

Arguments for planning to facilitate encounter and disorder are often based on critiques of planning for redistribution and recognition. For instance, certain forms of redistributional planning have been taken to task for their inattention to the importance of small-scale, casual and unpredictable encounters in cities. The now-classic work of Jane Jacobs in *The Death and Life of Great*

American Cities was primarily concerned with the impact of urban renewal programs (such as those discussed by Gans to which we referred in Chapter 3) on this aspect of city life. Jacobs wrote in defence of neighbourhood forms which were under-valued by the dominant modes of redistributional planning, on the grounds that they sustained 'sidewalk contacts' which were fundamentally important to urban life. 'Lowly, unpurposeful and random as they may appear, sidewalk contacts are the small change from which a city's wealth of public life may grow' (Jacobs, 1961, p. 72). In addition to her observations about the life of the urban street, Jacobs made suggestions for planning:

> [M]ost city diversity is the creation of incredible numbers of different people and different private organizations, with vastly differing ideas and purposes, planning and contriving outside the formal framework of public action. The main responsibility of city planning and design should be to develop – insofar as public policy and action can do so – cities that are congenial places for this great range of unofficial plans, ideas and opportunities to flourish, along with the flourishing of the public enterprises. City districts will be economically and socially congenial places for diversity to generate itself and reach its best potential if the districts possess good mixtures of primary uses, frequent streets, a close-grained mingling of different ages in their buildings, and a high concentration of people (Jacobs, 1961, p. 241–2).

Likewise, writing a decade or so after Jacobs, Richard Sennett condemned planners' obsession with ordering the urban environment for pre-defined uses – an obsession he considered to be the harmful consequence of fear-driven desires to 'free the individuals of the community from the need to confront and interact with each other directly' (Sennett, 1970, p. 83).

Alongside these critiques of planning efforts to redistribute through urban renewal, new critiques have also begun to emerge about the harmful impact of certain forms of planning for recognition. In particular, affirmative forms of multiculturalism (such as those discussed in Chapter 4) have been accused of stifling encounters among diverse urban inhabitants. Multiculturalism is seen in some places and by some analysts to have over-emphasized the boundaries between people, both in its philosophy and its practice. Alain Touraine (2000, p. 187), for instance, has found identity politics to be acting 'solely in the name of its difference' rather than in the interests of interaction. He is critical of the static nature

of the group identities promoted in some forms of multiculturalism he observes in Europe:

> In a world ... where no culture is really isolated, and where women and
> men from all continents, societies and all forms and stages of historical
> development mingle on the streets of the cities, on television screens
> and on cassettes of world music, it is both ludicrous and dangerous to
> attempt to defend a timeless identity ... we therefore have to assign
> a positive value to these fusions and encounters which allow us all
> to expand our own experience and to make our own culture more
> creative (Touraine, 2000, p. 182).

He sees a successful multicultural society as one in which 'the greatest
possible number of individual lives are constructed' (2000, p. 181),
in a process in which individuals design their own communications
and interactions according to how they perceive their similarities to
others and their differences from others. Ulrich Beck (2002, p. 21) is of
a similar mind. Like Touraine, he objects to the way multiculturalism
(as he sees it) 'fosters a collective image of humanity in which the
individual remains dependent on his cultural sphere' (p. 36), and in
which the individual is 'protected' from change to that identity. Both
Touraine and Beck, then, are proposing a more fluid interpretation
of identity. They are critical of policies which are premised on reified
cultural groups, and suggest a move towards policies which recognize
(and encourage) individual distinctiveness produced through everyday encounters with others in globalizing cities.

These critiques of (certain forms of) redistribution and recognition
in planning, then, share a hostility towards separation and confinement as strategies for dealing with the messy diversity and disorder
of city life. The desire to confine and separate certain activities and
groups of people to pre-defined parts of the city (characteristic of
urban renewal and 'modernist' land use zoning more generally)
is roundly rejected. Rejected also is the desire to group people
according to pre-defined group identities (characteristic of affirmative multiculturalism). In place of separation and confinement, these
critiques suggest that the inherent hybridity of both places and people ought to be acknowledged and embraced as a condition of urban
life. That is, places should be viewed as capable of sustaining a range
of different activities rather than being defined through functional
segregation, and people should be treated as capable of sustaining
a range of identities and identifications in different situations.

In contemporary urban studies, critiques of planning through separation and confinement are increasingly articulated with reference to cosmopolitan visions of the city. As Tajbakhsh (2001, p. xv) puts it, 'the idea of cosmopolis is a radical alternative to both social homogeneity and a plurality of mutually exclusive enclaves – which in the end are the same'. For Tajbakhsh (and others such as Sandercock (1998; 2003)), in the ideal cosmopolis, hybridity is both acknowledged and valued over homogeneity, in order to contest 'enclave consciousness' (Tajbakhsh, 2001, p. 182). Cosmopolitan visions of the ideal city are also offered as responses to the complex changes to urban life wrought by the increasing global movements of people, ideas, cultures and commodities along a dizzying array of trajectories. Such movements are said to have further deepened the diversity of people and places. The 'internalised globalisation' (Beck, 2002, p. 17) of nations and cities mean that people are increasingly 'place polygamists': 'They are married to many places in different worlds and cultures. Transnational place-polygamy, belonging in different worlds: this is the gateway to globality in one's life' (Beck, 2002, p. 24). The point here is that some kind of cosmopolitanism is a lived reality for many, particularly in the global cities. Dürrschmidt (2000) concurs, concluding from his study of individuals in London that:

> people's familiar routines, their feeling of belonging, and their meaningful relationships to significant others, are increasingly delinked from the primacy of locality and local community. Relatedly, there is a complementary story-line articulating the individual's active effort to generate and maintain situatedness and familiarity within a field of action and experience that stretches across distance and beyond the definition power of local settings (2000, p. 17).

The consequences of this 'place-polygamy' for urban life are profound. In particular, when (some) people's feelings of belonging are increasingly delinked from locality and local community, then they might experience localities and local communities not as 'locals' but as 'strangers'. And of course, this implies that the places in which people do feel that they belong as 'locals' are also likely to be shared with others who they consider to be 'strangers'. From this perspective, the disorderly presence of strangers is therefore a condition of everyday urban life. Any attempt to render urban life totally predictable and ordered through planning for separation and confinement is thus a 'war declared on strangers' (Bauman, 1995, p. 128).

There are interesting tensions to be explored in considering the role that planning might play in embracing hybridity and fostering encounters among 'strangers'. To embrace and plan for the presence of strangers is to embrace and plan for a degree of disorder in the city. But is it possible to plan for disorder, or is this a contradiction in terms? While we acknowledge the role that urban planning has often played in inhibiting rather than fostering the kinds of disorder that facilitate encounter, we nonetheless want to insist on the important role of planning (often from within the state) in facilitating this creative and disorderly encounter. Like Jacobs (1961), Wilson (1991) and more recently Sandercock (2003) and Keith (2005), we do not see spaces of encounter as beyond the claim of planning, when planning is carried out as a mode of governance in which the state is a major player. As Wilson (1991, p. 115) points out, commenting on Jacobs's work, while the condition of urban streets and activities might seem creatively disordered if left alone and unplanned by public agencies, they may well be under orchestration by purposeful actions in the privately run housing market and other forms of 'unfettered capitalist development'. Gentrification, notes Wilson, was what happened in Jacobs's areas of 'rich street life' when they were left alone, unplanned, in their diversity. Indeed, like Michael Keith (2005), we find it unhelpful to imagine the spaces of encounter as wholly outside either the state *or* the market, in some pure conception of 'civil society'. As he (2005, p. 43) notes, 'such space exists principally in romanticised narratives of city life'.

Now, our assertion that planning has an important role to play in fostering those forms of disorder which facilitate encounters among strangers raises many questions. As we articulate a planning for encounter, it is important to suggest the scale at which such disorder is desirable, what it achieves by way of creative and productive encounter, and who benefits and loses from it in different contexts. Most importantly, planning for *encounters* among *strangers* requires us to articulate what we mean by, and what we value in, both concepts. As Goffman (1961, p. 7) pointed out in his classic studies of 'encounter', if one defines an encounter simply as a situation in which 'people effectively agree to sustain for a time a single focus of cognitive and visual attention', then encounters can clearly take many forms – not all of which we may want to embrace in efforts to promote just forms of diversity. '[C]ard games, ballroom couplings, surgical teams in operation, and fist fights provide examples of encounters' (Goffman, 1961, p.298): so which kinds of encounters should planning seek to foster, and why?

Important concepts: the stranger and conviviality

Central to planning for encounter are two concepts – the stranger (the individual who is to be welcomed or accommodated by such planning), and conviviality (which is the form of encounter among strangers to be facilitated by such planning). In this section we will first discuss the characteristics of the stranger, for the stranger is the imagined object of planning for encounter. Where the uniform or homogeneous citizen is the object of redistributive planning, and groups of identified people are the object of planning for recognition, the individual stranger is the person at the centre of planning for encounter. We will then examine the form of contact or conviviality to be achieved in planning for encounter, which will occur at particular local sites.

The stranger

The figure of the stranger, as we have seen above, has been key in efforts to theorize the importance of encounter for urban life. Estrangement is indeed a condition of urban life, generated by the incessant mobility of urban inhabitants (see for example Certeau, 1984; Bauman, 1995; Dikeç, 2002). Urbanites are constantly on the move – between cities, within cities – in pursuit of everyday activities such as work, leisure, care, study, shopping, eating and so on. Thus, in one sense, 'we' are all strangers at some time and place or another. And there can be no place without strangers, for all localities are populated by inhabitants with social spheres of different horizons, such that each local 'reality is constituted by the intermeshing and interrelating of these spheres' (Albrow, 1997, pp. 47–8). For some theorists of the city, this condition of estrangement literally defines urban life. For example, Iris Marion Young (1990, p. 240) defines city life as 'a being together of strangers'.

Likewise for Richard Sennett (1994, pp. 25–6), 'the city brings together people who are different, it intensifies the complexity of social life, it presents people to each other as strangers'.

But the notion that urban inhabitants share a condition of strangerhood is not to say that everyone experiences this stranger-hood in the same way. While the claim that 'we' are all strangers can be sustained at one level, it begins to break down when we take account of the very different experiences of mobility that character-ize urban inhabitants. Urban populations are in fact stratified by their different mobilities (Bauman, 1995, p. 130). For one thing, the resources required for movement are not equally shared. Nor are choices about where and when we move unconstrained – for instance, some movements may be forced rather than voluntary (think here, for example, of the mobility forced on recipients of unemployment benefits with job-search requirements), and some pathways may be restricted for some people and not others (think here, for example, of border controls and requirements designed to keep 'economic migrants' from moving internationally between cities in search of work).

Furthermore, not only do different strangers have different opportunities for movement – the hospitality extended to differ-ent strangers in different circumstances can also vary enormously. When somebody is constructed as 'strange' by those claiming the status of 'host' in a particular locale, they may experience this strangerhood in a range of ways (Diken, 1998). Some strangers may be warmly welcomed, their particular attributes valued as exotic and desirable. But even here, this welcome may take the form of an indifference and appreciation from a distance – that is, even when a locale is apparently hospitable to strangers and open to diversity, 'the sheer fact of diversity does not prompt people to interact' (Sennett, 1994, p. 357). Some strangers, on the other hand, may be viewed with hostility, 'treated as detestable strangers with no "right to the city"' (Deutsche, 1999, 176). For instance, racist responses to the presence of individuals of particular bodily appearance, in certain places, are not uncommon in cities. This hostile response is often associated in the literature with communitarian desires to overcome the estrangement characteristic of urban life through the creation of boundaries which will facilitate harmony, consensus and mutual understanding (Young, 1990, p. 229: see also Donald, 1999; Deutsche, 1999; Tajbakhsh, 2001).

So, while some urban inhabitants might be in the fortunate position to be 'connoisseurs of metropolitan life' who move around the city in order to 'meet the stranger or experience the strange on [their] terms and in settings [they are] able to choose and feel comfortable in' (as was the case for one of the individuals studied by Dürrschmidt, 2000, p. 150), not all are so fortunate. Indeed, to say that urban inhabitants are all strangers is certainly not to say that they are all 'flâneurs' – those characters who freely and randomly wandered the city in nineteenth century Paris without any purpose other than taking pleasure in the 'beauty' to be found in the everyday, in 'streets, factories and urban blight', and in the 'trivial, fragmented aspects of street life' (Wilson, 1991, p. 5). Rather, there are quite different experiences of estrangement. Given these different experiences, the task of planning is to identify and facilitate opportunities for positive experiences of strangerhood. This is not a matter of becoming (just like) a 'local', but rather, a matter of having opportunities to move around the city as a 'stranger' and thus to have a full range of experiences of urban life. How, we ask, might planning help to create the conditions in which urban inhabitants can move within/between cities, participating in encounters with others which allow them to 'glimpse their own hybridity, their own contingency' (to paraphrase Tajbakhsh, 2001, p. 183), alongside their more fixed identities as group members and citizens?

This is not, we would emphasize, simply a matter of demanding that all urban inhabitants be 'open' to the arrival of strangers. Nor do we argue that any differentiation among the many strangers we encounter is inherently unethical, as if one could treat everybody as a 'stranger' rather than making distinctions between people based on particular characteristics. Where some cosmopolitan visions of the good city tend to demand such openness (see Iveson, 2006b), for us, a different strategy is required. We agree that encounters among strangers (rather than indifference or hostility) are a desirable goal for urban life, in order that all urban inhabitants have opportunities to explore their own hybridity through experiencing a variety of different situations and people in the course of their everyday lives. But we argue that such encounters are most likely to take place as a consequence of engagement in shared projects and labour, rather than as a consequence of some virtuous 'openness' to strangers which is informed by an appreciation of our shared 'strangerhood'. In other words, rather than expecting urban inhabitants to approach others either on the basis of their 'commonality (a community of friends) or uncommonality (a community of strangers)' (Ahmed, 2000, p. 179), we believe that encounters take place through the *identifications* which characterize everyday interactions in different situations. As Laurier *et al.* (2002, p. 353) note, while the figure of 'the stranger' has a certain use in urban theory, we should not assume that it is a concept that can be used in the course of ordinary urban interactions. Rather:

> the massively apparent fact is that people in cities do talk to one another as customers and shopkeepers, passengers and cabdrivers, members of a bus queue, regulars at cafés and bars, tourists and locals, beggars and by-passers, Celtic fans, smokers looking for a light, and ... as neighbours (Laurier *et al.*, 2002, p. 353).

Facilitating encounters and hybridity, then, is a matter of enhancing the number of opportunities for people to experiment with these different identifications with others in a range of different situations. These identifications and the encounters they sustain can be fleeting and temporary, but they are vital resource for opening up opportunities for all to experience 'strangerhood' without rejection and/or indifference. As we shall see in the next chapter, for instance, it is precisely through their use of a library newspaper reading room that a variety of individuals – who may also be identified as 'young', 'old', 'homeless', etc. – can adopt a shared identification as a 'library user' which allows them all to glimpse another dimension of themselves and each other. This is not a matter of being *either* a homeless person *or* a library user, but a matter of being a homeless person *and* a library user. Planning for encounters among strangers, then, is a matter of working towards a kind of *conviviality* in urban life, where diverse individuals can work together on shared activities, projects and concerns which don't totally reduce them to fixed identity categories either as 'citizen' or 'group member' (even as such identity categories will always remain important, for reasons we have explored in previous sections).

Conviviality

Conviviality is the state of encounter we seek in our suggestions for local planning. It is more than the free mingling of people in large public squares and spaces. It is more than the apparently aimless wandering of the flâneur, being pleasant to those strangers s/he may see. Rather, conviviality as we see it describes encounters with a certain intent or purpose. These forms of encounter may be quite fragile and often fleeting. They depend for their existence on the availability or construction of certain settings in which urban inhabitants can explore shared identifications (in addition to identities) through shared activities. The conviviality that can emerge through such encounters is certainly distinct from 'community' characterized by shared identities. As Paul Gilroy (2004, p. xi) puts it, the concept of conviviality 'introduces a measure of distance from the pivotal term "identity". ... The radical openness that brings conviviality alive makes a nonsense of closed, fixed, and reified identity and turns attention toward the always-unpredictable mechanisms of identification.' As such, the concept of conviviality offers an alternative to more communitarian frameworks for approaching urban encounter such as 'social cohesion' and 'social capital', both of which tend to privilege lasting relationships and bonds established through shared values.

To flesh out our concept of conviviality, let us turn first to the writings of Ivan Illich. Writing more than 30 years ago about conviviality and how it might come to exist, Illich (1973) saw a 'convivial' society as one in which the tools or technologies needed for modern life were controlled by individuals rather than by large and powerful organizations. His was a view of conviviality that saw it as the product of purposeful individuals determining their own fates, having access to technologies and means of being productive at their own choosing. Illich opposed the monopoly of the professions over the ways to do things, and also of course the control of people's endeavours by major corporations and institutions. He eschewed expert knowledge, in particular, arguing that '[o]verconfidence in "better knowledge" becomes a self-fulfilling prophecy. People first cease to trust their own judgement and then want to be told the truth about what they know' (Illich, 1973, p. 86). His view of the individual as an agent able to resolve his or her similarities and differences with others in order to work or socialize with them has some similarity to the views on this subject held by Beck and Touraine discussed earlier. Illich's is clearly a perspective of convivial interaction, which is about people being productive together, but it is about formed individuals making their own choices in the way this productive activity is carried out. While his perspective did locate conviviality outside both market and state institutions in a rather romanticized vision of civil society, it is nonetheless particularly suggestive for our efforts to articulate the role of planning in facilitating encounter.

The eminent planner Lisa Peattie has taken up Illich's ideas recently, and written of their applicability to planning in public spaces and social activities. She sees the idea of conviviality, as developed by Illich, as an alternative to 'community', for the way it recognizes the 'sociable pleasure in many kinds of purposeful activities'. Rather than viewing people's interactions as about sharing interests developed over the long term and for permanence, as the idea of community usually does, conviviality stresses people 'remaking their world' and being creative even in very small ways (Peattie, 1998, p. 247). Peattie includes as well in her discussion the more common-sense meaning of conviviality, as sociability often over eating and drinking. And she points to ways planning can facilitate conviviality:

> Conviviality can take place with few props: the corner out of the wind where friends drink coffee together, the vacant lot which will become a garden. But it must have some sort of material base – the right-shaped corner, the piece of vacant land and a couple of rakes – and it must have the rules that permit it. Conviviality cannot be coerced, but it can be encouraged by the right rules, the right props, and the right places and spaces. These are in the domain of planning (Peattie, 1998, p. 248).

One of the things Peattie emphasizes is the presence of 'third spaces' – places like coffee shops, community or drop-in centres, bars, even post offices and general stores – which are the out-of-home and outside-work sites that 'get you through the day' because they offer sociability and familiarity (1998, p. 249). Conviviality can occur in a range of guises, as Peattie says, and can be more or less bounded – that is, more or less exclusionary. Street festivals in public space are unbounded occasions. Around the edges of public squares, however, one often finds cafés, in which one must pay to sit and consume. There are economic limitations to conviviality in such third spaces; the relationship between commerce and conviviality, as Peattie notes, is important and varied. There are also boundaries relating to like-mindedness, or to having similar characteristics, that limit other types of gatherings – child care centre working bees, or political meetings, for example.

The concept of 'conviviality' can also be further developed with reference to recent interventions in debates about the future of multiculturalism in Britain. Ash Amin (2002), for example, has suggested that successful, intercultural interaction among strangers is most likely to take shape through 'micro-publics' – that is, through sites of purposeful and organized group activity like workplaces, schools, and community organizations where people might interact in pursuit of common projects and goals that are not defined with reference to ethnic identities and differences. In a similar vein, Paul Gilroy (2006, p. 40) suggests that participation in such sites and activities is a very ordinary part of everyday life for residents of British cities:

> Conviviality is a social pattern in which different metropolitan groups dwell in close proximity, but where their racial, linguistic and religious particularities do not – as the logic of ethnic absolutism suggests they must – add up to discontinuities of experience or insuperable problems of communication.

Conviviality, in other words, is fostered by 'institutional, demographic, generation, educational, legal and political commonalities as well as elective variations' (2006, p. 40) which have worked to produce and sustain alternative identifications alongside those based on fixed identity categories (such as 'race'). Like Illich, Gilroy celebrates the capacity that urban inhabitants have demonstrated to work together and identify with one another in a range of situations, thereby challenging (if not entirely eradicating) racism and its associated segregation. And like Peattie's concept of the 'third space', Amin's concept of 'micro-publics' directs us to find ways our planning can enhance the development of sites of conviviality.

But alongside the more purposeful versions of encounter, like those discussed by the likes of Illich and Amin, there is something to be said for conviviality as neighbourly greeting, of a mutually non-interfering kind as described by Dürrschmidt (2000). Often convivial encounters occur on a very casual, relatively detached, basis. As Dürrschmidt says (2000, p. 155), there is great value in cities in sharing with neighbours the 'non-intrusive presence of certain nearest others'. This means being pleased to have others about, and speaking with them occasionally because one sees them from time to time, but living close to them on the basis of 'civil inattention' or 'mutual non-interference'. This form of sociability can occur in third spaces, as these are the places where one often bumps into those living round about. Perhaps this is best termed 'contact' – and perhaps in many situations it may be beyond the control of planning to facilitate, lest one stray into the 'urban conduct' campaigns of some contemporary governments.

Delany (1999) has penned a fine account of 'contact' in New York City, and how it has been threatened for some groups by the redevelopment of Times Square in the late 1990s. He sees occurrences like occasional chats in supermarket lines, and being pleasant in greeting people living round about whom one often then notices again and again, as part of the operation of healthy cities. He regards the inter-class nature of such interaction as part of its particular importance. As was the case with Dürrschmidt's contemporary flâneur, he is clear that we cannot see these interactions as random, and without selection – for we choose, after all, which areas to live in, where to shop and where to walk. Certain urban redevelopments, Delany argues, destroy such inter-class interactions: this is his assessment of the redevelopment of Times Square. (Deutsche (1999) shares his view, being critical of a range of homogenizing urban redevelopments carried out under the banner of 'quality-of-life' improvements to cities). So, says Delany (1999, p. 43), making the redevelopment of Times Square sound like some of the examples of mid-twentieth century urban renewal we discussed in Chapter 3:

> The current transformation of Times Square is a Baron Haussmann-like event. But like Haussmann's rebuilding of Paris, this event comprises many smaller ones, among them the destruction of acres of architecture, numerous commercial and living spaces, and, so far, the permanent obliteration of over two dozen theater venues, with (as of May 1997) more than a half-dozen other theater demolitions planned within the next three months. With this dies a complex of social practices, many of which turned on contact, affecting hundreds of thousands of men and women a year, some native to the city, some visitors.

Delany comments in his writing particularly on the removal of contact opportunities for street sex workers and for gay men in their sexual activity. (Warner (2000), whose analysis of this period in the governance of New York City was discussed in Chapter 5, regrets this change, as well). Contact, casual though organized as it is, means different things to different people. To those who argue that the redevelopment of Times Square is to enhance women's safety, Delany comments that there have always been women in the area – living, working and strolling through it. It is just that current concerns are being expressed about women of a different class background from those now being displaced by the redevelopment.

If we are to imagine that place-making is a planning strategy that might facilitate local public sites of encounter – of contact and of conviviality – then these questions of whether and how contact and conviviality occur between certain individuals and certain groups is of great significance. Common to all of the articulations of contact and conviviality we have discussed above is a strong emphasis on the need for urban life to provide opportunities for people to construct temporary *identifications* with others alongside their fixed *identities*, either via fleeting encounters or more purposeful activities with 'strangers'. Contact and convivial encounter, then, are not simply matters of unbounded, all-inclusive mingling in the large public spaces of the city. Indeed, as Peattie (1998) says, all encounter is bounded in some ways, even though we might like in theory to eliminate all exclusions. This is where planning for redistribution and for recognition helps us to analyse the implications of any measures to plan for encounter we might devise. Questions of redistribution force us to look at the possibilities for inter-class contact or conviviality, of the kind Delany observes being removed in certain American urban redevelopments. Questions of recognition of group differences and identities urge us to examine who the people we are planning for, those individuals who are often strangers, actually are, and whether we 'know' them adequately. In Chapter 3, discussing Gans's work on urban renewal in 1950s Boston, we remarked on the importance of knowing those for whom one plans. The same point pertains here.

Decision rules and discourses: ways of crafting a just diversity through encounter

In this section we consider the question of what 'rules of thumb' and discourses can be used to plan for convivial encounters among 'strangers', thereby facilitating opportunities for people to identify with one another in the course of shared activities and labours. As has been clear in earlier chapters, the appropriateness of certain decision rules and discourses will vary in different contexts. And through the discussion to follow, it will be clear that redistributive and recognition-related matters criss-cross these ways of implementing planning for encounter.

As noted earlier in Chapters 2 and 4, decision rules are statements of the form of specific planning measures. They indicate how a situation is understood because they state the means by which it is to be tackled. In the examples used in Chapter 2, we saw decision rules about the spatial distribution of certain public facilities and the way resources were to be directed to certain income or neighbourhood groups; these were decision rules in planning for redistribution of public resources so as to achieve more equitable outcomes. In Chapter 4 the decision rules associated with planning for recognition either identified 'groups' clearly and ensured their interests were represented in planning decisions, or chose to limit specific single-group identifications by seeking cross-group rather than single-group strategies. In this section, we set out three decision rules that might be taken to facilitate convivial forms of contact and encounter. Often these rules are focused on a local level, as encounter (excluding that via the internet and other forms of long-distance communication, which probably are not able to be planned by urban planners) is about face-to-face interaction and physical presence in a place. The interpretation or scale of the relevant 'local', however, varies according to context. Sometimes planning for encounter will involve the social and spatial arrangements within a particular building or organization; on other occasions the relevant scale may be a streetscape or the routes and stations of a public transport network.

The first decision rule we note is: provide a variety of social and economic infrastructure. With planning for encounter we are talking about planning meeting places – either places and situations intended for meetings (like drop-in centres), or places and situations in which meeting occurs in infrastructure intended primarily for something else (like public transport or public libraries). Local infrastructure may be developed for use by diverse individuals, all together, or for use by specific groups at certain times and in limited cross-group interaction. A specific or a general stranger can be kept in view. A variety of infrastructures of all these kinds needs to be planned for – and one decision rule for encounter is to arrange specifically to do this in a designated local place.

This first decision rule is illustrated though an examination of European (and some Australian) approaches to facilitating encounter between artists and other 'creative professionals' in run-down but affordable premises in inner cities. It draws on the research of Kate Shaw (2005). Here, heritage and planning regulations have been invoked so as to allow purposeful, convivial (in Illich's sense) encounter amongst members of that particular group to occur, in relatively 'disorderly' environs in bounded locales and in relatively non-controlling ways.

Alternative cultures in run-down inner city areas have, in many places, been subject to pressures from gentrification and other forms of redevelopment. But those spaces have hosted convivial encounter over long periods, amongst musicians and other artists, in interaction with passers-by, purchasers of artworks and interested onlookers. If one imagines that participants in alternative cultures are a group, identified by their resistance to the dominant cultural mainstream, then this 'group' must be understood to be large and itself diverse. Says Shaw (2005, p. 151):

> The concept of 'scene' thickens that of alternative culture by including not only all the arrangements of proponents, participants, audiences, supports and infrastructures involved in cultural production, but the connections between particular forms (music, film, theatre, literary, art, etc).

The alternative 'scene', though it is rooted in local places, also has networks at far greater than the local scale. In Berlin, Amsterdam and Melbourne, Shaw analyzes the ways governments, aware of the threat to these vibrant areas of creative activity in their central cities, have sought to keep these activities alive both because of their cultural production but also because they draw interested onlookers into the city. This requires strategies to keep affordable premises available, even as these inner city areas are under pressure of redevelopment. (In this emphasis on the availability of affordable premises, decision rule one is implemented.) Strong discursive positioning of this planning decision rule has been necessary for planners to succeed with its development and implementation.

We describe Shaw's case study of the Breeding Place Project in Amsterdam, as evidence of the sorts of decision rules and supportive discourses that can facilitate and underpin continued encounter amongst participants in an alternative inner city scene. Soon after it became clear, through the activism of squatters and artists, that appropriate premises for alternative culture were disappearing in central Amsterdam, the city government concluded that these cultural forms would not persist without 'cultural refuges'. Such places were necessary for creativity (and, we say, encounter) to occur. Shaw (2005, p. 161) quotes one of the City of Amsterdam's recent reports on this:

> It is precisely these combinations of homes, workplaces and studios that are often the breeding ground for new art and cultural innovation. And in doing so, they bring colour and vitality to the city. A cosmopolitan city such as Amsterdam cannot exist without cultural refuges.

And, continues Shaw (2005, p. 161):

> the breeding place project intended to introduce or retain 2000 living and working spaces in inner-Amsterdam by 2005. It operates by purchasing existing 'breeding places' (illegal squats where their future is threatened) from their private or public owners at the lowest prices [negotiable] ... The buildings are then sold or leased at heavily subsidized rates to collectives of artists and 'non-commercial cultural entrepreneurs – small-scale, largely culture-oriented activities including visual and performing artists'.

Of course, there are some rules about the conditions under which cultural workers can retain these working and living spaces – these conditions are necessary in order to prevent the spaces becoming the subsidized sites of commercially successful artistic operations. This introduces our second decision rule: encourage stakeholder or participant agency in the encounter occurring in places. What this decision rule requires is that planning sets general expectations of the use of a physical facility or space, but allows those involved in the interactions there to form those interactions and use the facility or space according to their own needs. It allows for the tension to be sustained between planning that keeps in mind both order and disorder, in the manner suggested by Amin and Thrift (2002). In the Breeding Places Project, broad expectations are set by planners, even as they avoid micro-management of outcomes, because outcomes are determined by participants. Shaw interviewed one participant in the management of the Breeding Places Project, who said of these conditions:

> certain guidelines have to be met – their incomes have to be limited, they have to show that they are really active in this world of subcultural art and entrepreneurship. After that, we let it loose. We are creating the conditions for continuing cultural production. On the artistic level, in terms of what is happening in these buildings, we leave it to the groups themselves (Shaw, 2005, pp. 163–4).

Here, then, are general decision rules that accept the need for planning to provide those material spaces identified by Peattie (1998) as requirements for conviviality. For the form of encounter being underpinned here is conviviality, as Illich, Peattie and Gilroy saw it – it is productive encounter in which individuals are making their own decisions and designing their own forms of creativity and productivity. And as Shaw says, it is planning that sets loose rules – that leaves it to the individuals and groups to organize themselves, and that gives them 'room to move'. There is capacity for the individuals to chart their own ways forward, in the encounter being facilitated by this planning.

The example of Amsterdam's Breeding Places Project contrasts with certain claims about the recent redevelopment of Times Square in New York City, in which critics have alleged that 'quality-of-life' policies (or planning decision rules) have been used to produce the 'deadly serious effects' of excluding certain 'different people' (certain strangers) from areas whose residents and businesspeople find them undesirable or not longer appropriate for the area (Deutsche, 1999, p. 197). Such 'quality-of-life' interventions have often been justified on the grounds of improving public safety. Certainly, we do agree that the question of safety is crucial in our thinking about planning for encounter. If urban environments are to facilitate encounter, participants in that encounter must not find the experience entirely threatening and fearful, even as it may involve risks and uncertainty. But the concept of safety takes on a different look when viewed from the perspective of 'conviviality' rather than 'community'. This leads us to our third decision rule: create safe and transparent spaces for interaction, both physically and socially (of course the creation of these spaces will draw on the expert knowledge of locals).

To illustrate how planners might approach the issue of safety from the perspective of conviviality, consider Wekerle and Whitzman's (1995) account of Canadian efforts since the 1990s to design safer cities for women. Here the decision rules of facilitating encounter by creating safe and transparent spaces, and of encouraging stakeholder agency by using local knowledge to design the spaces, are employed. Acknowledging the reality of women's fear of crime in city streets and public spaces, and how this fear (often of strangers) may limit encounter there, this work develops a way of seeing the problem broadly, and treating the issue of urban safety as one that can be enhanced by planning local surroundings more effectively. It does draw on the thinking of Jane Jacobs (1961) that social activity and frequented third spaces in city streetscapes are effective in producing safer environments. And it takes a positive view that women should be out and about in cities, rather than fearfully limiting their forays and mixing only with their familiars. Its discourse is positive and seeks to empower planners and local citizens to facilitate encounter by organizing their urban contexts so as to increase activity in public spaces. Its decision rules give rise to a set of very practical strategies for undertaking such a task.

What this work does is remind us that encounter is not just something had in one's spare time – when attending street festivals in public spaces, or relaxing after work in cafés, or meeting strangers in recreational jaunts to new parts of the city. Encounter is also part of daily life, because it is what happens when one is shopping, travelling, socializing and working in the micro-public spaces we have already discussed. Wekerle and Whitzman (1995, p. 3) describe the effect of fear of crime, in limiting encounter:

> Fear of crime keeps people off the streets, especially after dark, and out of parks, plazas, and public transit. It is a substantial barrier to participation in the public life of the city. ... Women worried most about such unavoidable situations as going to the laundromat, using public transit, and walking by bars, parks, or empty lots. For many women these are necessary activities that they must engage in on a day-to-day basis. Women often limit their activities because of fear of crime. They stay home at night; they don't take night courses; they don't go to the grocery store; they don't visit friends or socialize. Many women will not take jobs that keep them out at night. As a response to fear of crime a large number of women isolate themselves in their own homes.

Clearly, if planning can assist in reducing fear of crime, through improving the environments in which people carry out their activities, the contact and conviviality that is part of people's every activity beyond their immediate private space may be enhanced. Forming a proactive and positive discourse about the possibilities for planning to help reduce fear of crime and therefore to reduce women's disempowerment in the city, Wekerle and Whitzman position 'safer cities' as an alternative to the standard crime-reducing strategies of increased 'law and order' and 'fortress security'. People in local areas, working with planners, can do something about their feelings of insecurity by creating spaces that are safer, is the message. Further agency is given to local people by the safer cities approach, which stresses that individuals in local areas are the experts on the nature of violence and crime in their daily lives, and therefore these people are best placed to develop plans and solutions for their particular area, in partnership with city agencies.

From decision rules two and three of those we have listed above, guidelines for good practice in devising a safer city's agenda are developed by Wekerle and Whitzman. The guidelines are organized according to three principles and with reference to typically 'unsafe' sites in cities. The three guidelines for planning safe environments (which could be seen as additional, more specific, decision rules) are that: (1) the user of the environment should find it easy to be aware of the characteristics of that environment, with clear sightlines and lighting providing transparency as to what is going on in the area. (2) The user of an area should be visible to others, and there should be others around to see that person. (3) There should be means of assisting oneself in an area, through a range of escape and exit routes, ways of attracting attention to get help (like alarms), and good signage. The typically 'unsafe' places, that is those that generate particular fear of crime, to which special attention should be directed in planning for safety, include: transportation sites like parking lots, isolated bus stops, pedestrian underpasses; commercial sites like empty shopping streets and malls, at night; industrial parks and sites, usually also deserted at night; parks; residential areas of different housing environments; and university and college campuses. If plans to produce safer cities can apply the principles outlined to the sorts of areas listed here, say Wekerle and Whitzman, then that is a good place to start. Progress can be made; fear of crime can be reduced; encounter can seem and be safer. Designing more readable environments is accompanied by encouraging 'activity generators' as land uses in urban environments, in many of their recommendations. In a description reminiscent of Jane Jacobs (1961), though not of those advocates of quality-of-life redevelopment who seek to reduce inter-class contact, they say:

> Active, vital urban spaces that attract diverse groups of people are perceived as safe places. But many urban spaces lack a sense of activity and liveliness. Activity generators include everything from increasing recreational facilities in a park, to placing housing in a previously commercial area, to adding an outdoor café to an office building. They can include, on a small scale, mixing land uses, but can also include intensifying a particular use. Generating more activity often involves planning for different uses and users rather than design changes. The purpose of activity generators is to add 'eyes' to the street or open space: to make a place more secure by populating it. Activity generators do not operate in isolation. It is not enough to add housing to a commercial area if the housing is isolated and without services. Placing a hot dog vendor in a huge parking lot will only make the hot dog vendor scared (Wekerle and Whitzman, 1995, p. 46).

The authors' last comment makes another important point, which is that planning for safer cities, and therefore for readier encounter, is most successful when it becomes a way of thinking underpinning all interventions in the built environment. It is less successful when it must be used to somehow refashion existing built environments that already function poorly and generate fear of crime.

Now, such an approach to naming and then seeking to plan to reduce women's fear of crime in urban environments is not without its critics. Wilson (1991, p. 10) makes one feminist point particularly clearly. She finds that emphasizing the need to provide 'safety, welfare and protection' for women in cities is honouring the 'traditional paternalism of most town planning'. Furthermore, it is anti-urban:

> Yet it is necessary also to emphasise the other side of city life and to insist on women's right to the carnival, intensity and even the risks of the city. Surely it is possible to be both pro-cities and pro-women, to hold in balance an awareness of both the pleasures and the dangers that the city offers women, and to judge that in the end, urban life, however fraught with difficulty, has emancipated women more than rural life or suburban domesticity (Wilson, 1991, p. 10).

Responding to Wilson's point, it is probably fair to say that the sorts of safer cities being proposed by Wekerle and Whitzman are more truly the sorts of cities Wilson envisages as benefiting women, than are the urban environments whose poor planning causes them to be perceived as 'unsafe'. Beyond criticisms of making women seem the victims of cities, by naming them as particularly fearful in those cities, there are many accounts in the literature of analysts who have found the safer cities framework useful and powerful. Kallus and Churchman (2004), for example, have considered its applicability to the context of women's safety in Israeli cities. Having discovered a variety of policies and strategies being used in cities across Canada, though all of these have been inspired by the Toronto experience reported by Wekerle and Whitzman (1995), the possibilities for transferring such programs to Israeli cities are limited (the authors say) by the patriarchal nature of many ethnic groups there, and the fact that involvement in a national security struggle means that political interest in local issues of women's safety is limited. Nevertheless, Kallus and Churchman make a series of recommendations for local safer cities initiatives, drawing particularly from the Canadian material the need for local stakeholders to be proactive about this rather than dismissing it from the first. In another assessment, Shaw and Andrew (2005), themselves from Canada, evaluate the safer cities initiatives against an international environment in which relatively little attention is paid to gender in crime prevention strategies. They find the safer cities approach proactive and wide-ranging, compared for example to approaches to violence against women that focus only on domestic violence by intimate partners. They note the particular strength of safer cities strategies in seeking decision-making partnerships between grassroots organizations and local government authorities. The innovative methods used in developing recommendations for local, safer cities, plans are particularly praised by Shaw and Andrew – safety audits and exploratory walks in which women (who have been found to be more willing to talk about their fears than are men) identify places they find fearful and why, are a fine way of devising locally specific recommendations to improve the environment. This is a strategy using local knowledge for the development of policy and policy tools, rather than relying on the knowledge of distant 'experts' so decried by Illich (1973).

Examples of three decision rules (and their supporting discourses) in planning for encounter have been discussed. Planning practices using these rules have been identified in Amsterdam, in planning providing a variety of forms of infrastructure (especially affordable premises) for the continued presence of alternative cultures in the city which supports those cultures, and in planning supporting stakeholder agency that allows participants 'room to move'. In Toronto and elsewhere in planning for more transparent and therefore safer cities for women, local individuals and groups have been engaged in providing their expert local knowledge for the plans devised. In both cases, the value of contact and conviviality is acknowledged for city life, and the value also of these forms of encounter being between diverse groups and individuals. In the case of urban redevelopments of prominent public spaces based on quality-of-life discourses, which have involved the clearing away of undesirable strangers from the new consumption sites of the middle classes, a different kind of evaluation may be made. As was observed in Chapters 2 and 4, planning for encounter requires the clear maintenance of values about distribution and recognition by planners and the pursuit of those values in practice.

Conclusion

It is perhaps no coincidence that discussion of encounter, that seemingly unable-to-be-planned-for matter, should surface so strongly in discussions of cities in the present period of neoliberal discourses about reducing the involvements of government. In one political reading, though probably not one favoured by most interested in encounter as an urban planning strategy to facilitate rights to the city, reducing regulation and letting events and activities shape and locate themselves might be equated with letting the market decide on urban outcomes. This is certainly a strategy used by some governments who favour public-private partnerships for the implementation of particular developments, rather than strategic planning of whole areas (see Sandercock and Dovey (2002) on Melbourne in the 1990s, for such a view on anti-planning there, at that time). A planning-oriented (rather than a market-oriented) solution to such a dilemma is difficult to prescribe closely. As Amin and Thrift (2002, p. 131) put it: 'One thing we are clear about is that the goal cannot be prescribed or an end-point legislated. But this does not mean that we can leave things entirely to the free play of the current political system. In other words, we need to be normatively non-normative.' In the same vein, Keith (2005, p. 170) wishes to find the way to 'plan the cosmopolitan, seeking a reconfiguration of the politics of city change and the notion of the city planner'. Keith, as we have noted already, stops short in his deliberations of conceiving of planning as somehow separate from the state and its bureaucracies.

Yet we have described examples of locally oriented planning, which have identified encounter as a vital part of city life and have used planning strategies and methods (what we have termed decision rules) to underpin it. In both the Amsterdam Breeding Place Project, and the Toronto Safer Cities Program, the importance of local participants in the forms of encounter in question deciding how they would participate in the planning and how they would react to it, was crucial. In 'quality-of-life'-based redevelopments, public planning was replaced by market forces, with the consumption behaviours of the middle classes taking priority. Planning for encounter, it is clear, is locally focused and locally defined, even as we recognize that perhaps it frequently engages the wide range of people who may use these localities for different purposes.

In the early 2000's climate of fear about terrorism, being ramped up by the 'war on terrorism' now being waged internationally, the matters of the stranger and encounter in the city that we have discussed take on a whole new and politicized dimension. Wekerle and Jackson (2005) have listed ways that the anti-terrorism agenda of Western nations has implications for dissent and difference in cities, particularly in the United States. Existing programs to promote urban security and safety, like those analyzed by Wekerle and Whitzman (1995), have been taken up under the anti-terrorism banner:

> At the local level, the focus on community crime prevention in urban areas that emerged in the 1990s has ... been appropriated for the anti-terrorism project. Neighborhood Watch, started in 1972 on a volunteer basis by the National Sheriffs Association, has now taken on a citizen terrorist watch role. ... The Crime Prevention Association of Michigan ... now associates safe homes and communities with anti-terrorism (Wekerle and Jackson, 2005, p 43).

In this political climate of fear, fanned by governmental discourses and use of repression, there is plenty of scope for the 'villainization of "others"' (p. 38). Wekerle and Jackson quote Stephen Graham's comment that the Bush Administration's War on Terror 'problematized the urban cosmopolitanism and "hybrid" transnational identities of many neighborhoods and communities in American cities' (2005, p. 36). What the limits will be on local planning to facilitate encounter, especially of the 'disorderly' kind favoured by urban theorists and exemplified by the Amsterdam Breeding Place project, will be an issue of concern. The importance of developing oppositional discourses to those which see diversity and dissent as automatically unpatriotic and to be suppressed, will be of paramount importance.

How can encounter be transformative, in cities, even given the limitations of the current political climate? When the welcoming and/or accommodation of strangers creates a form of convivial inclusion and identification, that is transformative. It can lead to the working and socializing together of individuals with different characteristics and identities, as they connect briefly over a project or matter of fleeting but common interest. When an expansion in opportunities for convivial encounter leads to new ways of being in the city, that is transformative, for it provides a life that could not previously have been lived. In doing this, it works towards the 'right to the city' that we discussed in Chapter 1, with its emphasis on the city life as a project of exploration and change. And if planning for encounter can facilitate 'room to move' as Shaw (2005) noted in contemporary Amsterdam, by providing the material supports for such room without micro-managing the outcomes, that will have been transforming for planning practice as well as for the individuals in the place in question.

7 Planning for Encounter in Practice

In Chapter 6 we focussed conceptually on the aim of planning to foster encounter, viewing encounter as interaction between unlike individuals and groups occurring in local places such as streets, public spaces and 'third spaces' like coffee shops and drop-in centres. The conviviality sought, as a result of encounter, can be the product of quite casual contact within one's neighbourhood, or more purposeful interaction through an organized activity or micro-public. No encounter, planned or not, can be envisaged without some form of exclusion being associated with it. So one of the tasks of planning for encounter is to make sure that the forms of inclusion and exclusion that might arise from such planning are anticipated insofar as this is possible, acknowledged and compensated for if they privilege certain groups and behaviours over others. The decision rules devised for planning practice that facilitates encounter may incorporate thinking about redistribution and recognition, to help ensure this. In addition, as we saw with decision rule number two discussed in Chapter 6, a light planning touch is expected in planning for encounter. With planning approaches that aim not to micro-manage outcomes, the particular forms of exclusion may be difficult to predict. Nevertheless, using the social logics of redistribution and recognition together with that

Box 7.1: Case studies in Chapter 7		
Encounter	*Encounter and redistribution*	*Encounter and recognition*
Festivals	Public libraries	Drop-in centres

of planning for encounter, it is possible to interrogate planning approaches that seek to facilitate interaction, asking questions, for example, about the degree to which they impede or encourage inter-class interaction and the extent to which they are built on an actual knowledge (or recognition) of those who might be participating in the interaction. Note that planning for increased interaction between like individuals – that is planning for community – is not our focus here, though it is possible that one outcome of successful planning for encounter is that individuals discover similarities with others that they had not anticipated and form some sustained sense of community with them.

In this chapter, we discuss three examples of planning for encounter. Understanding that our three social logics – redistribution, recognition and encounter – are not independent from each other, we follow the practice of previous chapters to consider first an example in which we focus primarily on encounter, followed by examples in which planning for encounter has a redistributive bent, and a recognition emphasis. Our example of planning for encounter *qua* interaction is planning for street festivals. Our example of planning for encounter with a redistributive purpose is that of planning for public libraries. And our example of planning for encounter with a recognition emphasis is planning for drop-in or community centres. These examples show the different forms that planning for encounter may take in different contexts, though the values that underpin it persist.

Encounter: street festivals

A relatively strong current in radical urban scholarship has celebrated the power of festivals and carnivals as disruptive events in which the everyday hierarchies and norms of urban life are momentarily suspended, or even inverted. Henri Lefebvre, for instance, whose work on the 'right to the city' has been influential for us in this book, imagined un-alienated urban life as a kind of permanent festival. For him, urban everyday life had become alienated, and the very taken-for-grantedness of certain rhythms and routines was one of the principal means through which power was inscribed in urban life. As such, the radical transformation of urban life would necessarily mean that the 'antithesis between the quotidian and the Festival – whether of labour or of leisure – will no longer be the basis of society' (quoted in Elden, 2004, p. 119). Through participation in festive or canivalesque moments, urban inhabitants could produce a more authentic form of being together against the taken-for-granted rhythms and routines of everyday life. Lefebvre's influential account of the Paris Commune of 1871 as a 'revolutionary carnival' in turn helped to inspire the activists involved in the events of May 1968 in Paris (Shields, 1999). One of Lefebvre's aphorisms for capturing the radical potential of everyday life which could be unlocked in a festive moment – 'beneath the cobblestones, a beach!' – appeared as graffiti across Paris during these events. More recently, contemporary activist group Reclaim the Streets have also embraced the power of festival and carnival for radical politics. Indeed, during one of their illegal parties conducted on a motorway in London, they dumped a tonne of sand on the road to make a beach, just to reinforce the point! As the Reclaim the Streets activists rather romantically put it:

> The great moments of revolutionary history have all been enormous popular festivals – the storming of the Bastille, the uprisings of 1848, the Paris Commune, the revolutions of 1917–9, Paris '68. Conversely, popular festivities have always been looked on by the authorities as a problem, whether they have banned, tolerated or semi-institutionalised them. Why does power fear free celebration? Could it be something to do with the utopian urges which seize a crowd becoming aware of its own power? From the middle ages onwards the carnival has offered glimpses of the world turned upside down, a topsy turvy universe free of toil, suffering and inequality. Carnival celebrates temporary liberation from the prevailing truth and the established order; it marks the suspension of all hierarchical rank, privileges, norms and prohibitions [http://rts.gn.apc.org/prop14.htm#revolutionary].

This concern with the radical potential of festivals has some clear connections with our concern for encounter in urban life. The notion that festivals offer 'glimpses of the world turned upside down' conveys a hope that through participating in a festive disruption to everyday life, people are not confined to prescribed identities and roles but rather are free to explore potential identities and to share this experience with strangers. Consider, for example, Kristin Ross's (2002, pp. 24–5) description of the events of Paris, May 1968:

> May '68 in fact had very little to do with the interests of the social group – students or 'youth' – who sparked the action. What has come to be called

'the events of May' consisted mainly in students ceasing to function as students, workers as workers, and farmers as farmers. May was a crisis in functionalism. The movement took the form of political experiments in *de*classification, in disrupting the natural 'givenness' of places; it consisted of displacements that took students outside of the university, meetings that brought farmers and workers together, or students to the countryside – trajectories outside of the Latin Quarter, to workers' housing and popular neighbourhoods, a new kind of mass organizing ... that involved physical dislocation. And in that physical dislocation lay a dislocation in the very idea of politics – moving it out of its place, its proper place. ...

Ross's notion of 'political experiments in declassification' captures a key element of our notion of encounter, in the sense that we are interested in how planners might work to facilitate opportunities for people to explore different identifications, through encounters with strange others in the city. So, perhaps festivals can sustain forms of conviviality which, even if they are only temporary, allow people to become 'strangers to themselves' in the shared time-space of the festival? Of course, the festival itself may not be 'permanent' in Lefebvre's sense, and indeed it achieves its significance as a temporary moment which stands out from the 'everyday' – but this does not necessarily reduce the importance of moments in which new perspectives and possibilities are experienced, as a catalyst for new explorations and collaborations.

However, before we get too carried away with ourselves here, we should also note that these very same scholars and activists who celebrate the radical potential of festivals have also argued that festive and carnivalesque events are not necessarily radical of themselves. Indeed, they point out quite correctly that festivals and carnivals also have the potential to support dominant power arrangements and inequalities. Guy Debord (1995) and the French Situationists famously referred to such events such as officially sponsored festivals as 'spectacles' – stage-managed festive events where the powerful experience of participating in an interruption to everyday life is mobilized not in the service of radical change, but rather in the service of state- or corporate-defined goals. In such spectacles, the radical potential of the festival is thereby 'hijacked' to reinforce, rather than disrupt, the status quo:

Feelings of belonging to place may be constructed through positive feelings of celebration or the negative emotions of fear. In either case, spectacle is an effective means of social control, and the social elite who controls such events exerts a strong influence in the social realm and within popular consciousness (Duffy, forthcoming-a).

Debord went so far as to argue that we now live in the 'society of the spectacle', and this perspective continues to have strong resonance in recent radical social analysis (see for example Retort, 2005). Orchestrated political gatherings, sporting events like the Olympics or football matches, pop concerts and music festivals, and planned events like neighbourhood multicultural festivals could all be considered as 'spectacles' from this perspective.

As will no doubt be apparent from this critique of the festival as 'spectacle', planners and festivals are not conventionally thought to be a particularly good mix in the radical scholarship on festivals! The implication of this critique is that festivals only have a radical edge to the extent that they remain to a large degree unlicensed and unplanned. As such, when planners get involved in officially sponsoring/regulating/certifying festivals, their motivations are likely to be subject to critical scrutiny. As we shall see, the ways in which festivals have been mobilized in the service of urban planning goals have come under sustained attack from a range of critics. In particular, the use of festivals as tools for place-marketing and building tolerance of difference have been heavily criticized.

Nonetheless, we want to argue in this section that even planned festivals can create opportunities for encounters which can work towards a just diversity in cities. While the distinction between unplanned and planned festivals captures some important distinctions in the nature of different festival events, it is a dichotomy that we believe is also unhelpful in some ways. In particular, such a distinction can serve to obscure the ways in which planning can work to open up opportunities for unscripted encounters in festival events, as well as close them down, depending on the planning approach adopted. Planned festivals, then, can also work in the service of progressive agendas for urban change – 'beneath the festival, an encounter', we might say!

So, in developing our argument about festivals, we proceed in the following steps. First, we consider the ways in which festivals have been embraced by urban planners in recent times, and explore the existing critiques of the festival impulse. Second, we consider the implications of these critiques for the kind of encounters that are sustained in festival events. After noting some of the problems with the critiques of planned festivals, we then conclude the discussion by offering some thoughts on the ways in which planners can shape festivals so that they do offer possibilities for encounters which are not fully scripted or pre-determined.

Festivals of one kind or another have become an established part of the repertoire of contemporary urban planning. Festivals which have become commonplace in many cities and urban neighbourhoods around the world include: thematic festivals (such as comedy, film, or music festivals); festivals which celebrate a particular place (whether that be a neighbourhood or a city); festivals which celebrate a particular culture and/or community (such as gay and lesbian festivals and ethnic cultural festivals), etc. Indeed, some cities are globally renowned for their festivals – think, for example, of Cannes (for its film festival), Edinburgh (for its International and Fringe festivals), Sydney (for its Gay and Lesbian Mardi Gras) and Rio (for its Carnivale).

The formal embrace of festivals by urban authorities can be explained with reference to at least two commonly-held priorities. First, festivals are increasingly being mobilized by urban authorities in the service of place-marketing. A successful festival, it is hoped, might help to put a neighbourhood or a city 'on the map', making it distinctive and thereby drawing in tourists and investment from elsewhere. Thematic and place-focused festivals are obviously particularly important here. So, for example, Jamieson (2004) notes that the City of Edinburgh has an explicit 'Festival Strategy', designed to promote Edinburgh across Europe (and indeed the rest of the world) as Europe's 'City of Festivals'. For a six week Festival season, the city hosts *The Edinburgh International Jazz and Blues Festival, The Edinburgh Fringe Festival, The Edinburgh International Book Festival, The Edinburgh International Film Festival, The Edinburgh Tattoo, The Edinburgh International Festival,* and *The Guardian Edinburgh International Television Festival.* As Jamieson (2004, p. 65) notes:

> In the race to win investment and tourism, Edinburgh mines its cultural resources and charismatic urban images, defining itself visually by either images of the castle or the city during its festival season. ... Within today's competitive urban context, Edinburgh's culture, heritage, and public spaces are regarded as assets that add rich social references to the lexicon of city marketing campaigns.

And of course, such strategies are replicated in countless places on a much smaller scale. For instance, the regional city of Parkes in Australia now hosts an annual Elvis festival which organizers believe makes an important contribution to local economic development through the generation of tourism-related revenues (Brennan-Horley, Gibson *et al.*, 2006).

Second, festivals are often supported as a means to celebrate a particular way of life and/or community which is perceived to be stigmatized or marginalized in the wider public sphere. So, for example, municipal governments across a wide range of cities have actively embraced festivals as a way of promoting multiculturalism, hoping that such festivals will promote greater tolerance and understanding of ethnic minority communities. In Australia, Dunn *et al.* (2001) surveyed Australian local governments about the actions that they were taking to foster good intercommunal relations between cultural groups. They found that 'the most often reported programmes took the form of cultural festivals, food fairs, multicultural days, fiestas, and arts projects' (2001, p. 1581). Such festivals are used as 'strategies for celebrating diversity, sharply contrasting with the pathologising of difference that deviates from a presumed cultural norm (an Anglo-Celtic norm in the case of Australia)' (2001, p. 1577).

It should also be noted here that a given festival might shift in emphasis over time – Sydney's Gay and Lesbian Mardi Gras is a good example here. This event started off as a radical and highly contested march in support of gay and lesbian rights in the late 1970s, and is now a relatively mainstream attraction which is explicitly embraced as part of the City of Sydney's economic development strategies. The parade is broadcast on television, and tourism associated with the Gay and Lesbian Mardi Gras is estimated to contribute millions of dollars to the local economy (Duffy, forthcoming-a).

Now, festivals which are planned with either or both of these two goals in mind have attracted widespread criticism for failing to advance the cause of a more just diversity. Indeed, critics of festivals designed to advance these goals argue that they work to reinforce existing inequalities in cities as 'spectacles' rather than genuinely open festival events with radical potential. Most obviously, the place-marketing impulse behind festivals has been attacked on the grounds that it inevitably privileges only those activities and places that can be marketed to tourists and other spectators *as consumers.*

As such, the image of the city portrayed in the festival becomes of paramount importance, and people, places and activities which do not fit with the desired image are excluded from the festival time-space. In her analysis of Edinburgh's festival season, for example, Jamieson documents the careful construction of a 'festival gaze' by urban authorities which significantly restricts both the spaces in which festival events are staged and the kinds of encounters that can take place:

> To participate in the city's festivals is also to participate in the city's pub-lic relations, which necessarily guarantees protection from the socially incompatible and visually irreconcilable and solicits complicity from the urbane visitor (Jamieson, 2004, p. 71).

In the case of Edinburgh, the festivals are staged in the highly demarcated space of the old city, and the forms of festive stranger-sociability fit with 'the city's dominant visual logic of bounded flamboyance and spontaneous street activities' (2004, p. 71) within this demarcated space. As she goes on to note:

> Edinburgh's festival spaces have both social and geographic boundaries, which if absent, would discourage the visitor sought by the service economy stakeholders and city marketing consortiums (2004, p. 71).

The celebratory impulse behind multicultural festivals has also been attacked by critics who argue that it tends to pursue a weak kind of tolerance by exoticizing minority cultures and ethnici-ties in order to make them 'safe' for the majority. In Australia, critics of dominant forms of multiculturalism have argued that multicultural festivals are often premised on the logic that they provide minority ethnic groups with opportunities to demonstrate the value of their culture to the white 'host' culture (for example Hage, 1998, pp. 117–18). As such, they work to reinforce the posi-tion of Anglo-Australians as 'host', who may 'enrich themselves' through their participation in the festival experience. Further-more, such festivals can tend towards overly simplistic presenta-tions of ethnic minority cultures, overlooking their dynamism and internal diversity. As Permezel and Duffy (2007) summarize this critique:

> the performances that make up the multicultural festival are viewed as shallow representations of the complexities of cultures, with an emphasis on costume, food and music, rather than demonstrating the dynamic nature of culture, as well as the response of groups to the dynamics of displacement and readjustment.

The implication of these critiques, then, is that:

> 'Ethnic festivals', food fairs, and community arts exhibitions provide only a spatially limited and temporally confined challenge to everyday cultural norms of Anglo-Celtic Australia. While exposing the wider community to an array of cultural displays, such celebratory events can trivialise cultural differences as well as issues of serious social inequality (Dunn *et al.*, 2001: 1579).

These critiques of place-marketing and celebratory multiculturalism share some common themes. The first of these themes concerns the centrality of *consumption* to the planned festival. Planned festivals designed to market places or celebrate cultures inevitably seem to interpolate festival-goers as consumers – either of place and/or of culture. The centrality of consumption means that planned festivals would appear to be overwhelmingly concerned with a particular vision of *safety*. This is either the safety of 'ordered disorder' in a street-based festival such as Edinburgh which meets a touristic 'appetite for safe yet unexpected encounters' (Jamieson 2004, p. 71), or else the safety of reducing ethnic others to 'exotic' elements safe for mainstream consumption such as food, dress and performance, rather than demands for measures to address social injustice and racism. In turn, such attempts to create safe experiences for consumers tend to mean that festival locations are *spatially circumscribed* and bounded, chosen more for their visible appeal (in terms of marketability and/or exoticism) rather than for their potential to stimulate unpredictable encounters which might disrupt everyday routines and separations. And finally, even when festivals still might manage to offer some opportunities for encounters despite the concerns listed above, such opportunities are *temporally circumscribed* and are therefore said not to offer much potential for long-term change. All of this would appear to have deleterious effects for festivals as time-spaces of unscripted encounters. As Jamieson (2004, p. 68) puts it, the planned festival seems the opposite of the 'revolutionary carnival' valued by the likes of Lefebvre:

> When licensed, as most events are today, the festival is bounded to a specific time and space where spontaneity and bodily encounters are guided by bureaucratic structures that are believed to disempower the *disordering* and *reordering* potential of the carnivalesque spirit.

However, we think that this rather negative reading of planned festivals neglects some of the ways in which even planned festivals can establish opportunities for unscripted encounters that can contribute to just diversity in cities. Here, we are particularly influenced by some of Michelle Duffy's recent research on festivals, conducted both individually and in collaboration with a number of colleagues (see Duffy, forthcoming-a; Duffy, forthcoming-b; Duffy, Waitt *et al.*, 2007; Permezel and Duffy, 2007; Wood, Duffy *et al.*, 2007). There are at least three ways in which even planned festivals can operate as alternative or 'liminal' spaces which offer opportunities to step out of everyday routines and rhythms in unscripted ways. People who go to festivals can have fleeting encounters *as festival-goers* sharing an out-of-the-ordinary experience in the city, thereby potentially escaping or ignoring other identifications which might shape their everyday lives.

First, as noted in Chapter 6, we do believe that safety is an important component of conviviality. Certainly, the emphasis on 'locking-down' festival spaces ahead of the event (for example, through the forced removal of homeless people from festive spaces) will significantly reduce the scope of encounters that are possible. Nonetheless, the radical potential of the festival also rests to some degree on the 'safety' established by temporal and spatial boundaries of the event. These boundaries, in other words, can give a kind of 'license' for people to set aside their everyday identities and expectations in order to explore alternative identities and experiences. As Duffy *et al.* (2007, pp. 7–8 in manuscript) put it, the anthropolitical concept of 'liminality' often associated with festivals suggests a:

> time-space where conventional social rules are temporarily suspended, and where differences drawn by social categories such as age, faith, ethnicity

or sexuality are less important. This is argued to sustain a 'safe' time and space that may enable opportunities to celebrate notions of shared communal identity or to explore contentious social concerns.

Second, and closely following our first point, we believe that criticisms which point out the transitory nature of festival events also miss the mark when they imply that temporary suspensions of norms are of little consequence. The festival does not have to become a 'permanent carnival' in order to have some progressive political effects. As noted in Chapter 6, 'fleeting' encounters can be of profound significance for urban inhabitants where they provide opportunities to step out of a given identity or function in order to explore new possibilities. Indeed, the fact that festivals are by their nature temporary suspensions of everyday routines and rhythms is part of their significance for urban encounters, as well as part of their limitation. Michelle Duffy (forthcoming-a) puts it this way:

> the transitory nature of the event – the brief encounters and exchanges occurring within the festival space – produces different and often conflicting configurations of identity, place and belonging.

This, indeed, is the paradox of festivals:

> these events function as a form of social integration and cohesion *while simultaneously* they are sites of subversion and protest. This paradox is the source of such an event's socio-spatial and political significance [emphasis added].

Festivals share this paradoxical nature with other temporary uses of urban space, such as the temporary occupation of abandoned buildings or public spaces. Such uses can radically reshape the possibilities of the city and open up new spaces of encounter and conviviality, or they may not. As Haydn and Temel (2006) note, 'the spectrum of interests behind temporary uses is broad', and temporariness belongs neither to the radical nor the bureaucrat or developer.

Third, and perhaps most importantly, we also believe that the practice of festival-going can escape the intentions of festival planners, even when such intentions are narrowly prescriptive.

Permezel and Duffy's (2007) account of one multicultural festival in suburban Melbourne is particularly suggestive here. In response to the existing critiques of multicultural festivals, they argue that in fact even multicultural festivals intended as celebrations and consumption of the 'exoticism' of others nonetheless share the paradoxical nature of festivals described above. As they note, it is important not to simply take the intentions of planners as given, as if they wholly determine the outcome of festival-going. Instead, it is important to look at what people actually do at festivals. Through such an analysis, they argue, it is possible to see that people's mode of participation 'often exceeds the way local government attempts to manage cultural difference through its multicultural policies' (Permezel and Duffy, 2007). Music and food, for example, can be much more than 'shallow signifiers of culture'. By engaging the senses, such activities can help to ensure that festivals become 'a place of experimentation', such that 'the structure of the local festival allows and enables dialogue in potentially collaborative and innovative ways' (Permezel and Duffy, 2007). Participation in a musical festival element (as performer or audience member), for example, is a kind of non-verbal encounter which can establish profound emotional connections:

> Musical performances are, then, about 'intimate' encounters with others; they are about sharing an emotional experience with other people, most of whom will never see each other again, let alone exchange the time of day. These are encounters where feeling, sensing and tacit understanding are more prevalent than articulation and explanation (Wood, Duffy *et al.*, 2007, p. 25).

Once again, we want to be careful to note here that the meaning of these encounters is not necessarily progressive nor outside deliberate attempts to engineer them for a particular purpose – our point is again to note that regardless of such intentions, the encounters themselves remain unpredictable.

Our analysis here, then, suggests that 'planning' and 'festivals' are not necessarily mutually incompatible, even for those who would wish to see festivals establish opportunities for encounters which are not simply scripted interactions characteristic of spectacles for consumption. As such, we would suggest at least three ways in which planners involved in festival planning might work to avoid some of the pitfalls identified by critics and maximize the progressive potential of festivals for conviviality and encounter. First, the spatial location of festivals is very significant for the kinds of encounters they might sustain. Will the location of festivals in the city ensure that festival-goers have opportunities to share a time-space only with others 'like them', or it will it help to expose urban inhabitants to strangers through initiating forms of spatial dislocation? One of the problems with the Edinburgh festivals noted by Jamieson (2004) was that festival-goers were never encouraged to leave their comfort zone in the inner (old) city, and so they were unlikely to be exposed to some of the diverse groups who inhabit other parts of the city. So, for example, planners could work with community groups to stage festival events outside the 'usual' places. In the annual *Sydney Festival*, for example, planners have worked to stage festival events outside the tourist-friendly CBD. Some events have been staged in suburban locations, others in public housing estates, and others in so-called 'no-go' areas like 'the Block', a concentration of Aboriginal-owned housing in inner city Redfern. The imprimatur of the Sydney Festival can help to make visits to such places 'safe' for people who might not otherwise visit them, thereby establishing new opportunities for encounter. Likewise, planners in Leicester in the UK have recently realized that while support for festivals such as Diwali, Christmas and the Caribbean carnival can help to 'celebrate diversity', to be effective in addressing the segregation of different groups such festivals need to be embedded in a range of cultural spaces (see Singh, 2004, p. 49).

Second, Duffy, Waitt *et al.* (2007) suggest that the effectiveness of festivals in sustaining an atmosphere conducive to encounter relies not just on creating an effective interruption to everyday rhythms and routines, but also in creating a temporary 'festival rhythm'. Deploying a musical metaphor, they argue that a successful festival creates a momentary 'groove' which is shared by festival participants. While this might be done through the use of music, the 'groove' they are describing here is not restricted to musical practices. Rather, the point is that a good festival will create situations which make it easier for participants to step out of their conventional stances towards each other, enabling fleeting moments of encounter based on their shared status as participants in a festival.

Conversely, in a bad festival, one with no groove, participants are likely to remain distant witnesses to events, emotionally unengaged from the event. If they are right here, then some form of planning or even 'stage-managing' would appear to be crucial to the success of a festival as a time-space of encounter. This is a point which has not been lost on radicals over the years – to return to the example of activist group Reclaim the Streets from the beginning of this section, a tonne of sand does not simply 'arrive' on a freeway without considerable planning!

Third, and perhaps slightly at odds with our point about planning, we believe that planners must nonetheless work hard *not* to micro-manage all potential forms of disorder at festivals. In particular, it is vital that the planning of festivals is not organized so as to completely avoid disagreement and discord in order that festivals present a 'united front' to their intended audience. So, in the case of multicultural festivals, this might mean that organizers work hard to include second generation young people alongside established community leaders in the planning of festival events. Or in the case of place-based festivals, it might mean acknowledging the potential for levels of discomfort among those who visit spaces beyond their 'comfort zone', such that 'safety' is not interpreted as a complete absence of the potential for confrontation. As Permezel and Duffy (2007) argue, there is a need for festival organizers to establish less formal activities and spaces as part of the festival, and to explicitly acknowledge (and even embrace) the notion that not all festival activities can be pre-determined by their organizers:

> There is an important interplay between the formal institutional expectations and outcomes, and creating less formal and structured environments where people can come together.

In this section, we have focused almost exclusively on 'encounter' in relation to festivals. But it will no doubt have become clear to readers that the encounters sustained in festivals are also shaped in part by issues of recognition (in the form of multiculturalism, for example) and redistribution (in the form of strategies for local economic development, for example). As such, some of the issues discussed in the subsequent examples in this chapter would be highly relevant for further thinking about the planning of festivals as a means for facilitating encounter.

Encounter and redistribution: public libraries

Networks of city centre and suburban public libraries are one of the great legacies of modernist planning in many Western cities. In this section, we consider planning for public libraries as an example of planning for encounter that also aims, and long has aimed, at progressive redistribution.

By the close of the twentieth century, public libraries in many urban contexts faced two major challenges – the changing role of the state in direct provision of urban infrastructure and 'public services' such as libraries (see Chapter 2), and the rise of the 'information superhighway' which threatened to bypass libraries altogether. On top of this, many public libraries serve urban communities that are experiencing rapid demographic change through factors such as international migration and economic restructuring (as indeed they always have). In response to these challenges, public library advocates have sought to secure the future of libraries by developing new visions for public libraries in the twenty-first century designed to inform efforts to adapt and/or construct library infrastructure. The new visions for libraries are sometimes articulated with reference to rather functionalist arguments concerning public libraries' contribution to neighbourhood economic regeneration and/or social cohesion. However, contained within some efforts to renew public libraries is a vision of the library which connects with our concerns about the importance of encounter in urban life. As we shall see, librarians, planners and designers have worked together in both the United Kingdom and Australia to foreground the significance of public libraries as a space of encounter through which particular forms of conviviality can emerge. In this section, we elaborate on the forms of conviviality that are sustained in and through public libraries. Importantly, we suggest, the conviviality facilitated by public libraries is fundamentally premised on free and equal access. As such, we will argue that public libraries are an instance of planning for encounter which is also an instance of planning for redistribution – library users should simultaneously be conceptualized as 'strangers' and 'citizens'.

Increasingly, supporters of public libraries are beginning to emphasize the role that these institutions can play in urban life – not simply as repositories of knowledge, but also as *spaces* with a diversity of uses and users. That is to say, there has been a renewed interest in *going to the library* as an important activity for a wide range of urban inhabitants and visitors. This marks a significant shift in approaches to understanding the role of libraries in urban life:

> In available studies of community library usage, the ways in which libraries function as community centres is notably under reported. These include patterns of regular usage, (i.e. attendance and using the space, rather than borrowing rates or information seeking activities), and various formal and informal activities that draw people to the library (University of Technology Sydney and State Library of New South Wales, 2000, p. 7).

Recently produced accounts of what different people actually do when they go to the library draw our attention to the significant contribution that public libraries can make to encounter in cities. Indeed, as we shall see, a consideration of the forms of conviviality which characterize public libraries demonstrates the importance of looking to spaces beyond the street and other open spaces conventionally associated with urban encounter (a point we made in Chapter 6).

In considering public libraries as spaces of encounter, our account draws upon new visions for public libraries currently being developed in the United Kingdom and Australia. In the UK, the Commission for Architecture and the Built Environment (CABE) has gathered together existing research and case studies to produce two important reports on the future of public libraries in the UK's towns and cities –*Better Public Libraries* (2003) and *21st Century Libraries* (Warpole, 2004). Most importantly for our purposes here, these two reports make the case for treating public libraries as a matter of fundamental significance for urban planning and governance. In Australia, the State Library of Victoria (2005) and the State Library of New South Wales (University of Technology Sydney and State Library of New South Wales, 2000) have initiated research projects which seek to identify and promote the role played by libraries in community life. The State Library of Victoria's *Libraries/Building/ Communities* project is particularly significant for its attempt to outline a vision for public libraries.

As advocacy research, all these reports tend to place particular emphasis on the ways in which public libraries might be mobilized to address specific government policy objectives – in the case of CABE's work, the role of public libraries in neighbourhood economic regeneration is a particular emphasis (see for example Warpole, 2004, p. 5), while the Australian reports are particularly concerned with the role played by public libraries in building 'social capital' (University of Technology Sydney and State Library of New South Wales, 2000; State Library of Victoria, 2005b). As we noted in Chapter 6, our vision of encounter does not wholly conform to either of these objectives. So, while we might agree with CABE that, 'We need to stop seeing libraries as dusty repositories of books,' we are not sure that it follows that we should 'start seeing them as part of the glue that holds society together' (Commission for Architecture and the Built Environment, 2003, p. 28). Nonetheless, we believe that the findings and recommendations presented in these reports are also suggestive of how public libraries can provide spaces for the kinds of encounter and conviviality that we believe to be an important goal for planning.

So, reading these reports very slightly against the grain, we now want to consider the particular forms of encounter and conviviality that can be sustained by public libraries, and reflect on the kinds of decision rules that have worked to sustain them.

To step into a public library is to step into a space that is shared with 'strangers', in the form of other library users and library staff. As such, the forms of encounter that might occur between these strangers are mediated by the normative expectations about how a library should be used that are extant in any given library – what we might call a library's 'library-ness' (Bryson *et al.*, 2003). One of the most remarkable features of 'library-ness' most commonly identified in research on contemporary public libraries concerns the diversity of uses and users that libraries can accommodate. Reading newspapers, checking community notices, checking email, surfing the Internet, doing homework, relaxing with a coffee, attending lectures and community meetings, listening to live or recorded music, discussing a book with staff or other users, flirting, meeting and making friends ... all of these activities are taking their place in many public libraries alongside more conventional activi-ties such as consulting reference material and borrowing books or audio-visual resources.

In the course of these various activities, forms of encounter can vary enormously. Users might remain silent for their entire stay and have only non-verbal interactions with one another, they might have brief chats with other users and staff whom they may or may

not recognize, they might form more regular or lasting connections and relationships with others. All of these encounters are
significant. Following our discussion in the previous chapter, we
want to resist privileging more extended connections and relationships over the more fleeting forms of conviviality that occur among
library users. Rather, it seems to us more productive to recognize
that *all* library encounters are premised on the capacity of those
who use the library to mutually negotiate their common status *as
library users* in the moments of their encounters. This is not to say
that users stop being 'young people', or 'elderly', or members of a
particular ethnic community or community association, etc, when
they use a library – indeed, it is precisely in relation to such identities that people may in fact come to the library in the first place.
But once they are there, they also become library users. And as
such, people who may otherwise be very different from one another,
and who may not encounter each other in any other context, are
drawn into a momentary relationship as they share library space.
As the State Library of New South Wales (NSW) Report (University
of Technology Sydney and State Library of New South Wales, 2000,
p. 4) notes:

> Library users will often share the space with groups they do not usually
> encounter. In the sharing of the resources and physical space, people will
> meet others outside their close circles and recognise both commonalities
> and differences in familiar surroundings which are seen as safe space.

Similar claims are repeated in the wider international literature on
public libraries. In the United States, for instance, Goulding (2004,
p. 4) argues that:

> libraries are used by a wider cross-section of the local population than
> almost any other public, commercial or retail institution. Use and visi-
> tor statistics show that people of all ages mix in the public library and
> it could be said that it is one of the few public places where both
> old and young are welcome and encounter one another on a regular
> basis.

Reading across the UK and Australian reports, a number of
attributes associated with public libraries are said to foster such
encounters.

First, the resources, facilities, activities offered by public libraries have the potential to draw in an enormous variety of people with different identities, capacities, needs and interests. The UK and Australian reports draw our attention to a dizzying array of ways in which libraries work to attract and maintain heterogeneous user populations. To start with the most obvious point, library collections appeal to a massive range of potential users. This is not only a matter of maintaining a 'general' collection of popular fiction and non-fiction, but in some instances it is also a matter of establishing specialist collections (such as foreign language books and newspapers, children's books, popular music CDs, etc.) which may have particular appeal to some groups. Further, library facilities like computers with free Internet access might be used by a range of groups, such as travellers and migrants seeking to keep in touch with friends, family and news from 'back home' or school students participating in homework clubs. Staff with specialist expertise might be on hand to assist people with a passion for particular issues such as genealogy, or to support those who need assistance in developing their computer skills. Many libraries stage special events to draw in different user groups, such as exhibitions by local artists, displays of local historical material, musical performances, lectures and talks on a variety of themes.

Second, the physical layout, design and location of public libraries can also work to draw in a wide mix of users. Interestingly, given the discussion of drop-in centres we will have in the section to follow, in which we make a similar point about the meaning of the physical spaces of the centres, both the UK and Australian reports place a high value on the capacity of public libraries to serve as a kind of 'living room in the city' (Commission for Architecture and the Built Environment, 2003, p. 8) or 'community loungeroom' (State Library of Victoria, 2005a. p. 13). That is, libraries are identified as spaces where people might simply relax or socialize away from home but in a 'homely' environment which can support long and comfortable visits. Here, the UK and Australian approach has echoes in the US, where some new public libraries have explicitly embraced the notion of the public library as an 'urban room' (Mattern, 2007, p. 88). In interior design terms, this can be achieved through the provision of facilities such as armchairs and sofas, toilets, interactive zones, and food and drink facilities. For CABE (Warpole, 2004. p. 9), libraries are therefore 'a civil and education alternative to the frenetic commercial world of the modern shopping mall or the themed bar' – although it is interesting to note that contemporary commercial bookshops have in some instances provided the inspiration for such interior design efforts in public libraries (Commission for Architecture and the Built Environment, 2003, p. 14). In programming terms, this can be achieved through programming of events such as lectures and performances, or regular meetings such as children's reading sessions and book clubs. The diversity of library users and uses can also be supported in design terms through the provision of 'libraries within libraries', or 'specific areas for special types of users, for example children, teenagers study areas and quiet areas' (Commission for Architecture and the Built Environment, 2003, p. 26). Both the UK and Australian reports also argue that public libraries have had considerable success in attracting a mix of users through co-location with other commercial, government and non-government services. Examples of successful co-location which have drawn new users to libraries include: establishing an independently owned coffee shop run out of a library building which offers catering services to groups using library meeting rooms (Bryson *et al.*, 2003, p. 31); co-location with an art gallery to diversify the users of both spaces by encouraging movement from one to the other (State Library of Victoria, 2005a, p. 13); and 'one-stop-shop' co-location with other community and government services such as employment assistance schemes (State Library of Victoria, 2005a, pp. 17–19). Finally, the construction of new library buildings with exciting architectural features can also help attract attention to libraries. One of the most high-profile examples of such a strategy can be seen in Peckham (London), where a new library with a striking design contributed to a tripling of library attendance and loans in the first year after it opened (Commission for Architecture and the Built Environment, 2003, p. 17; see also Mattern, 2007, on the new Rem Koolhaas-designed public library in Seattle).

Thirdly, public libraries attract a diversity of users because they are viewed as safe spaces for a variety of groups who find other 'public spaces' in the city to be unsafe or inhospitable. Indeed, the State Library of NSW report on public libraries was called *A Safe Place to Go*, in recognition of the importance of this aspect of public libraries. This report, in line with other research internationally (Alstad and Curry, 2003; Goulding, 2004), suggests that many (although not all) libraries are felt to be safe spaces by children and their parents, by women, by the elderly and by the homeless – all groups who may experience marginalization from streets and other forms of open public space. Most interesting for our purposes here is the manner in which these feelings of safety are successfully established in (some) libraries. Significantly, feelings of safety in public libraries do not appear to depend on the existence of surveillance and security technologies – indeed, some research goes so far as to argue that the use of such technologies can actually detract from the perceptions of safety associated with libraries (University of Technology Sydney and State Library of New South Wales, 2000, p. 5). Rather, the survey of library users and non-users in NSW found:

> an almost universal perception that libraries are places where all people have a right of access, regardless of their circumstances or backgrounds. ... The heritage of free use and the public ownership of libraries mean that nobody is turned away, and users feel that all others have a right to be there, creating a sense of equity and entitlement, and thereby neutralising any sense of marginalisation or exclusion (University of Technology Sydney and State Library of New South Wales, 2000, p. 8).

This would appear to suggest that libraries do not need to embrace some of the more exclusionary approaches to the governance of conduct discussed in Chapter 6 in order to create a feeling of safety. While some libraries have taken this exclusionary approach (Lees, 1997), they would be better served by working to maintain a shared commitment to open access. Such a commitment is more likely to be sustained when libraries allow for user-staff negotiation of what it means to be a 'good library user' at various times/places.

The encounters that take place in libraries are not only those of the face-to-face kind. Indeed, one of the key contributions that public libraries make as spaces of encounter is to provide various media through which users can encounter a diversity of people who are not physically present in the library space. Good public libraries have always been prized because they offer 'a window onto the world of the imagination and of raised intellectual horizons' (Commission for Architecture and the Built Environment, 2003, p. 4), where users can explore different issues and interests, and experience different perspectives, in a self-directed manner.

Most obviously, libraries provide windows onto the wider world through their book and media collections, and now increasingly through networked computing facilities. So, while we agree that libraries are more than just repositories of knowledge, this is not to say that their role as repositories of knowledge is not still important! But approaches to the on-going acquisition of library materials are changing. There is an increasing recognition of the need to democratize library collections. That is, just as the activities offered by public libraries might be developed in collaboration with users, so too collections can be shaped with reference to the particular needs and/or desires of library users and staff in any given context. This means breaking down traditional hierarchies between library staff and users, and also breaking down traditional hierarchies between 'central' and 'branch' libraries which allocate collections and facilities according to externally derived criteria (Warpole, 2004, p. 20). (Recall in Chapter 2 that the equitable allocation of resources to different neighbourhoods and population groups, in a study in Oakland, California in the 1970s, was examined with just such a democratization of library collections in mind.)

As noted above, free Internet access also establishes the library as a networked space through which people can explore the wider wired world. Indeed, the increasing significance of Internet access in many people's lives has given libraries a new relevance in many contexts, particularly (but not exclusively) in those urban communities where Internet access is poorly provided and/or unaffordable for many. Through making networked computer technology accessible and offering support for users, public libraries in fact are playing a central role in efforts to address the so-called 'digital divide' (State Library of Victoria, 2005b, p. 9). As CABE (Warpole, 2004, p. 5) noted, the on-going importance of public libraries in the age of the Internet confounds earlier predictions of their demise:

> The technological revolution of the 1980s and 1990s was widely seen as sounding the death knell for the public library as we knew it. Why would people bother to borrow books when they could get all the information they needed from their home computers? These predictions have proved unfounded. Indeed, ironically the Internet has proved to be one of the saviours of today's public library.

Certainly, some public libraries have also established themselves as 'virtual libraries', providing Internet portals through which users can access collections and databases remotely, 24 hours a day. But, as Bryson *et al.* (2003, p. 11) have argued:

> Although the virtual library has a role to play, ... in the 21st Century libraries must also be buildings. The commitment of the politicians and professionals responsible for the libraries involved in this project demonstrates the value and impact these buildings can have on local communities.

'Library-ness', in other words, continues to be positively associated with a physical building – not least for some of the reasons outlined in the discussion of face-to-face encounters above.

Finally, beyond their collections and Internet access, libraries are full of physical traces of other users with whom one only 'shares' the library at different times. In particular, library noticeboards are also windows onto the world, displaying a wide range of activities that are conducted in the library itself and in the community outside. In some cases, participation in the activities advertised on library noticeboards might result in future face-to-face encounters with others. But even if users never take part in any of these activities, the mere fact that their attention is drawn to the existence of such activities constitutes a form of mediated encounter which is significant in demonstrating the diversity of interests held by those who share the library space over time.

Through all the mediated forms of encounter on offer at public libraries, users might become 'strangers to themselves' (Kristeva, 1991; see also Deutsche, 1999; Tajbakhsh, 2001). That is, in using a library, users have a chance to explore different identifications, even to discover interests, desires and capacities that they did not even know they had until the moment of encounter. Of course, readers should not be surprised that we hold such a view of the possibilities and romance of the library – obviously, we would not be bothering to read and write articles and books if we did not have some faith in the power of mediated encounters with other people and perspectives! And importantly, it seems to us that both the face-to-face and the mediated encounters sustained by public libraries connect very strongly with Henri Lefebvre's notion of the 'right to the city' (see Chapter 1), which he understood as a dynamic right to become someone else through urban exploration and encounter, not just a more static and formal right to 'be yourself' in the city. Here, we support the emphasis given to 'lifelong learning' through public libraries, so long as this concept is not reduced to a more functionalist concern with 'job-readiness' and labour market status.

Given the incredible diversity of encounters sustained through public libraries, we suggest that the provision of public libraries ought to remain a strategic priority for municipal, regional and national governments committed to working towards just diversity in cities. As such, there are several ways in which the forms of encounter sustained through public libraries are also fundamentally a matter of *redistribution*.

We have noted above that free and open access to libraries and their resources, facilities, activities and spaces is fundamental to the forms of 'library-ness' we have discussed above. As Alstad and Curry (2003) note, in the end, supporters of public libraries must resist the logic of commercialization which has been applied to other forms of urban infrastructure provided by the state – any introduction of a 'user pays' logic would significantly undermine the convivial aspects of library-ness we have discussed. It is crucial that access to public libraries is simultaneously understood as a matter of *citizenship*, with its associated notions of universal rights of access, as well as strangerhood, with its associated notions of encounter. Furthermore, public libraries must also resist market-driven models of service provision in their efforts to meet diverse community demands and form partnerships. The vision of the public library articulated here, as Alstad and Curry (2003) argue, is much more than 'a specialized, demand-based materials distribution service in the style of the private sector but with a public subsidy' (McCabe, 2001; quoted in Alstad and Curry, 2003). Maintaining public libraries as spaces of encounter must involve on-going commitments to state funding.

Of course, we acknowledge that such commitments are always difficult to secure, and this is certainly the case in the current period of rapid change for public libraries. For public libraries to provide many of the resources, facilities, activities and spaces we have discussed above, existing library infrastructure may need to be considerably altered, upgraded or even constructed from scratch. As CABE (Warpole, 2004, p. 8) puts it, existing library buildings 'pose both opportunities and problems', and addressing some of the problems will require significant levels of public investment. In both the UK and Victoria, governments have established designated library infrastructure funds to assist in the updating of existing libraries and the construction of new library facilities. According to Bryson *et al.* (2003, p. 27), such funding is most effective 'when it is supported and even driven by the overall strategic agenda of the local authority'.

Additionally, as we have noted in Chapters 2 and 3, questions of redistribution are fundamentally spatial. Equality of access is a key issue in relation to library services, and the provision of public libraries facilities can in fact help to address spatial disadvantage. We have already referred, for example, to the role that public libraries can play in addressing the so-called 'digital divide', as discussed in the Victorian *Libraries/Building/Communities* project. In summarizing the findings of this project, the authors noted that:

> People and geographic areas already suffering social and economic disadvantage were said to have more restricted access to information and computer resources. Public libraries were seen as having a crucial role in ensuring that people on low incomes and from other disadvantaged groups are able to access information and technology and develop the necessary skills to use these (State Library of Victoria, 2005b, p. 9).

Interestingly, it would appear that levels of support for on-going government spending on public libraries vary in different places. In the UK, CABE (Warpole, 2004, p. 10) sound a word of caution about the need to maintain a diverse support base for public libraries in order to secure their future:

> the threat which the private sector posed to the traditional library service, through the growth of more user-friendly bookshop chains, online information services to the office and home, allied to the perception of the library service as part of a failing municipal sector, has temporarily been arrested, and in some places reversed. Nevertheless, there is evidence that certain key groups of opinion-formers and age groups – particularly young trend-setters and middle class professionals – have deserted the library service, and unless their support and interest is re-captured, the service will struggle to advance its cause and sustain a positive public and media profile in the corridors of power.

This concern echoes the situation Mattern (2007, p. 34) reports in the United States, where supporters of public investment in downtown public libraries have had to overcome scepticism about whether they will be used only by the inner city poor and homeless. The NSW public library study in Australia (University of Technology Sydney and State Library of New South Wales, 2000), on the other hand, found extremely high levels of support for state-funded provision of public library facilities among both users *and non-users*. And of course, research reports such as those discussed here play an important part in securing political commitments to such funding.

The need to secure state funding is by no means the only problem to be addressed by those who support the new visions of public libraries being articulated in the UK and Australia. In concluding our discussion of encounter in public libraries, we want to reflect on a couple of emerging tensions and conflicts that will pose further challenges for public library staff, users and supporters.

There are at least two elements of the 'new' public library discussed above that remain contentious for those concerned with the kinds of encounters sustained by public library use. The first relates to the interior design of library spaces. Some libraries have embraced a 'libraries within libraries' approach to library use, by establishing different spatial zones for different activities (such as computer use, group discussion, quiet reading and contemplation, etc.). Such a strategy is justified on the grounds that it can help to diversify the user groups who come to public libraries. As CABE (2003, p. 26) notes:

> One of the major challenges in designing a library is handling the conflicting demands – solitude versus interaction, quiet versus noise, order versus mess, openness versus security and limited hours versus '24/7' expectations. One solution is the concept of zones and libraries within libraries. This provides a specific area for special types of users, for example children, teenagers study areas and quiet areas.

But as they note in another report, this strategy presents its own problems, with regard to finding a balance between the library as a space for citizens and a space for strangers:

> How is the historic universalism of the public library to be squared with managerial requirements to separate out different user groups and their needs, particularly in a more culturally segmented and multi-media society? (Warpole, 2004, p. 22)

Functional segregation may in fact work to *prevent* some of the forms of encounter that have been associated with public libraries in the discussion above:

> the library may also represent the only place where ... different social and age groups come into contact, and this contact may well have more positive than negative consequences. Total segregation is unlikely to represent the best solution (Warpole, 2004, p. 20).

This tension has no simple solution. Certainly, as Mattern (2007, p. 9) notes, 'the shaping of a library building is, in effect, the shaping of the publics it serves'. As such, the design process raises questions of recognition alongside those matters of encounter and redistribution already discussed with respect to libraries. There is a fine balance between the use of design to foster diversity, and the use of design to 'solve' conflict by separating different user groups in a way that isolates them from one another. Certainly, where distinct zones are created, they should not be so clearly defined and bounded that they become 'no-go' areas for other users (University of Technology Sydney and State Library of New South Wales, 2000, p. 23). A similar dilemma is inherent in efforts to manage potential user conflicts via temporal strategies, by encouraging different user groups (such as teenagers and the elderly) to use the library at different times. And where libraries decide to establish distinct zones, such spaces should be established in conjunction with shared open spaces which have a life of their own, through which all users are likely to pass and/or linger, and which are by definition not associated with any one user group. Most importantly, library designers and staff should not attempt to head off all potential conflicts through design 'solutions', which would undermine the capacity of different user groups to negotiate their use of the library *as library users*.

The second contentious element of the new vision for public libraries concerns the co-location of public libraries with other commercial, community and government services. As with the 'libraries within libraries' concept, co-location is often considered a useful way to heighten the exposure of public libraries to a variety of potential users who may not otherwise use the library (and the converse is of course true for those services with which libraries co-locate). Furthermore, co-location can create interesting synergies

(Bryson *et al.*, 2003, p. 30). But, once again, this spatial strategy potentially has significant drawbacks. Co-location might compromise the highly-valued neutrality and accessibility of libraries, which are fundamental parts of their library-ness (Goulding, 2004, p. 5). For instance, where public libraries are co-located with government agencies, levels of trust/mistrust in government among some users may deter them from visiting the library. Similarly, where public libraries are co-located in commercial premises (such as retail arcades or entertainment quarters), tensions may arise when ideals of universal access confront commercial concerns for establishing secure spaces for consumption. Bryson *et al.* (2003) suggest that some co-location arrangements are more appropriate in this context than others – in particular, they note that some commercial, non-government and government agencies are engaged in activities which 'support the social and information remit of the library' (p. 35). For example:

> Education and Training organisations use the information and resources provided by the library; restaurants and cafés offer refreshment and communal activities that invite people into the establishment and keep them there (p. 35).

Certainly, as Mattern (2007, p. 7) points out in the US context, libraries have always had at least some commercial element, so blanket criticism of any new commercial arrangement is not necessarily productive or realistic:

> we may find ourselves measuring modern day public libraries against a mythical yardstick and concluding that today's public libraries have fallen short in upholding ideals that have always been out of reach.

Mattern (2007, p. 89) prefers to see some of the new commercial arrangements (such as cafés) as akin to the inclusion of romance novels on library shelves one hundred years ago:

> commercial activities and commercial literature both draw patrons who might not otherwise come to the library, and it is hoped that they will serve as a stepping stone to something better, whether that be entering the library itself, rather than simply mingling ... outside, or choosing reading material of higher quality. Marketing and merchandising have for years influenced librarianship.

Despite such difficulties, the provision of public libraries informed by the new vision of libraries discussed has considerable potential to facilitate encounters in cities. As we have seen, the potential does not require the wholesale rethinking of public libraries. Indeed, as Mattern (2007, p. 7) notes, some of the questions raised above about the future of public libraries are variations on perennial questions facing libraries:

> The contemporary public library is wrestling with the same issues it always has: how to accommodate multiple media formats; how to promote public access to those media while ensuring security; how to successfully accommodate nonmedia functions, including commerce; how to be a public space committed to free, universal access while also acknowledging that the library is subject to the same financial pressures that any non-profit organization or institution is subject to; and how to balance its obligations to function well internally as a library and its external responsibilities as a civic icon and an anchor in urban development.

As such, what is required to sustain public libraries as spaces of encounter is an acknowledgement and on-going adjustment of 'a core library service and culture which has proven to be highly resilient through many decades, and is likely to continue to be so' (Commission for Architecture and the Built Environment, 2003, p. 4).

Encounter and recognition: drop-in centres and community centres

Drop-in centres and community centres, though their name suggests they are open to all comers, in fact are usually directed at certain individuals and groups. They recognize the assistance that would be given to these individuals and groups by having access to an informal meeting place. Often the individuals and groups in question are strangers to the locality. Often they are marginalized as well. They may be newcomers – often immigrants whose lives in their new place of residence would benefit from improving their language skills and meeting other local residents; they may sometimes be homeless or very poor people requiring respite from the street; they may be people with disabilities who receive support from the workers in the centre. In most cases, the location and characteristics of a drop-in centre are planned on the basis of knowledge of which particular 'strangers' in the locality need assistance, and offer a targeted even if informal approach to assisting these strangers to make their lives in the locality. Sometimes centres provide a link to the more formal social services sector, but often the informal interaction they offer is as valuable for itself.

We see drop-in centres, targeted as they are to encounter between members of particular sets of strangers, as meeting places that are planned by linking strategies about encounter with strategies about recognition. They are not 'community centres' of the kind aimed at one group, from (say) a checklist of self-identified groups. They aim for interaction between individuals who may be differently grouped, and emphasize the diversity of the participants in their activities. Nevertheless, the forms of encounter sustained in drop-in centres do depend upon recognizing the need amongst people with certain characteristics in the locality. So, paradoxically, drop-in centres at once foster interaction between anyone who 'drops in', but also aim to cater to particular needs and therefore set boundaries by making themselves less attractive to groups or individuals not having those needs.

Consider first the provision of drop-in centres for people who are economically marginalized, who may be unemployed, homeless or destitute, possibly having arrived at that circumstance from a process of deinstitutionalization or at least due to the reduction of social supports from the state associated with deinstitutionalization. These individuals are often isolated from social networks that might otherwise have supported them. What does encounter mean for such individuals or groups, and how is it planned for? Recall the important point made in Chapter 6, in the discussion of safe cities, that encounter is something that should be part of everyday life, rather than merely something one has from time to time when one attends a special event. Encounter is eased, we saw in the decision rules identified in Chapter 6, when it occurs in apparently safe, because they are transparent, spaces, and when participants have some control over the activities in which they are engaged and the types of interaction they have.

A central feature of planning drop-in centres for economically marginalized groups and the relatively isolated individuals within them is that the centres are home-like in their size, internal physical features and the informal social behaviours they allow. (In this, they have some similarities with the home-like atmospheres developed within some public libraries.) In these ways, such centres exhibit in their features thinking of the kind exhibited in the decision rules noted above. Being home-like, they seem safe and their form is transparent or readily comprehended, and the expectation of informal social behaviour there (though the centres are always run by an organization, and clearly so) gives a degree of control by participants over their interactions, different from what would occur in a formal classroom for example. This is the nature of their spatiality, the combined spatial and social features that make them (successfully) what they are. (Particular forms of spatiality have been discussed by Watson, (2004) with reference to their importance in the effective workings of a range of community organizations.) Encounter in this context means social interaction of a relatively informal kind, at a relatively small scale, which can become quite familiar with repeated visits to the centre. It is neither the incidental, occasional contact of casual interactions in more public spaces (in events in city squares, or meeting up with a friend in a local store), nor the purpose-defined socializing that occurs in the organized micro-publics identified by Amin (2002) (in adult education classes, for example, or sports or artistic clubs). Planning for encounter of this kind in these sorts of centres is planning the arrangements of a particular physical structure, usually one building, and the activities within it. Two of the decision rules we saw in Chapter 6 are relevant here, as noted above, but the decision rule about providing a variety of infrastructural sites for people of different social and economic capacities is planning at a different scale from that being exercised within such a centre.

Close analyses of the characteristics and workings of individual drop-in centres illustrate the way they have been planned for encounter that emphasizes homeliness and informality. We draw on examples of: a drop-in centre for 'street youth' in Toronto (Canada); a drop-in centre for people with mental health problems in Nottingham (UK); a community drop-in centre in outer Bristol (UK); a neighbourhood house in Melbourne (Australia) which includes in the groups for which it caters people with intellectual disabilities, immigrants and isolated women; and Playcentres for children and their parents in New Zealand.

Physically, the internal spaces of these centres are home-like, in that they are arranged for informal and small-scale social interaction, tempered by the comforts of refreshments prepared in a home-sized kitchen. The layout of the internal space of the Nottingham centre is shown by Parr (2000, p. 230). This centre, located in an area with many hostels and rented accommodation for lower-income people, is open during the day for all but has some of its evening sessions limited to people identified by the staff as having mental health problems. Though in a church hall, its space is organized around a kitchen from which food is provided through a food hatch, and two different kinds of seating – a set of round tables, grouped together, with four chairs around each, and a set of chairs and benches along two walls edging a pool table. Different sorts of interaction are catered for in this arrangement of furniture – there is conversation around the small tables, and also observation of pool games where observers are alone but still part of the activity by locating in the spectator seats along walls. Unlike in some other centres, however, access to the kitchen area is limited to staff of the centre. The Toronto centre for street youth opens during weekday afternoons to provide 'daytime shelter' for isolated young people and also adults without homes. Dachner and Tarasuk (2002) describe its physical resources as including a kitchen, pool table and common area with tables and chairs (like the Nottingham centre), but also a laundry, bathroom with a shower, and a range of other resources like telephones, a computer and a photocopying machine. Unlike the Nottingham centre, the kitchen of this one in Toronto may be used by those coming to the centre to make themselves tea and coffee and to prepare meals with food they have brought to the centre themselves. In the Melbourne neighbourhood house, Permezel (2001, p. 168) notes that for the isolated women it serves locally, who use the centre for making initial social contacts in their suburbs, the home-like and familiar physical form of such houses (for these are ordinary suburban houses in suburban locations) and their location nearby in residential streets, make them comfortable places for anxious women to visit as they start to extend their social interactions beyond the family home. In all the cases cited here, the finding is that centre users find that these home-like settings seem 'safe' and welcoming, as well as familiar.

Of course the planning of the form and location of these drop-in centres is only important because of the social interaction this particular form encourages. Close attention has been paid by analysts to this matter; though in the case of the centres catering to people with intellectual disabilities or mental health problems, the analysis has often been of the 'behaviours' of those attending the centres, as much as the encounters people have with others. In the case of the centre in outer Bristol, located in an area of high unemployment and poverty, and catering during the day to local people, the idea is to provide a 'supportive and welcoming space where local people can meet and socialise' (Conradson, 2003, p. 513). Conradson sees this centre as a 'therapeutic space' because it provides practical opportunities for people to demonstrate an interest in the well-being of other individuals. He describes how different individuals found the centre useful and helpful, because it allowed them to develop (not necessarily easily) friendly relationships with a range of local residents and a selection of volunteer workers who were there to provide support and the occasional advice and referral. The Toronto centre for homeless youth and adults is, more than the other centres described here, about survival of the centre's users, but it also serves as a social space for the young people who use it to interact around its tables.

In the Melbourne neighbourhood house catering to people with intellectual and mental health disabilities and the Nottingham centre whose group of visitors is people with mental illnesses, the encounters between centre users are mediated by the behaviours individuals exhibit and how acceptable they are to others, and by the interactions between centre users and the staff who seek to 'manage' centre users to a considerable degree. Parr (2000, pp. 232–3) describes how the Nottingham centre allows for interaction amongst people with unusual behavioural and bodily habits:

> the use of space [by centre visitors] in highly personalised ways, whether as a result of an institutionalised identity or a fantastical spatial displacement – indicates a micro-geography of inclusion. These are safe spaces where such mind/body characteristics can be revealed away from both the diagnostic gaze of more clinical-institutional geographies and the threat of 'othering' in mainstream public space. There is an implicit recognition of the other members' different emotional and mental states by the tolerance of what might be constituted outside of the drop-in as 'not normal', 'strange' and 'bizarre' behaviour.

But in the Melbourne neighbourhood house, visitors with intellectual and mental health disabilities and unusual behaviours use the centre at the same time as those without such characteristics and identities. Interaction between centre users does not occur as freely between those with intellectual disabilities and mental health problems and those without, as it does between those with particular identities of gender, language and culture, according to Permezel (2001, p. 201). Permezel quotes one centre user, a person with mental health problems, saying: 'this is the only social outlet I have each week. I don't go to clubs or anything ... it's nice to mix with people who are different from those I normally mix with ... it passes the time coming here, an escape from your own things, and I can do volunteer work' (2001, p. 201). But in addition, in this centre, anxiety amongst other users about the behaviour of people with intellectual and mental health disabilities frustrates informal interaction. For this reason, Permezel regards informal encounter as less possible when centre participants with intellectual disabilities and mental illnesses interact with a broader range of identity groups. She regrets the way that neighbourhood houses with such a varied set of users have sought to 'manage' the behaviour of those with disabilities, corralling the latter into certain areas of the houses at certain times, and making these 'potentially empowering spaces' reproduce some of the characteristics of more confined institutional settings (2001, p. 215).

Besides the physical arrangement of drop-in centres, in attempts to make these centres home-like in scale and facilities, an important planning issue is how to treat informality in these centres. To what extent should interaction be managed? How do we interpret this matter in light of the decision rule we have noted about facilitating stakeholder or participant agency and 'room to move'? This matter is thrown into sharp relief by the inclusion of people with intellectual and psychiatric disabilities in the centres, either in groups alone or with other identity groups. In addition, to what extent should drop-in centres become places principally offering organized programs to people using them – either social service programs and referrals, or adult education courses? Analysts of such centres agree that the informal nature of interaction, that it is not programmed and not particularly purposeful, is a real benefit. As Conradson (2003, p. 321) remarks, for example, such centres should not be held to account because they don't offer more 'services' – it is significant that there are such places where people can just 'relate to others and simply be'. Certainly, participant agency is perhaps limited when formal and programmed interaction (such as classroom teaching) is mandated.

Considering the question of the management of interactions, it seems obvious that management of centres by their staff is needed to keep the centres operating smoothly, and to ensure that the needs of certain groups and individuals don't override those of others, thereby acting to exclude some people. If centres are hosting people with intellectual disabilities and mental illnesses, then the question of the ways to 'manage' differences in behaviour and forms of interaction amongst centre uses can be more complex. In the situation described in Nottingham by Parr (2000), evening sessions specifically for people with disabilities seemed to provide 'spaces of inclusion'; on the other hand in the Melbourne case the provision of special sessions of this kind was criticized as overly controlling (Permezel, 2001) and as pandering to the anxieties about unusual behaviour held by other users of the neighbourhood house in question.

In relation to the question about the degree to which centres' informal interactions should be supplanted by the offering of formal programs, the answers are equally unclear. Programs offered by centres do help local users of those centres, and can be tailored to their particular needs. In locations where there are immigrants without much facility in the language of their new country, then language classes are of benefit; employment readiness programs may assist as well; referrals to specialist health or social services providers may be a useful aspect of centres' operations. But making drop-in centres primarily service providers, and part of the social services system, is frowned upon by analysts. Permezel (2001, p. 191) describes how a trend in the relevant government authorities towards making adult education programs more formal by, for example, insisting that they be accountable for more precisely measured outputs, and making them take place in more classroom-like settings, has threatened the home-like and supportive environments on offer in neighbourhood houses. Neighbourhood houses are pushed towards becoming part of the formal educational sector, and the social interactions they facilitate informally are made to seem less significant than this formal role. Similarly, in the case of the Nottingham centre, Parr (2000, p. 227) describes how:

> The 'informality' of the drop-in was deemed to be threatened in part by new administrative practices being brought in by the social services manager. These practices involved keeping attendance records and

creating formal lines of communication between individual members' 'care workers' and the drop-in. In some ways, this can be seen as an attempt by the local state to 'seal' any 'leaks' in the community care net, and thus ensuring that people with mental health problems were well cared for. A more interpretive (and less positive) conclusion is that the state was seeking to extend its means of surveillance of this problematic population, thus ensuring discipline and management in spaces outside the walls of formal institutions.

In both these cases, the informal encounters able to be had in drop-in centres were deemed by governmental funding agencies to be less significant than the more directed encounters between service providers and service users that might result from making the centres into social servicing sites. Workers in the centres, if funded by government agencies, were obliged to be accountable to those employing them, by complying with such expectations.

Centres catering to a broader population as informal, drop-in places have as their principal purpose the facilitation of interaction, as we have seen. But in addition, establishments directly serving particular populations may become places of encounter for a broader population. This is one characteristic of schools and other educational establishments for the young, where it often happens that such facilities become sites of interaction for the parents and grandparents of the children using the service. Every kind of service-providing facility would not have the same potential for developing interaction between a broader population as do educational services for the very young; the relevant aspect of educational services for the young, causing them to facilitate widespread local encounter, is that the young must be brought there by adults each day and those adults are actively encouraged to participate in the activities of the educational establishment. So there is meeting, with a purpose, amongst a broad group of adults whose major common concern is that they are in a family with young children.

A long-established example from New Zealand is the country's Playcentres. The first Playcentre was begun as a parent cooperative in the 1940s, and the New Zealand Playcentre Foundation formed as a national organization in 1948. Now, these centres are found throughout the country. The twin aims of the centres are to educate children and to support their parents and extended families. Parents are responsible for maintaining the centre, holding working bees to maintain the buildings and equipment. Parent

and extended family involvement in the provision of early childhood education is described in one account as follows: 'a typical
Playcentre session will have children from birth to school age playing together with their parents and other adults, engaged in a wide
range of learning experiences' (http://www.pplaycentre.org.nz).
In such a setting, adults meet other adults whom they would, under
other circumstances in their lives, never come across, and engage
in purposeful activity with them. This is a 'micro-public' of the kind
that Amin (2002) described and can become a valuable point of
connection for participants. A recent report to the New Zealand
Playcentre Foundation indicates the positive effect of Playcentres
in generating broad interaction and community feeling in New
Zealand localities (Powell, 2005).

Now, in Playcentres, interaction between ethnic and cultural
groups is variable, despite the opportunity often taken up by parents
to work together cooperatively to maintain the centres physically
and to participate in educational sessions. The Playcentres do stress
culturally inclusive practices and introduce into their activities the
ways of both Maori and Paheka (white settler) cultures. Nevertheless, studies have found that even when a local area has a population from a mix of backgrounds, this does not translate necessarily
into wide-ranging and sustained multicultural interaction in all
Playcentres there. Rather, particular ethnic groups tend to frequent
particular Playcentres (Witten, McCreanor and Kearns, 2005). (This
is a point we noted theoretically in Chapter 6, in the argument of
Beck (2002) that a cosmopolitan setting does not make of all its
residents cosmopolitan subjects.) In the past, some Maori parents
have experienced racism at Playcentres (Ritchie, 2003, p. 12) and
therefore have avoided them. There are in the reports of immigrant
mothers, however, examples of the ways that encounter fostered in
Playcentres has greatly aided the settlement of those women and
their families, even if the range of ethnic groups participating in
the Playcentres has been limited. A range of newly arrived Asian
groups have benefited from their children's grandparents attending educational sessions during weekdays, with parents participating in night-time business meetings of the centres and weekend
working bees (Tse and Liew, 2004). 'Magnet' playcentres have thus
emerged that attract other Asian children. The authors find that
material about Asian cultures, to be included in the educational
sessions of these Playcentres, needs to be negotiated with the range

of non-Asian parents using the centres. In another example, Goan women, otherwise isolated new immigrants in Auckland, found participation in Playcentres important to the new social networks they were needing to establish (DeSouza, 2005).

In contemporary New Zealand, the strong focus in local governance on partnerships between communities and their organizations and the institutions of government, is building on longstanding, grassroots organizations such as Playcentres (Larner and Craig, 2005). Not only are such organizations being called upon to help coordinate locality based service delivery, but in addition the people (often women) who have honed their skills in community development and negotiation through participation in voluntary programs like Playcentres are being called upon to staff newly emerging regional and community partnership programs. Larner and Craig quote the comments of one community development manager, talking about the importance of her volunteer experience with Playcentre, and the training programs offered by Playcentre, for her capacity to undertake her current role: 'Playcentre gave me, and many other women in the community, the opportunity for personal growth through the training programme. That was a major turning point for me and set me off on an unintended career path' (Larner and Craig, 2005, p. 411). There are ironies in the dependence of contemporary service delivery and governance on such organizations, however. Volunteer-run organizations like Playcentres often produce community activists, skilled at politicizing their needs in the local context. If such activists are now collaborative members of governing and service-providing partnerships, their role has changed. They are no longer activists, primarily. People working in the new partnership arrangements, who have 'trained' through grassroots organizations like Playcentres, are now in their new roles required to shape their previously political claims into the technical formats of strategic planning. This is a matter akin to the challenges to informality of drop-in centres for the economically marginalized, which we have mentioned already.

Drop-in centres for strangers who are new arrivals to urban localities, often immigrants, are a little different from the ones for the economically marginalized groups described above and indeed from those like Playcentres which, somewhat incidentally to their major function of educating the young, become important sites of encounter for adults. Those centres established purposefully for new arrivals may be for immigrants as a group – that is to say, centres recognizing the need of new arrivals to a place to have opportunities for encounter – or they may cater to a particular immigrant group that is nationally or ethnically specific. In the latter case, where the immigrants being catered for are, for example, from a particular country, the case might be made that the drop-in centre in question is not encouraging broad encounter but rather is advancing the needs of that particular group. This is a blurry distinction, but important to note. Perhaps even making such a point represents too strongly the 'group checklist' thinking described and criticized in Chapter 3. Like centres facilitating encounter for marginalized groups such as the deinstitutionalized and the homeless, centres for immigrants have a range of partnerships and relationships with government service-providers, and therefore emphasize encounter rather than service provision to different extents. As Mitchell (2001) has described in Vancouver in the 1990s, immigrant organizations can be amongst those sub-contracted to provide social services to immigrant communities at a time that governments are withdrawing from direct provision of social services. Such centres may differ from those established for marginalized groups like the deinstitutionalized and the homeless, however, because their resources can be sourced from overseas, when immigrants from particular countries sponsor organizations for their compatriots who have migrated to the place where the centre is located (Mitchell, 2001).

There are some drop-in centres for immigrants that do not specify so precisely the national origins of participants. In inner Melbourne, churches – both their services and their bible study sessions – fulfil this function for newly arrived tertiary students from overseas (often from countries in South-east Asia) who identify as Christians (Fincher and Shaw, 2006). These are clearly not organizations planned by urban planners and policy-makers. But it is possible that in their ministry and in the interaction they foster between newly arrived people, they are performing, albeit temporarily and at a far more limited scale, some of those functions of a 'shadow state' community organization that Mitchell (2001) has described for the immigrant organization in Vancouver. These organizations put a great deal of effort into welcoming newly arrived but known strangers into their group, not only singling them out at church services for special attention but also allocating them to small bible study groups that meet at least weekly, often in the homes of members. The strangers are known because the churches are well aware of the large number of new students from overseas who will be in the area, recently arrived, each year, and their places of origin and characteristics. The churches are aware also that if such welcoming is done effectively, in the absence of much other activity of this special kind, many students will enrol in the congregations and perhaps remain in them. The form of encounter being organized here by the churches is not limited to any particular 'group', being open to all who wish to attend.

So here, then, is that attention to welcoming newcomers to a home-like atmosphere, that we observed in the drop-in cities for marginalized people. Here, in addition, is the attempt to form friendship groups and to host social activities (which the bible study units do, in addition to being study sessions). Like the situation with the drop-in centres though, these organized encounters do often end up being patronized by groups with certain interests and characteristics, despite being ostensibly open to all comers. In the case of the Melbourne churches with a special mission to tertiary students from overseas, it does happen that Southeast Asian students tend to cluster at certain churches and European students at another. It also happens that students from particular churches in the overseas countries of their origin cluster at certain churches.

This last example is not one about urban planners organizing encounter for groups recognized as having particular kinds of characteristics. It is offered here to show how the planning of such activity does focus on the scale of the home-like and the personal. This is evidently a strategy that planners and urban policy-makers in this line of social planning work might emulate.

Conclusion

In this chapter three case examples of planning for encounter have been presented. Our first example was planning for street festivals. Here we considered planning for encounter and sociality alone, with less emphasis on redistribution and recognition than was the case in the other examples (although it could always be that some street festivals do cater for, and recognize or include, particular groups more than others). Implementing a new vision for public libraries was a second example, in which the interaction between library patrons and between patrons and library staff is designed for, even as the longstanding tradition of providing free access for the public to library collections is continued. Here is planning for encounter that emphasizes redistribution, in which, as we have described, users of library services and spaces are envisaged both as citizens (in the unfettered access they have to the libraries) and as strangers (in that their identities are not prescribed in any way, nor is there any suggestion that one sort of person is a better 'fit' in library spaces than others). Our third example was planning for drop-in centres, places where even as the stranger is encouraged to 'drop in', the characteristics of likely centre users in the local area are recognized or known. This is planning for encounter that aligns with recognition, for it does understand the characteristics of those who are likely to visit the centre, and does provide particularly to welcome those centre users.

We have emphasized the way that planning for encounter requires, for success, a 'light touch' – here is no micro-management of individual participants, nor the close specification of group interests or identity. Rather, planning creates the opportunity for sociality, and then allows the form of that interaction to be largely determined by the participants themselves. In addition, we have emphasized that planning for encounter requires that such opportunities arise in everyday contexts, rather than in infrequent special events. Informal, observably safe, spaces are those in which planning for encounter will be most viable.

Drawing out these emphases further, two issues come to mind, in concluding this chapter of case examples of planning for encounter. The first is to elaborate on how encounter does thrive when situated in 'home-like', everyday, spaces. In both public libraries, in which designers of new library spaces have created 'living rooms in the city' for encouraging the sharing of spaces between strangers, and in drop-in centres in which rooms with functions like those of domestic homes have been created for the comfort of visitors to the centres, we observe a conscious planning for the familiar, the everyday, the domestic scale. Even in the example of street festivals, the planned activities are relatively informal and casual rather than formal celebrations – in their informal nature they extend an everyday type of sociality to a one-off, somewhat different, though still familiar setting. In seeing how encounter thrives in surroundings reminiscent of our everyday lives, we set some limits to the idea that fleeting encounters are unbounded.

The second matter to develop is that of the tension that can arise when attempts are made to have other activities, more closely managed, co-located with those of relatively unfettered interaction in familiar spaces. This we see as an attempt to plan for encounter with a heavier rather than a lighter approach, which is likely to be less productive. Or rather, it may be an attempt to load on to situations facilitating encounter extra functions that will reduce the opportunities for informal sociality overall. In public libraries, we have remarked this in efforts to manage the co-existence of different groups of users, particularly by designing spaces or zones for those with certain characteristics or interests. One outcome of this, of course, is that the broad co-presence of strangers is limited, whilst the planning is promoting certain groups' interests. With drop-in centres, attempts to provide referrals to social services agencies from within the centres, or to require as a condition of their funding that they offer classes in formal classroom settings, have been criticized as defeating their very important 'drop-in' purpose. To allow places of successful encounter in cities to be what they are, using a light planning touch to ensure this, is important. To load these places up with other more purposeful activities is a temptation to be avoided.

Transformation in the social relationships of cities is a theme to which we have alluded throughout the book. In the case of the social logic of encounter, we see its transformative potential to lie particularly in its unsettling of identities and of group certainties, so that a range of features or forms of belonging of every individual urbanite are brought into view. It is important to acknowledge and debate the ways encounter is achieved in planned places, and whether those settings of sociality can be 'improved' with more explicit recognition of groups and with more overt redistributional aims and practices.

8 Conclusion

In Chapter 1, we laid out a rationale for seeking a just diversity in cities, which would both conceptualize the social ambitions of planning and examine ways in which they have been put into practice. This intention we framed in terms of three social logics – redistribution, recognition and encounter – which we argued were useful in drawing our attention to different, though related, dimensions of the 'right to the city'. Trying to form a more just diversity in cities is obviously a normative activity. It is a quest to put in place what should be done. But through the chapters of the book it will have become evident that norms may be simply expressed, but they are never straightforwardly achieved or even defined readily in real-world planning contexts. For in every place in which planners try to improve the social conditions of urban built or serviced environments, they must contend with contests, power relations, shifts in government and governance, and the sheer inertia of old ways of proceeding.

Further contextual complexity arises because interpretations of the three social logics, through the decision rules associated with their implementation, vary between places and times. As we have seen, for example, redistribution in social services planning now often means targeting the very poorest people for service provision, and tying their use of a service to their participation in 'workfare' programs. In previous decades redistributive planning of service provision did not take this precise form. Recognition in local planning may, for example, in some more homogeneous local contexts like residential outer suburbs, mean that immigrants' applications to build different public buildings become mired in processes monopolized by longstanding residents' objections to change. In cases in which visionary frameworks are established to guide local planning thought and practice, however, like the UNESCO child-friendly cities framework, then new ways of using the local built environment for recognition can occur.

The decision rules we have observed from the varied planning interventions described in the book, are the following. (They are merely a few of many, but are those that were evident in the cases we chose to discuss.)
In planning for redistribution:

- provide equity in allocation of expenditure on different areas and income groups
- create social mix.

In planning for recognition:

- make a checklist of social or identity groups and allocate resources between them
- devise cross-group projects and allocate resources to these.

In planning for encounter:

- provide a variety of social and economic infrastructure locally
- encourage stakeholder agency in encounter
- create safe and transparent spaces for encounter.

What can be said about these decision rules? How do they assist with planning for redistribution, recognition and encounter in practice? As we observed in Chapter 4, decision rules guiding practice are needed to demonstrate that conceptual thinking in planning can extend beyond critique. What these decision rules do is to show us some 'rules of thumb' that planners in different contexts have tried to use, even in the face of power struggles, political shifts and inertia. Each set of rules is an attempt to unpack a more abstract idea, forming the basis of practical actions to take that are related to the central idea in question. We regard these decision rules as useful ways of thinking about how to approach situations, though clearly they are far from a complete guide to planning action. They still leave open matters of interpretation – what is equitable allocation, for one thing? The production of a longer list of such decision rules is desirable, and would be a useful basis for discussion of the interpretations being made of the broader social logics around which we have structured the book.

In addition, these decision rules show how fundamental to planning is an attempt to grapple with the nature of the 'groups' in the population of concern, and how these groups interact with each other. Of course this is a principal concern of social planning for a just diversity. But the matter bears remarking. In each of the decision rules listed, planners may be seen making judgements about group characteristics, boundaries between them, similarities, competition between them and ways they might be brought together under certain circumstances. The decision rules associated with redistribution, for example, are about income groups, both the presence of particular income groups in distinct neighbourhoods and their mixture in other areas. With recognition, the decision rules are frequently about the grouping of people according to the attributes of immigrants that are often bunched together and labelled as ethnicity. We see in planning strategies attempts to allocate resources according to whether groups identify themselves and claim resources on that basis, or whether they suppress those identities and work together with other 'identity-suppressed' groups. In planning for encounter, a 'group' of strangers, or individuals unknown to each other and sharing some characteristics that make them somehow unfamiliar in that context, have to be comprehended by planners if spaces and places can be devised keeping them in mind.

The book, and the decision rules it lists, however, progress from forms of thinking about planning that envisage people as having fixed identities to a perspective that unsettles those fixed identities. Approaches concerned with redistribution view people as homogeneous agents of equivalent need but divergent incomes. Approaches concerned with recognition view people and groups as having fixed identities of a wider range of attributes. But planning perspectives seeking to facilitate encounter are much less stringent in their thinking about groups' characteristics and the manner in which individuals identify strictly and permanently with those characteristics. Seeking encounter through planning means facilitating fleeting interactions as well as more stable ones, and it is a planning strategy that acknowledges urban inhabitants as strangers with a variety of attachments and group-based identities that might be adopted in a variety of contexts during their lives.

In thinking about the ways in which these different logics understand urban inhabitants – as citizens, as group members and as strangers – it becomes apparent that planning thought and practice are informed by particular ways of understanding the city and its people. Our examples show how planners and urban policy-makers working in different contexts have tried to understand the nature of their local populations, and how they have conceived of various strategies in response to these understandings. As Fainstein (2005) has argued, effective planning must be informed by these wider theorizations of the city. As we have hopefully demonstrated throughout this book, such knowledge can be drawn from work being conducted across a range of disciplines, not just the technically focused planning literature.

Indeed, the view of planning taken in this book has been anything but narrow. A focus on the presence of social logics in planning thought and practice demands this. Far from examining only land use planning, the provision of social services has been placed firmly within the scope of planning. Negotiating over national policy frameworks as well as their local implementation has been seen as part of a planner's task, in different settings. Though planners themselves have been envisaged as actors in a range of organizations – governmental, business and community in source – we have nevertheless stressed their strong relationship to the public sector and its interpretations of the public interest. It has been our intention, in drawing from a wide range of examples in the book and in elaborating in some detail the decision-making contexts in which planners are situated there, to demonstrate the variety and complexity of the planning task. In addition, we have tried to suggest in our examples the importance of political positioning in the work of planners, because the politics of public sector institutions are matters in which they become adept players.

In concluding the book, we wish to make five points about the material covered in the previous chapters, reflecting on its arguments and features.

First, from the example chapters, Chapters 3, 5 and 7, it is evident that planning practice rarely exhibits one social logic alone. It is invariably the case that planning for recognition acknowledges some aspects of redistribution and encounter, for example, the more so when local detail and knowledge are sought for the planning matter in question and when the emphasis is on locality as the scale of relevance. The fact that issues of redistribution, recognition and encounter are so intertwined does not mean, however, that the analytical separation of these issues and logics is problematic. Indeed, it is precisely through analytical separation that the relation among these logics has been rendered visible. Awareness analytically of the three social logics allows it to be evident how, in a situation of some apparent success in planning practice, that success might have been due to sensitivity to all three logics in that situation; less success might be in part the product of a failure to act upon diversity understood in all three ways.

We are aware, however, that the approach poses challenges, because examples used to illustrate one conceptual logic could in fact often illustrate another if their stories were to be told in a slightly different way. Indeed, in some contexts, planners might see a new planning framework or a local action as an example of recognizing the interests and needs of one group, whereas we as analysts might interpret the framework and action as evidence of redistributing certain resources more equitably across numerous groups in the population. In Chapter 5, the examples of child-friendly cities and provision of services and planning permissions to immigrants are a case in point. In that chapter, we chose to use services for immigrants as an example of planning for recognition that seeks to redistribute resources across the population, acknowledging that immigrants are disadvantaged when settling in a new location and benefit from receiving specialized assistance. We have considered child friendly cities as an illustration of planning for recognition that is grounded in recognition alone, a situation in which a new framework in local planning is devised to take account of the interests of a 'disenfranchised' group, children. But it is possible that we as analysts could have used each of these examples to illustrate what the other is illustrating. That is, child friendly cities could be interpreted as a redistributive planning measure, in which resources are directed through planning at enhancing the development of an under-resourced life-course group (children). And land use planning giving permission for immigrants to place visually evident symbols (public buildings) of their priorities on the urban landscape could be seen as an act of recognition alone. So be it. Arguments may be made one way or the other. We have selected our empirical distinctions on the basis of the evidence at hand in our sources, and our conceptual distinctions in the light also of our rejection of what Fraser (2003, p. 60) terms 'post-structuralist anti-dualism' (the belief that matters are so complexly intertwined that it is worthless to try to separate them conceptually). That having been said, however, it is clear that in planning scenarios matters are complexly intertwined in reality, and that the post structural anti-dualists have a conceptual point about the significance of this!

Second, whilst conceptualizations of the three social logics are significant for establishing an analytical frame of reference against which planning actions can be judged, it is plain that it is in planning practice that the range of interpretations of these logics is developed. And it is in practice, of course, that redistribution, recognition and encounter actually occur and a just diversity is formed (or not) in everyday uses and experiences of cities. As planners, together with publics, craft policies and practices they use logics in practical ways to amend outcomes that are often highly politicized. Contingency and context play a part in outcomes, as we have seen in the examples of the book. Governments are elected on more or less stringent economic platforms; national policy frameworks like multiculturalism from which planning can draw may have political support or not; other policy settings may enhance or hinder the possibilities of using the three social logics. This is one reason that our broad sweep of examples in the book is useful. From the examples we can derive insights into the ways planners have handled shifts in policy settings and still maintained their practical connections to redistribution, recognition and encounter, even though they are located in different institutional and spatial contexts.

Examples of how shifts in broad policy frameworks affect the possibilities of on-the-ground planning practice using the three social logics are found in numerous chapters of the book. In Chapter 5, it is evident that in the minds of some planning analysts (e.g. Qadeer, 1994) the national framework of multiculturalism (in Qadeer's case, in Canada) has helped the introduction of land use planning practices in Ontario that support immigrant groups in their efforts to establish public buildings of meaning to them. There is some question now as to what will happen with such 'progress' if this national policy framework is less enthusiastically supported. Taking another example from that chapter, the United Nations' Child Friendly Cities framework has recently been hailed as another framework of value in drawing planners' and policy-makers' attention to positive planning to enhance children's lives in cities, and not at all by segregating them into facilities designed for them alone. In previous decades, as we saw in Chapter 3, national policies supporting local child care provision were able to be used by planners in localities, through their skilful use of local-national relationships within government, to improve the circumstances of working parents, especially women. It is interesting to consider which social groups, to which planning efforts might be directed in the interests of creating a just diversity, might possibly find support in national policy frameworks. Children are one group for which it can be imagined that national frameworks might be widely supported. Immigrants in some countries have had that status. Other groups, such as same-sex groups, might at present be more likely to find planning support from a local political base rather than a national one. This is clearly a question of national politics, and planning for a just diversity is sometimes able to tap into progressive national politics when it appears.

This brings us to our third point. There are some powerful criticisms of the view that a local focus in planning, which engages locals and grassroot organizations in achieving goals, is necessarily a negative symptom of neoliberal small government. A local focus is not necessarily synonymous with the foregoing of responsibility by senior levels of government for broader issues of spatial redistribution. McGuirk (2005), for example, argues that the apparent coherence of the narrative of neoliberalism does not disguise the fact that actual modes of governance still have great variety, and that states retain the capacities for spatial planning that they have always had even if they now exhibit different political values than in the days of welfare state Keynesianism. Examining the history of metropolitan planning in Sydney, she states:

> Neoliberalist metropolitan planning has seen decidedly new sets of desired spatial and social outcomes implanted. Yet it would be a mistake to view this retreat from social democratic policy aims as a hollowing-out of state political and institutional capacity to effect desired distributional outcomes (McGuirk, 2005 p. 64).

In an account with some similar arguments, Larner (2005) shows from her examination of 'neoliberal', place-based planning in New Zealand that we may be 'telling partial, and possibly unduly pessimistic, stories' about it, and that 'a whole new set of social relations is coming into being, only some of which are the direct offshoot of neoliberalism' (p. 11). Looking at the local arrangements made in response to the Stronger Communities Action Fund established in New Zealand in late 2001, in which (as in the Safer Cities initiatives discussed in Chapter 6) government agencies are combining with local citizens and community organizations to tackle social problems using 'local knowledge', Larner (2005, p. 14) contrasts the reduction of welfare state-style social programs with the design of local solutions to local problems, partly determined by local people. And she finds that new 'experts' are emerging in the local community, through these partnerships, rather than expertise being centred outside the local area and in central institutions of government. Many individuals in the locality are pleased with this new self-determination. Others will be excluded from membership in the local 'expert' group, as is always the way when policy approaches shift.

Certainly, the 'rescaling of attention from metropolitan to local-scale processes', especially the place-management approach which has sought to bring about 'holistic planning for urban social and economic development and environmental sustainability', can hide 'the inevitable spatial inequities in the development outcomes of such an approach' McGuirk (2005, p. 64). So, for example, if we focus on the conditions within places, then the redistributional questions we would ask if we were comparing places in a regional or metropolitan planning framework are not so readily asked.

Nonetheless, it should also be clear that the scope of localized planning actions to pursue redistribution, recognition and encounter is not wholly determined by extant national and regional policy frameworks. As we saw with the example of child care provision in Chapter 5, local actors can act in different ways in response to these extra-local constraints and opportunities, achieving quite different results in their localities. In crafting these different responses, an awareness of approaches adopted in other places can be powerful. Indeed, 'local' planners need to network across their localities, both as a means to try to have an impact on trans-local processes which shape possibilities for their own localities, and as a means to develop new ideas. Hopefully, the benefits of this trans-local awareness and connection are apparent in the comparative nature of the examples we have considered in this book, drawn as they are from a variety of national contexts.

Fourth, however, we note that redistributive planning seems not to provide such ready examples of 'success' as planning for recognition and encounter may do. This may be because of the scale at which redistribution has to occur before it is noticeable. Examples of successful planning for recognition and encounter can be evident in relatively minor amendments to local built environments or relatively infrequent social events in public spaces – an annual street festival or the building of a mosque on a major street may demonstrate recognition and encounter. But examples of redistribution are rarely of such local temporal or spatial scale, and even when they are, collecting evidence so as to know that interventions like the provision of a new public library have in fact redistributed resources is difficult. In recent discussion of the provision of new public libraries in relatively disadvantaged areas of UK cities, for example, discussed in Chapter 7, considerable emphasis has been placed in some disadvantaged localities on the construction of library buildings of arresting architectural design. These buildings certainly provide new opportunities for encounter, in high-quality learning spaces. Evidence of their redistributive impact would be more difficult to determine, and would rely on collection of evidence about who the users of the new buildings actually are (are they, for example, people from out of the area now coming into it, rather than locals), and whether the collections of material housed within the building are being used (or whether, instead, the buildings are used as hanging-out, drop-in spaces, in the absence of other collectively available spaces locally, and if this matters).

Fifth, have the chapters and cases discussed shed any light on which planning practices and conceptualizations have been merely affirmative, keeping things as they are, or transformative in their effects? We accept of course that the forms of affirmation or transformation will vary with context and that unintended consequences will often be present. And we accept as well that the future cannot be predicted, so that transformations may occur that would not have been envisaged earlier. It does seem to us that in those cases in which all three social logics have been used consciously in planning, the results are more likely to have been transformative and enduring. Or, rather, that in situations in which the three social logics have been understood to be important, the greatest learning about what should be done or what should have been done has occurred, even if the outcome of the planning intervention in question is deemed to be lacking. So, taking a look back to Chapter 2, and considering the cases of urban renewal in Boston and Beijing about whose outcomes the analysts quoted were very critical, learning based on the three social logics has been extensive. In response to what has happened in each of those cities, urban renewal of an appropriate kind is understood now to require commitment to redistribution towards poorer existing residents, aided by knowing in detail the characteristics and aspirations of the groups of people who are being planned for (recognition), including their views about privacy and appropriate uses of public space in their locality (encounter).

There is another point to make here, about mixing the three social logics in particular ways for best effect. Perhaps it is in planning for encounter, where a conscious effort is made not to anticipate fixity in group characteristics, that participants may more usefully be 'known' or recognized for the way they are in that precise context, although the frame of redistribution is still needed to ensure that resources are delivered appropriately. Poverty, and extreme variations between rich and poor, are always an unacceptable accompaniment to encounter and in fact preclude opportunities for encounter of the most thoroughgoing kind. In addition, the interplay of the three social logics, their use together to understand and plan in particular contexts, may demonstrate the manner in which successful planning can be paradoxical, seeming to run counter to what focussing on any one social logic might suggest would be the right way to go. An obvious example of this, from Chapter 7, is how successful planning for encounter in place requires setting some boundaries around any given interaction rather than opening up an event or place to all forms of instant access and communication. Accordingly, drop-in centres, we have observed, have home-like physical characteristics and sessions of operation often restricted to certain sets of strangers. Public libraries, though they are open to all members of 'the public', nevertheless maintain certain forms of sociality and do not permit others, so that it is possible for any person to be in that same space with any other. Street festivals, though they offer perhaps the broadest access to an event, are temporally limited, rarely lasting more than a couple of days. So, rather than planning for encounter assuming that all forms of interaction are to be encouraged at an event or public place over a limitless time, in fact the forms of interaction that will occur between the strangers recognized, or known as likely to be present, need to be carefully anticipated and planned for.

The three social logics of redistribution, recognition and encounter are useful norms and tools for planning that has progressive social intentions. These social logics, and the decision rules that can be derived from them, allow questioning of planning strategies and the formulation of alternatives. If this conceptual apparatus is wielded alongside learning from the practices and thinking of planners in other contexts, noticing how very much effective planning requires astute negotiation across national and local settings of the public sphere, we need not be so concerned that the longstanding social norms of planning have been set aside.

Bibliography

Ahmed, S. (2000) *Strange Encounters: Embodied Others in Post-Coloniality* (London and New York: Routledge).

Aitken, S. C. (2000) 'Mothers, communities, and the scale of difference', *Social and Cultural Geography*, Vol. 1(1), pp. 65–82.

Albrow, M. (1997) 'Travelling beyond local cultures: socioscapes in a global city', in J. Eade (ed.), *Living the Global City: Globalization as a Local Process* (London and New York: Routledge), pp. 37–55.

Allmendinger, P. and Tewdwr-Jones, M. (2002) (eds), *Planning Futures: New Directions for Planning Theory* (London and New York: Routledge).

Alstad, C. and Curry, A. (2003) 'Public space, public discourse and public libraries', *LIBRES*, Vol. 13(1), (available at http://libres.curtin.edu.au/libres13n1/).

Amin, A. (2002) 'Ethnicity and the multicultural city', *Environment and Planning A*, Vol. 34(6), pp. 959–80.

Amin, A. and Thrift, N. (2002) *Cities: Reimagining the Urban* (Cambridge, UK: Polity Press).

Anderson, K. (1990) '"Chinatown re-oriented": a critical analysis of recent redevelopment schemes in a Melbourne and Sydney enclave', *Australian Geographical Studies*, Vol. 28(2), pp. 137–54.

Anderson, K. (1991) *Vancouver's Chinatown: Racial Discourse in Canada, 1875–1980* (Montreal and Kingston: McGill–Queen's University Press).

Anderson, K. (1998) 'Sites of difference: beyond a cultural politics of race polarity', in R. Fincher and J. M. Jacobs (eds), *Cities of Difference* (New York: Guilford Press,), pp. 201–25.

Arthurson, K. (2001) 'Achieving social justice in estate regeneration: the impact of physical image construction', *Housing Studies*, Vol. 16(6), pp. 807–26.

Arthurson, K. (2002) 'Creating inclusive communities through balancing social mix: a critical relationship or tenuous link?', *Urban Policy and Research*, Vol. 20(3), pp. 245–61.

Bauman, Z. (1995) *Life in Fragments: Essays in Postmodern Morality* (Oxford: Blackwell).

Beck, U. (2002) 'The cosmopolitan society and its enemies', *Theory, Culture & Society*, Vol. 19 (1–2), pp. 17–44.

Benhabib, S. (1996) *Democracy and Difference* (Princeton: Princeton University Press).

Benhabib, S. (2002) *The Claims of Culture: Equality and Diversity in the Global Era* (Princeton: Princeton University Press).

Benhabib, S. (2004) 'On culture, public reason, and deliberation: response to Pensky and Peritz', *Constellations*, Vol. 11(2), pp. 291–99.

Berlant, L. and Warner, M. (1998) 'Sex in public', *Critical Inquiry*, Vol. 24(2), pp. 547–66.

Berman, M. (1986) 'Take it to the streets: conflict and community in public space', *Dissent*, Vol. 33(4), pp. 476–85.

Binnie, J. and Skeggs, B. (2006) 'Cosmopolitan knowledge and the production and consumption of sexualised space: Manchester's Gay Village', in J. Binnie, J. Holloway, S. Millington and C. Young (eds), *Cosmopolitan Urbanism* (London: Routledge), pp. 246–53.

Blakeley, E. and Snyder, M. (1997) *Fortress America: Gated Communities in the United States* (Washington: The Brookings Institution).

Body-Gendrot, S. (2000) *The Social Control of Cities: A Comparative Perspective* (Oxford: Blackwell).

Brain, D. (1997) 'From public housing to private communities: the discipline of design and the materialization of the public/private distinction in the built environment', in J. Weintraub and K. Kumar (eds), *Public and Private in Thought and Practice: Perspectives on a Grand Dichotomy* (Chicago: University of Chicago Press), pp. 237–67.

Brennan, D. (2002) 'Australia: child care and state-centered feminism in a liberal welfare regime', in S. Michel and R. Mahon (eds), *Child Care Policy at the Crossroads: Gender and Welfare State Restructuring* (New York and London: Routledge), pp. 95–112.

Brennan-Horley, C., Gibson, C. and Connell, J. (2006) 'The Parkes Elvis Revival Festival: economic development and contested place identities in rural Australia', *Geographical Research*, Vol. 45(1), pp. 71–84.

Briggs, X. (2003) 'Re-shaping the geography of opportunity: place effects in global perspective', *Housing Studies*, Vol. 18(6), pp. 915–36.

Brodie, J. (2000) 'Imagining democratic urban citizenship', in E. Isin (ed.), *Democracy, Citizenship and the Global City* (London and New York: Routledge), pp. 110–28.

Bryson, J., Usherwood, B. and Proctor, R. (2003) *Libraries Must Also Be Buildings? New Library Impact Study* (Sheffield: The Centre for Public Libraries and Information in Society, Department of Information Studies: University of Sheffield).

Burnley, I., Murphy, P. and Fagan, R. (1997) *Immigration and Australian Cities* (Sydney: Federation Press).

Calhoun, C. (1994) 'Social theory and the politics of identity', in C. Calhoun (ed.), *Social Theory and the Politics of Identity* (Oxford: Blackwell), pp. 9–36.

Campbell, H. (2006) 'Just planning: the art of situated ethical judgment', *Journal of Planning Education and Research*, Vol. 26(1), pp. 92–106.

Campbell, H. and Marshall, R. (2000) 'Moral obligations, planning and the public interest: a commentary on current British practice', *Environment and Planning B*, Vol. 27, pp. 297–312.

Castells, M. (1983) *The City and the Grassroots* (Berkeley: University of California Press).

Castells, M. (2003) *The Power of Identity: The Information Age – Economy, Society and Culture, Volume 2* (Oxford: Blackwell).

Certeau, M. de. (1984) *The Practice of Everyday Life* (Minneapolis: University of Minnesota Press).

Chan, W. (2005) 'A gift of a pagoda, the presence of a prominent citizen, and the possibilities of hospitality', *Environment and Planning D: Society and Space*, Vol. 23, pp. 11–28.

Cohen, E. F. (2005) 'Neither seen nor heard: children's citizenship in contemporary democracies', *Citizenship Studies*, Vol. 9(2), pp. 221–40.

Commission for Architecture and the Built Environment. (2003) *Better Public Libraries* (London: Commission for Architecture and the Built Environment, Resource).

Conradson, D. (2003) 'Spaces of care in the city: the place of a community drop-in centre', *Social & Cultural Geography*, Vol. 4(4), pp. 507–25.

Considine, M. (2001) *Enterprising States* (Cambridge: Cambridge University Press).

Cox, E. (1995) *A Truly Civil Society* (Sydney: ABC Books).

Dachner, N. and Tarasuk, V. (2002) 'Homeless "squeegee" kids' food security and daily survival', *Social Science & Medicine*, Vol. 54(7), pp. 1039–49.

Dear, M. (2000) *The Postmodern Urban Condition* (Oxford: Blackwell).

Dear, M. and Taylor, M. (1982) *Not On Our Street: Community Attitudes to Mental Health Care* (London: Pion).

Dear, M. and Wolch, J. (1987) *Landscapes of Despair: From Deinstitutionalization to Homelessness* (Princeton New Jersey: Princeton University Press).

Debord, G. (1995) *The Society of the Spectacle* (New York: Zone Books).

Delany, S. (1999) '...Three, two, one, contact: Times Square Red, 1998', in J. Copjec and M. Sorkin (eds), *Giving Ground: the Politics of Propinquity* (London and New York: Verso), pp. 19–86.

DeSouza, R. (2005) 'Transforming possibilities of care? Goan migrant motherhood in New Zealand', *Contemporary Nurse*, Vol. 20(1), pp. 87–101.

Deutsche, R. (1999) 'Reasonable urbanism', in J Copjec and M Sorkin (eds), *Giving Ground: The Politics of Propinquity* (London and New York: Verso), pp. 176–206.

DeVerteuil, G. (2003) 'Homeless mobility, institutional settings, and the new poverty management', *Environment and Planning A*, Vol. 35, pp. 361–79.

Dikeç, M. (2002) 'Pera peras poros: longing for spaces of hospitality', *Theory, Culture and Society*, Vol 19, pp. 227–47.

Diken, B. (1998) *Strangers, Ambivalence and Social Theory* (Aldershot, UK: Ashgate Publishing).

Doherty, G., Friendly, M. and Forer, B. (2002) *Child Care by Default or Design? An Exploration of Differences between Non-profit and For-profit Canadian Child Care Centres Using the 'You Bet I Care!' Data Sets* (Toronto: University of Toronto, Childcare Resource and Research Unit, Occasional Paper No. 18).

Donald, J. (1999) *Imagining the Modern City* (London: Athlone).

Duany, A., Plater-Zyberk, E. and Speck, J. (2000) *Suburban Nation: The Rise of Sprawl and the Decline of the American Dream.* (New York: North Point Press).

Duffy, M. (forthcoming-a) 'Festival, spectacle' *International Encyclopaedia of Human Geography.*

Duffy, M. (forthcoming-b) 'The possibilities of music: "To learn from and listen to one another ..."', R. Bandt, M. Duffy and D. Mackinnon (eds),

Hearing Places: An Anthology of Interdisciplinary Writings (Cambridge: Scholars Press).

Duffy, M., Waitt, G. and Gibson, C. (2007) 'Get into the groove: the role of sound in generating a sense of belonging at street parades', *Altitude*, Vol. 8, http://www.altitude21c.com/, accessed Jan 30, 2008.

Duncan, N. (1996) 'Negotiating gender and sexuality in public and private spaces' in N. Duncan (ed.), *Bodyspace: Destabilizing Geographies of Gender and Sexuality* (London: Routledge), pp. 127–45.

Dunn, K., Hanna, B. and Thompson, S. (2001) 'The local politics of difference: an examination of intercommunal relations policy in Australian local government', *Environment and Planning A*, Vol. 33(9), pp. 1577–95.

Dürrschmidt, J. (2000) *Everyday Lives in the Global City: The Delinking of Locale and Milieu* (London and New York: Routledge).

Elden, S. (2004) *Understanding Henri Lefebvre: Theory and the Possible* (London: Continuum).

Fainstein, S. (2005) 'Planning theory and the city', *Journal of Planning Education and Research*, Vol. 25(2), pp 121–30.

Farouque, F. (2006) 'King of child-care castle pushes for bigger share', *The Age*, March 16, News, p. 2.

Feldman, L. C. (2002) 'Redistribution, recognition, and the state: the irreducibly political dimension of injustice', *Political Theory*, Vol. 30(3), pp. 410–40.

Fincher, R. (1991) 'Caring for workers' dependents: gender, class and local state practice in Melbourne', *Political Geography Quarterly*, Vol. 10(4), pp, 356–81.

Fincher, R. (1996) 'The demanding state: volunteer work and social polarisation', in K. Gibson, M. Huxley, J. Cameron, L. Costello, R. Fincher, J. Jacobs, N. Jamieson, L. Johnson and M. Pulvirenti *Restructuring Difference: Social Polarisation and the City* Melbourne, Australian Housing and Urban Research Institute, Working Paper 6, pp. 29–41.

Fincher, R. and Jacobs, J. M. (1998) (eds), *Cities of Difference* (New York: Guilford Press).

Fincher, R., Jacobs, J. M. and Anderson, K. (2002) 'Rescripting cities with difference', in J. Eade and C. Mele (eds), *Understanding the City: Contemporary and Future Perspectives* (Blackwell: Oxford), pp. 27–48.

Fincher, R and Shaw, K. (2006) 'Encounter by transnational and temporary residents in place', (Paper presented at the regional conference of the International Geographical Union, Brisbane, July).

Florida, R. L. (2002) *The Rise of the Creative Class: And How It's Transforming Work, Leisure, Community and Everyday Life* (New York: Basic Books).

Flyvbjerg, B. (1998) *Rationality and Power* (The University of Chicago Press: Chicago).

Forester, J. (1999) *The Deliberative Practitioner: Encouraging Participatory Planning Processes* (Cambridge, Mass.: MIT Press).

Fraser, N. (1989) 'Women, welfare and the politics of need interpretation' in N. Fraser *Unruly Practices: Power, Discourse, and Gender in Contemporary Social Theory* (Cambridge: Polity), pp. 144–60.

Fraser, N. (1995) 'From redistribution to recognition? Dilemmas of justice in a "post-socialist" age', *New Left Review*, Vol. 212, pp. 68–93.

Fraser, N. (1997a) 'A rejoinder to Iris Young', *New Left Review*, Vol. 223, pp. 126–9.

Fraser, N. (1997b) *Justice Interruptus: Critical Reflections on the 'Postsocialist' Condition* (New York: Routledge).

Fraser, N. (1998) 'Social justice in the age of identity politics: redistribution, recognition and participation' in *Tanner Lectures on Human Values*, Vol 19.

Fraser, N. (2000) 'Rethinking recognition', *New Left Review*, Vol. 3, pp. 107–20.

Fraser, N. (2003) 'Social justice in the age of identity politics: redistribution, recognition and participation' in N. Fraser and A. Honneth (eds), *Redistribution or Recognition? A Political-Philosophical Exchange* (London and New York: Verso), pp. 7–109.

Fraser, N. (2004) 'Institutionalizing democratic justice: redistribution, recognition and participation' in S. Benhabib and N. Fraser (eds), *Pragmatism, Critique, Judgement: Essays for Richard J. Bernstein* (Cambridge, Mass.: The MIT Press). pp. 125–48.

Fraser, N and Honneth, A. (2003) *Redistribution or Recognition*, (London and New York: Verso).

Freeman, C. (2006) 'Colliding worlds: planning with children and young people for better cities' in B. J. Gleeson and N. Sipe (eds), *Creating Child Friendly Cities: Reinstating Kids in the City* (London: Routledge), pp. 69–85.

Gans, H. (1962) *The Urban Villagers: Group and Class in the Life of Italian-Americans* (New York: The Free Press).

Gibson, K. and Cameron, J. (2001) 'Transforming communities: towards a research agenda', *Urban Policy and Research*, 19(1), 7–24.

Gilroy, P. (2004) *After Empire: Melancholia or Convivial Culture?* (London: Routledge).

Gilroy, P. (2006) 'Multiculture in times of war: an inaugural lecture given at the London School of Economics', *Critical Quarterly*, Vol. 48(4), pp. 27–45.

Gleeson, B. (1999) *Geographies of Disability* (London and New York: Routledge).

Gleeson, B. and Kearns, R. (2001) 'Remoralising landscapes of care', *Environment and Planning D: Society and Space*, Vol. 19, pp. 61–80.

Gleeson, B. and Low, N. (2000) *Australian Urban Planning* (Sydney: Allen and Unwin).

Gleeson, B. and Randolph, B. (2001) *Social Planning and Disadvantage in the Sydney Context*, Urban Frontiers Program Issues Paper Number 9, University of Western Sydney.

Goffman, E. (1961) *Encounters: Two Studies in the Sociology of Interaction* (Indianapolis: Bobbs–Merrill).

Gough, D. (2006) 'Fed-up parents push for child care choice', *The Age*, March 26, News, p. 5.

Goulding, A. (2004) 'Libraries and social capital', *Journal of Librarianship and Information Sciences*, Vol. 36(1), pp. 3–6.

Graham, S. and Marvin, S. (2001) *Splintering Urbanism: Networked Infrastructures, Technological Mobilities and the Urban Condition* (London and New York: Routledge).

Hage, G. (1998) *White Nation: Fantasies of White Supremacy in a Multicultural Society* (Sydney: Pluto Press).

Harvey, D. (2003) 'The right to the city', *International Journal of Urban and Regional Research*, Vol. 27(4), pp. 939–41.

Haydn, F. and Temel, R. (2006) 'Introduction', in F. Haydn and R. Temel (eds), *Temporary Urban Spaces: Concepts for the Use of City Spaces* (Berlin: Birkhauser).

Hayward, C. (2003) 'The difference states make: democracy, identity, and the American city', *American Political Science Review*, Vol. 97(4), pp. 501–14.

Healey, P. (1997) *Collaborative Planning: Shaping Places in Fragmented Societies* (Basingstoke and London: Macmillan).

Honneth, A. (1995) *The Struggle for Recognition: The Moral Grammar of Social Conflicts* (Cambridge, USA: Polity Press).

Huxley, M. (2002) 'Governmentality, gender, planning' in P. Allmendinger, M. Tewdwr-Jones (eds), *Planning Futures: New Directions for Planning Theory* (London and New York: Routledge), pp. 136–53.

Illich, I. (1973) *Tools for Conviviality* (New York: Harper & Row).

Imrie, R. and Raco, M. (2003) 'Community and the changing nature of urban policy', in R. Imrie and M. Raco (eds), *Urban Renaissance? New Labour, Community and Urban Policy* (Bristol: The Policy Press), pp. 3–36.

Isin, E. (2000) 'Introduction: democracy, citizenship and the global city', in E. Isin (ed.), *Democracy, Citizenship and the Global City* (London: Routledge).

Isin, E. (2002) *Being political: Genealogies of Citizenship* (Minneapolis: University of Minnesota Press).

Iveson, K. (2006a) 'Cities for angry young people? From exclusion and inclusion to engagement in urban policy' in B. J. Gleeson and N. Sipe (eds), *Creating Child Friendly Cities: Reinstating Kids in the City* (London: Routledge), pp. 49–65.

Iveson, K. (2006b) 'Strangers in the cosmopolis' in J. Binne, J. Holloway, S. Millington and C. Young (eds), *Cosmopolitan Urbanism* (London: Routledge), pp. 70–86.

Jacobs, J. (1961) *The Death and Life of Great American Cities* (New York: Vintage Books).

Jacobs, K., Kemeny, J. and Manzi, T. (2003) 'Power, discursive space and institutional practices in the construction of housing problems', *Housing Studies*, Vol. 18(4), pp. 429–46.

Jacobs, J. M. and Fincher, R. (1998) 'Introduction', in R. Fincher and J. M. Jacobs (eds), *Cities of Difference* (New York: Guilford Press), pp. 1–25.

Jamieson, K. (2004) 'The festival gaze and its boundaries', *Space and Culture*, Vol. 7(1), pp. 64–75.

Jans, M. (2004) 'Children as citizens: towards a contemporary notion of child participation', *Childhood*, Vol. 11(1), pp. 27–44.

Jenson, J. (2002) 'Against the current: childcare and family policy in Quebec', in S. Michel and R. Mahon (eds), *Child Care Policy at the Crossroads: Gender and Welfare State Restructuring* (New York and London: Routledge), pp. 310–32.

Jenson, J. and Sideau, M. (2001a) 'Citizenship in the era of welfare state redesign', in J. Jenson and M. Sideau (eds), *Who Cares? Women's Work,*

Childcare and Welfare State Redesign (Toronto: University of Toronto Press), pp. 240–65.

Jenson, J. and Sideau, M. (2001b) 'The care dimension in welfare state redesign', in J. Jenson and M. Sideau (eds), *Who Cares? Women's Work, Childcare and Welfare State Redesign* (Toronto: University of Toronto Press), pp. 3–18.

Jessop, B. (2002) *The Future of the Capitalist State* (Oxford: Polity Press).

Kallus, R. and Churchman, A. (2004) 'Women's struggle for urban safety: the Canadian experience and its applicability to the Israeli context', *Planning Theory and Practice*, Vol. 5(2), pp.197–215.

Kasson, J. F. (1978) *Amusing the Million: Coney Island at the Turn of the Century* (New York: Hill and Wang).

Katz, P. (1994) *The New Urbanism: Towards an Architecture of Community* (New York: McGraw–Hill).

Katznelson, I. (1992) *Marxism and the City* (Oxford: Clarendon Press).

Kearns, A. (2003) 'Social capital, regeneration and urban policy', in R. Imrie and M. Raco (eds), *Urban Renaissance? New Labour, Community and Urban Policy* (Bristol: The Policy Press), pp. 37–60.

Kearns, R. and Joseph, A. (2000) 'Contracting opportunities: interpreting post-asylum geographies of mental health care in Auckland', *Health and Place*, Vol 6, pp.159–69.

Keith, M. (1996) 'Street sensibility? Negotiating the political by articulating the spatial', in A. Merrifield and E. Swyngedouw (eds), *The Urbanization of Injustice* (London: Lawrence & Wishart), pp. 137–62.

Keith, M. (2005) *After the Cosmopolitan? Multicultural Cities and the Future of Racism.* (Abingdon and New York: Routledge).

Knopp, L. (1995) 'Sexuality and urban space: a framework for analysis' in D. Bell and G. Valentine (eds), *Mapping Desire: Geographies of Sexualities* (London: Routledge), pp. 149–64.

Knowles, C. (2000) 'Burger King, Dunkin Donuts and community mental health care', *Health and Place*, Vol. 6(3), pp. 213–24.

Knox, P. (1993) 'Capital, material culture and socio-spatial differentiation', in P. Knox (ed.), *The Restless Urban Landscape* (Englewood Cliffs, New Jersey: Prentice–Hall,), pp. 1–34.

Kristeva, J. (1991) *Strangers to ourselves* (New York ; London: Harvester Wheatsheaf).

Kulynych, J. (2001) 'No playing in the public sphere: democratic theory and the exclusion of children', *Social Theory and Practice*, Vol. 27(2), pp. 231–64.

Landry, C. (2000) *The creative city: a toolkit for urban innovators* (Near Stroud, U.K: Comedia: Earthscan).

Lanphier, M. and Lukomskyj, O. (1994) 'Settlement policy in Australia and Canada', in H. Adelman, A. Borowski, M. Burstein, and L. Foster (eds), *Immigration and Refugee Policy: Australia and Canada Compared*, Vol 2. (Melbourne: Melbourne University Press), pp. 337–71.

Larner, W. (2005) 'Neoliberalism in (regional) theory and practice: the Stronger Communities Action Fund in New Zealand', *Geographical Research*, Vol. 43(1), pp. 9–18.

Larner, W. and Craig, D. (2005) 'After neoliberalism? Community activism and local partnerships in Aotearoa New Zealand', *Antipode*, Vol. 37(3), pp. 407–24.

Laurier, E., Whyte, A. and Buckner, K. (2002) 'Neighbouring as an occasioned activity: "finding a lost cat"', *Space and Culture*, Vol. 5(4), pp. 346–67.

Lees, L. (1997) 'Ageographia, Heteropia, and Vancouver's New Public Library', *Environment and Planning D: Society and Space*, Vol. 15(3), pp. 321–47.

Lees, L. (2003a) 'The ambivalence of diversity and the politics of urban renaissance: the case of youth in downtown Portland, Maine', *International Journal of Urban and Regional Research*, Vol. 27(3), pp. 613–34.

Lees, L. (2003b) 'Visions of "urban renaissance": the Urban Task Force report and the Urban White Paper', in R. Imrie and M. Raco (eds), *Urban Renaissance? New Labour, Community and Urban Policy* (Bristol: The Policy Press), pp. 61–82.

Lefebvre, H. (1996) *Writings on Cities*, trans E. Kofman and E. Lebas (Oxford: Blackwell).

Lemon, C. and Lemon, J. (2003) 'Community-based cooperative ventures for adults with intellectual disabilities', *Canadian Geographer*, Vol. 47(4), pp. 414–28.

Levy, F., Meltsner, A. and Wildavsky, A. (1974) *Urban Outcomes: Schools, Streets and Libraries* (Berkeley, Los Angeles, London: University of California Press).

Ley, D. (1999) 'Myths and meanings of immigration and the metropolis', *The Canadian Geographer*, Vol. 43(1), pp. 2–19.

Low, N. (1994) 'Planning and justice', in H. Thomas (ed.), *Values and Planning* (Aldershot UK: Avebury), pp. 116–39.

McCabe, R. (2001) *Civic Librarianship: Renewing the Social Mission of the Public Library* (Lanham: Scarecrow Press).

McGuirk, P. (2001) 'Situating communicative planning theory: context, power and knowledge', *Environment and Planning A*, Vol. 33, pp. 195–217.

McGuirk, P. (2005) 'Neoliberalist planning? Re-thinking and re-casting Sydney's metropolitan planning', *Geographical Research*, Vol. 43(1), pp. 59–70.

Maher, C., Whitelaw, J., McAllister, A., Francis, R., Palmer, J., Chee, E. and Taylor, P. (1992) *Mobility and Locational Disadvantage within Australian Cities: Social Justice Implications of Household Relocation* (Canberra: Social Justice Research Program into Locational Disadvantage, Bureau of Immigration Research and Department of the Prime Minister and Cabinet).

Mahon, R. (2002) 'Gender and welfare state restructuring: through the lens of child care', in S. Michel and R. Mahon (eds), *Child Care Policy at the Crossroads: Gender and Welfare State Restructuring* (New York and London: Routledge), pp. 1–27.

Mahon, R. (2005) 'Rescaling social reproduction: childcare in Toronto/Canada and Stockholm/Sweden', *International Journal of Urban and Regional Research*, Vol. 29(2), pp. 341–57.

Mahon, R. and Phillips, S. (2002) 'Dual-earner families caught in a liberal welfare regime? The politics of child care policy in Canada', in S. Michel and R. Mahon (eds), *Child Care Policy at the Crossroads: Gender and Welfare State Restructuring*) (New York and London: Routledge), pp. 192–218.

Malone, K. (2006) 'United Nations: a key player in a global movement for child friendly cities', in B. J. Gleeson and N. Sipe (eds), *Creating Child Friendly Cities: Reinstating Kids in the City* (London: Routledge), p. 13–32.

Markell, P. (2000) 'The recognition of politics: a comment on Emcke and Tully', *Constellations*, Vol. 7(4), pp. 496–506.

Marshall, J. N. (2004) 'Financial institutions in disadvantaged areas: a comparative analysis of policies encouraging financial inclusion in Britain and the United States', *Environment and Planning A*, Vol. 36, pp. 241–61.

Mason, G. and Tomsen, S. (eds), (1997) *Homophobic Violence* (Leichhardt: Federation Press).

Mattern, S. C. (2007) *The New Downtown Library: Designing With Communities* (Minneapolis: University of Minnesota Press).

Meegan, R. and Mitchell, A. (2001) '"It's not community round here, it's neighbourhood": neighbourhood change and cohesion in urban regeneration policies', *Urban Studies*, Vol. 38(12), pp. 2167–94.

Merrifield, A. and Swyngedouw, E. (1996) 'Social justice and the urban experience: an introduction', in A. Merrifield and E. Swyngedouw (eds), *The Urbanization of Injustice* (London: Lawrence & Wishart), pp. 1–17.

Michel, S. (1999) *Children's Interests/Mother's Rights: The Shaping of America's Child Care Policy* (New Haven: Yale University Press).

Miller, M. (2003) *The Representation of Place: Urban Planning and Protest in France and Great Britain, 1950–1980* (Aldershot, UK: Ashgate).

Mitchell, D. (2003) *The Right to the City: Social Justice and the Fight for Public Space* (New York: Guildford).

Mitchell, K. (2001) 'Transnationalism, neoliberalism, and the rise of the shadow state', *Economy and Society*, Vol. 30(2) pp. 165–89.

Mitchell, K. (2004) 'Geographies of identity: multiculturalism unplugged', *Progress in Human Geography*, Vol. 28(5), pp. 641–51.

Moon, G. (2000) 'Risk and protection: the discourse of confinement in contemporary mental health policy', *Health and Place*, Vol. 6 (3), pp. 239–50.

Moran, L., Skeggs B., Tyrer, P. and Corteen, K. (2001) 'Property, boundary, exclusion: making sense of hetero-violence in safer spaces', *Social and Cultural Geography*, Vol 2(4), pp. 407–20.

Morrison, Z. (2003) 'Cultural justice and addressing "social exclusion": a case study of a Single Regeneration Budget project in Blackbird Leys, Oxford', in R. Imrie and M. Raco (eds), *Urban Renaissance? New Labour, Community and Urban Policy* (Bristol: The Policy Press), pp. 139–61.

Morrissey, M., Mitchell, C. and Rutherford, A. (1991) *The Family in the Settlement Process* (Canberra: Australian Government Publishing Service).

Moss, P. and Petrie, P. (2002) *From Children's Services to Children's Spaces* (London: Routledge).

Mountz, A. (2003) 'Human smuggling, the transnational imaginary, and everyday geographies of the nation-state', *Antipode*, Vol. 35, pp. 622–44.

Naylor, S and Ryan, J. (2002) 'The mosque in the suburbs: negotiating religion and ethnicity in South London', *Social and Cultural Geography*, Vol. 3(1), pp. 39–59.

Parr, H. (2000) 'Interpreting the "hidden social geographies" of mental health: ethnographies of inclusion and exclusion in semi-institutional places', *Health & Place*, Vol. 6, pp. 225–37.

Peattie, L. (1998) 'Convivial cities', in M. Douglass and J. Friedmann (eds), *Cities for Citizens* (Chichester: John Wiley & Sons), pp. 247–53.

Permezel, M. (2001) *The Practice of Citizenship: Place, Identity and the Politics of Participation in Neighbourhood Houses* (Unpublished PhD thesis: University of Melbourne).

Permezel, M. and Duffy, M. (2007) 'Negotiating the geographies of cultural difference in local communities: two examples from suburban Melbourne', *Geographical Research*, 45(4) (pp. 358–75).

Phillips, A. (1993) *Democracy and Difference* (University Park (PA): Pennsylvania University Press).

Phillips, A. (1996) 'Dealing with difference: a politics of ideas, or a politics of presence?', in S. Benhabib (ed.), *Democracy and Difference: Contesting the Boundaries of the Political* (Princeton: Princeton University Press), pp. 139–52.

Phillips, A. (1997) 'From inequality to difference: a severe case of displacement?' *New Left Review*, Vol. 224, pp. 143–53.

Podmore, J. A. (2001) 'Lesbians in the crowd: gender, sexuality and visibility along Montreal's Boulevard St Laurent', *Gender Place and Culture*, Vol. 8, pp. 333–55.

Podmore, J. A. (2006) 'Gone "underground"? Lesbian visibility and the consolidation of queer space in Montreal', in *Social and Cultural Geography*, Vol. 7(4), pp. 595–625.

Powell, D. (1993) *Out West: Perceptions of Sydney's Western Suburbs* (Sydney: Allen and Unwin).

Powell, K. (2005) *Executive Summary: The Effect of Adult Playcentre Participation on the Creation of Social Capital in Local Communities* (Report to the New Zealand Playcentre Federation: Massey University College of Education Research).

Preston, V. and Lo, L. (2000) '"Asian theme" malls in suburban Toronto: land use conflict in Richmond Hill', *The Canadian Geographer*, Vol. 44(2), pp. 182–90.

Preston, V., Kobayashi, A. and Siemiatycki, M. (2006) 'Transnational urbanism: Toronto as a crossroads', in V. Satzewich and L. Wong (eds), *Transnational Communities in Canada; Emergent Identities, Practices, and Issues* (Vancouver: UBC Press), pp. 91–110.

Putnam, R. with Leonardi, R. and Nanetti, R. (1993) *Making Democracy Work: Civic Traditions in Modern Italy* (Princeton: Princeton University Press).

Qadeer, M. (1994) 'Urban planning and multiculturalism in Ontario, Canada', in H. Thomas, and V. Krishnarayan (eds), *Race, Equality and Planning* (Aldershot, Hants, England: Avebury), pp. 187–200.

234   *Bibliography*

Quilley, S. (1997) 'Constructing Manchester's "New Urban Village": gay space in the entrepreneurial city', in G. B. Ingram, A.-M. Bouthillette and Y. Retter (eds), *Queers in Space: Communities, Public Places, Sites of Resistance* (Seattle: Bay Press), pp. 275–94.

Reeves, D. (2005) *Planning for Diversity: Policy and Planning in a World of Difference* (London; New York: Routledge).

Retort (2005) *Afflicted Powers: Capital and Spectacle in a New Age of War* (London: Verso).

Ritchie, L. (2003) 'Bicultural development in early childhood care and education in Aotearoa/New Zealand: views of teachers and teacher educators', *Early Years: An International Journal of Research and Development*, Vol. 23(1) pp. 7–19.

Rose, D. (1984) 'Rethinking gentrification: beyond the uneven development of marxist urban theory' *Environment and Planning D: Society and Space* 2(1) 47–74.

Rose, D. (1993) 'Local childcare strategies in Montreal, Quebec: the mediations of state policy, class and ethnicity in the life courses of families with young children', in C. Katz and J. Monk (eds), *Full Circles: Geographies of Women over the Life Course* (London and New York: Routledge), pp. 188–207.

Rose, G. (1997) 'Situating knowledges: positionality, reflexivities and other tactics' *Progress in Human Geography*, Vol. 21(3), pp. 305–20.

Rose, N. (2000) 'Government and control', *British Journal of Criminology*, Vol. 40(2), pp. 321–39.

Ross, K. (2002) *May '68 and Its Afterlives* (Chicago: University of Chicago Press).

Sandercock, L. (1998) *Towards Cosmopolis: Planning for Multicultural Cities* (Chichester: Wiley).

Sandercock, L. (2000) 'When strangers become neighbours: managing cities of difference', *Planning Theory & Practice*, Vol.1(1), pp. 13–30.

Sandercock, L. (2003) *Cosmopolis II: Mongrel Cities in the 21st Century* (London: Continuum).

Sandercock, L. and Dovey, K. G. (2002) 'Pleasure, politics, and the "public interest": Melbourne's riverscape revitalization', *Journal of the American Planning Association*, Vol. 68(2), pp. 151–64.

Sandercock, L and Kliger, B. (1998) 'Multiculturalism and the planning system, Part 1', *Australian Planner*, Vol 35(3), pp. 127–32.

Sennett, R. (1970) *The Uses of Disorder: Personal Identity & City Life* (New York: Knopf).

Sennett, R. (1994) *Flesh and Stone: The Body and the City in Western Civilization* (London: Faber and Faber).

Shaw, K. (2005) 'The place of alternative culture and the politics of its protection in Berlin, Amsterdam and Melbourne', *Planning Theory & Practice*, Vol. 6(2), pp. 149–69.

Shaw, M. and Andrew, C. (2005) 'Engendering crime prevention: international developments and the Canadian experience', *Canadian Journal of Criminology and Criminal Justice*, Vol. 47(2) pp. 293–316.

Shields, R. (1999) *Lefebvre, Love and Struggle: Spatial Dialectics* (London: Routledge).

Simmel, G. (1950) 'The stranger', in K. H. Wolff (ed.), *The Sociology of Georg Simmel* (New York: The Free Press), pp. 402–9.

Singh, G. (2003) 'Multiculturalism in contemporary Britain: reflections on the "Leicester Model"', *International Journal on Multicultural Societies*, Vol. 5(1), pp. 40–54.

Skelton, I. (1996) 'Child care services in Ontario', in K. England (ed.), *Who Will Mind the Baby? Geographies of Child Care and Working Mothers* (London and New York: Routledge), pp. 62–74.

Smith, D. M. (1994) *Geography and Social Justice* (Oxford: Blackwell).

Smith, N. (1996) *The New Urban Frontier: Gentrification and the Revanchist City* (London; New York: Routledge).

Smith, N. (1998) 'Giuliani time: the Revanchist 1990s', *Social Text*, Vol 57, pp. 1–20.

Soja, E. (1996) *Thirdspace: Journeys to Los Angeles and Other Real and Imagined Places* (Cambridge, Mass.: Blackwell).

Sommella, L. and Wolfe, M. (1997) 'This is about people dying: the tactics of Early ACT UP and Lesbian Avengers in New York City', in G. B. Ingram, A.-M. Bouthillette and Y. Retter (eds), *Queers in Space: Communities, Public Places, Sites of Resistance* (Seattle: Bay Press), pp. 407–38.

State Library of Victoria (2005a) *Libraries/Building/Communities – Report Four: Showcasing the Best* (Melbourne, State Library of Victoria, Library Board of Victoria, Victorian Public Library and Information Network).

State Library of Victoria (2005b) *Libraries/Buildings/Communities – Executive Summary* (Melbourne: State Library of Victoria, Library Board of Victoria, Victorian Public Library and Information Network).

Stretton, H. (1970) *Ideas for Australian Cities* (Adelaide: Hugh Stretton).

Tajbakhsh, K. (2001) *The Promise of the City: Space, Identity, and Politics in Contemporary Social Thought* (Berkley: University of California Press).

Takahashi, L. (1998) 'Community responses to human service delivery in U.S. Cities', in R. Fincher and J. M. Jacobs (eds), *Cities of Difference* (New York: Guilford Press), pp. 120–48.

Takahashi, L. (2001) 'Navigating the time-space context of HIV and AIDS: daily routines and access to care', *Social Science and Medicine*, Vol. 53, pp. 845–63.

Thompson, S. and Dunn, K. (2002) 'Multicultural services in local government in Australia: an uneven tale of access and equity', *Urban Policy & Research*, Vol. 20(3), pp. 263–79.

Tiesdell, S. and Allmendinger, P. (2001) 'Neighbourhood regeneration and New Labour's third way', *Environment and Planning C: Government and Policy*, Vol. 19, pp. 903–26.

Touraine, A. (2000) *Can We Live Together? Equality and Difference* (Cambridge, UK: Polity Press).

Tse, S. and Liew, T. (2004) 'New Zealand experiences: how is community resilience manifested in Asian communities?'. *International Journal of Mental Health and Addiction*, http://ijma-journal.com.

Uitermark, J., Rossi, U. and Van Houtum, H. (2005) 'Reinventing multiculturalism: urban citizenship and the negotiation of ethnic diversity in Amsterdam', *International Journal of Urban and Regional Research*, Vol. 29(3), pp. 622–40.

UNICEF (2004) *Building Child Friendly Cities: A Framework for Action* (Florence: UNICEF Innocenti Research Centre).

UNICEF (2005) *Cities with Children: Child Friendly Cities in Italy* (Florence: UNICEF Innocenti Research Centre).

University of Technology Sydney and State Library of New South Wales (2000) *'A Safe Place to Go': Libraries and Social Capital* (Sydney: University of Technology Sydney and State Library of New South Wales).

Valentine, G. (1993) '(Hetero)sexing space: lesbian perceptions and experiences of everyday spaces', *Environment and Planning D: Society and Space*, Vol. 11, pp. 335–413.

Wang, S. (1999) 'Chinese commercial activity in the Toronto CMA: new development patterns and impacts', *The Canadian Geographer*, Vol. 43(1), pp. 19–35.

Ward, C. (1978) *The Child in the City* (New York: Pantheon Books).

Warner, M. (2000) *The Trouble with Normal: Sex, Politics, and the Ethics of Queer Life* (New York: Free Press).

Warpole, K. (2004) *21st Century Libraries: Changing Forms, Changing Futures* (London: Commission for Architecture and the Built Environment, Royal Institute of British Architects, Museums Libraries Archives).

Watson, S. (2004) 'Cultures of democracy: spaces of democratic possibility', in C. Barnett and M. Low (eds), *Spaces of Democracy: Geographical Perspectives on Citizenship, Participation and Representation* (London: Sage), pp. 207–22.

Watson, S. (2006) *City Publics: The (Dis)enchantments of Urban Encounters* (London: Routledge).

Watson, S and McGillivray, A. (1995) 'Planning in a multicultural environment: a challenge for the nineties', in P. Troy (ed.), *Australian Cities: Issues, Strategies and Policies for Urban Australia in the 1990s* (Melbourne: Cambridge University Press), pp. 164–78.

Webster, C., Glasze, G. and Frantz, K. (2002) 'The global spread of gated communities', *Environment and Planning B: Planning and Design*, Vol. 29, pp. 315–20.

Wekerle, G. and Jackson, P. S. B. (2005) 'Urbanizing the security agenda: anti terrorism, urban sprawl and social movements' *City* Vol. 9 (1), pp. 33–49.

Wekerle, G. and Whitzman, C. (1995) *Safe Cities: Guidelines for Planning, Design, and Management.* (New York: Van Nostrand Reinhold).

Wilson, E. (1991) *The Sphinx in the City: The Control of Disorder, and Women* (Berkeley and Los Angeles: University of California Press).

Wilson, W. (1987) *The Truly Disadvantaged: The Inner City, the Underclass and Public Policy* (New York: Bantam Books).

Witten, K., McCreanor, T. and Kearns, R. (2003a) 'The place of neighbourhood in social cohesion: insights from Massey, West Auckland', *Urban Policy and Research*, Vol. 21(4), pp. 321–38.

Witten, K., Kearns, R., Lewis, N., Coster, H. and McCreanor, T. (2003b) 'Educational restructuring from a community viewpoint: a case study from Invercargill, New Zealand', *Environment and Planning C: Government and Policy*, Vol. 21, pp. 203–23.

Wood, N., Duffy, M. and Smith, S. J. (2007) 'The art of doing (geographies of) music', *Environment and Planning D: Society and Space*, Vol 25(5) (pp. 867–89).

Wood, P. and Gilbert, L. (2005) 'Multiculturalism in Canada: accidental discourses, alternative vision, urban practice', *International Journal of Urban and Regional Research*, Vol. 29(3), pp. 679–91.

Wotherspoon, G. (1991) *City of the Plain: History of a Gay Subculture* (Sydney: Hale and Ironmonger).

Wrigley, N., Guy, C. and Lowe, M. (2002) 'Urban regeneration, social inclusion and large store development: the Seacroft development in context', *Urban Studies*, Vol. 39(11), pp. 2101–14.

Wu, L. (1999) *Rehabilitating the Old City of Beijing: A Project in the Ju'er Hutong Neighbourhood* (Vancouver: UBC Press).

Yiftachel, O. (1995) 'The dark side of modernism: planning as control of an ethnic minority', in S. Watson and K. Gibson (eds), *Postmodern Cities and Spaces* (Oxford: Blackwell), pp. 216–42.

Young, I. M. (1990) *Justice and the Politics of Difference* (Princeton: Princeton University Press).

Young, I. M. (1997) 'Unruly categories: a critique of Nancy Fraser's dual systems theory', *New Left Review*, Vol. 222, pp. 147–60.

Young, I. M. (2000) *Inclusion and Democracy* (Oxford: Oxford University Press).

Zurn, C. F. (2003) 'Identity or status? Struggles over 'Recognition' in Fraser, Honneth, and Taylor', *Constellations*, Vol. 10(4) pp. 519–37.

Index